Unveiling of the model for Le Corbusier and Pierre Jeanneret's Palace of the Soviets of 1931–1932, their unexecuted project for the national parliament of the USSR in Moscow. Two collaborators lift the drape at left; Le Corbusier stands at right with a double bass.

Main

Makers of
Modern Architecture
Volume II

Tod Williams and Billie Tsien at work in their studio,
New York City, 1996, photograph by Michael Moran

Makers of
Modern Architecture
Volume II

Martin Filler

NEW YORK REVIEW BOOKS

New York

THIS IS A NEW YORK REVIEW BOOK

MAKERS OF MODERN ARCHITECTURE VOLUME II
Copyright © 2013 by Martin Filler
Copyright © 2013 by NYREV, Inc.

Published by The New York Review of Books
435 Hudson Street, Suite 300, New York NY 10014
www.nyrb.com

Library of Congress Cataloging-in-Publication Data

Filler, Martin, 1948–
    Makers of modern architecture / By Martin Filler.
    p. cm.
    ISBN-13: 978-1-59017-227-8 (alk. paper)
    ISBN-10: 1-59017-227-2 (alk. paper)
    1. Architecture, Modern — 20th century. I. Title.
NA680.F46 2007
724'.6—dc22

                                                                2007004176

ISBN 978-1-59017-688-7
Also available as an electronic book; ISBN 978-1-59017-701-3

Printed in the United States of America on acid-free paper

1 3 5 7 9 10 8 6 4 2

For
Robert Silvers
Editor, hero, and friend

Contents

ACKNOWLEDGMENTS   *ix*

INTRODUCTION   *xv*

1 Charles McKim, William Mead, and Stanford White   *1*

2 Frank Lloyd Wright   *17*

3 Le Corbusier   *31*

4 The Bauhaus   *45*

5 Ernst May and Margarete Schütte-Lihotzky   *59*

6 Oscar Niemeyer   *77*

7 Edward Durell Stone   *93*

8 Eero Saarinen   *105*

9 R. Buckminster Fuller   *121*

10 Carlo Scarpa   *133*

11 James Stirling   *147*

12 Renzo Piano   *161*

13 Rem Koolhaas   *177*

14 Bernard Tschumi   *195*

15 Tod Williams and Billie Tsien   *211*

16 Kazuyo Sejima and Ryue Nishizawa   *225*

17 Elizabeth Diller, Ricardo Scofidio, and Charles Renfro   *237*

18 Snøhetta   *251*

19 Michael Arad   *265*

ILLUSTRATION CREDITS   *277*

INDEX   *279*

ILLUSTRATIONS FOLLOW PAGE *120*

Acknowledgments

ALMOST ALL THE contents of this book originally appeared, in somewhat different forms, in *The New York Review of Books* between 2008 and 2013 and were edited by Robert Silvers, with the help of the *Review*'s remarkable editorial staff, whom I have consistently found to be unparalleled in their intelligence, diligence, and commitment— without question the finest group of professionals I have worked with during my four-decade publishing career. The one exception to my *Review* pieces is the chapter on Carlo Scarpa, which was first published in 1999 in *The New Republic* and was edited there by its longtime literary editor, Leon Wieseltier, who has my sincere appreciation.

For a wide variety of assistance, from helping me to gain access to buildings to generously sharing their ideas and research with me, I wish to thank John Anderson, Grant Bannatyne, Tim Benton, Barry Bergdoll, Francesca Bianchi, Sissel Breie, Ingrid Moe, and Aslaug Nygård of the Royal Norwegian Consulate General in New York; Larry Busbea, Jean-Louis Cohen, Joshua David, Gabrielle Esperdy, Octavia Giovannini-Torelli, Christopher Gray, Robert Hammond, Robert A. Heintges, Donald Hoffmann, Margot Jacqz, Bill N. Lacy, Rose-Carol Washton Long, Caroline Maniaque-Benton, Mary McLeod, Marco De Michelis, Stanislas von Moos, Guy Nordenson,

Süha Özkan, Peter Palumbo, Styliane Philippou, Leland M. Roth, Suzanne Stephens, Marco Venturi, Leslie Waddington, Elizabeth White, and Samuel G. White.

I am also indebted to the architects, critics, historians, and scholars whose works I quote in these pages, including Colin Amery, Rosemarie Haag Bletter, Adrian Ellis, Thomas Flierl, Mark Girouard, Jonathan Glancey, Robert Hammond, Susan R. Henderson, the late Ada Louise Huxtable, Charles Jencks, Richard Lacayo, George Packer, Bruce Brooks Pfeiffer, George Ranalli, Vincent Scully, Jorge Silvetti, Philipp Sturm, Dave Taylor, Robert Venturi, Nicholas Fox Weber, and Lynn Zelevansky.

I am tremendously grateful for the support of Angela Hederman of New York Review Books, who encouraged this second volume of my collected writings on architecture. She and her husband, Rea Hederman, the publisher of *The New York Review*, rank among the most admirable contemporary guardians of literary culture. The Hederman family's scrupulous and high-minded stewardship of the *Review* since they acquired it in 1984 has been a decisive factor in guiding the paper so successfully and uncompromisingly through a phase of profound difficulty and change for print publications.

To my great pleasure, New York Review Books was able to reassemble the same creative team that produced the first volume of *Makers of Modern Architecture* in 2007. Once again, Michael Shae, the editor of New York Review Collections, not only supervised this book but was also instrumental, in his parallel role as a senior editor at the *Review*, in preparing all but one of these essays for publication in their initial form. Michael has proven to be an ideal arbiter and collaborator, displaying the same consummate skill, equanimity, tact, and attentiveness that I experienced working with him the first time around.

Louise Fili has created a superb pendant to her elegant dust-jacket design for volume one of *Makers*, and Bordon Elniff's internal typographic scheme again impresses me as classic. Alaina Taylor has reprised her job as a responsive and resourceful photo researcher, equal to any I have worked with at major commercial publications. Duane Michals, an esteemed artist whose portraits of me and my family have marked the most important occasions in our lives over the past thirty-five years, has once again honored me by taking my author's photograph, an act of friendship, generosity, and continuity that touches me immensely.

Several of the chapters in this book have been augmented by material that originally appeared in the *NYRblog*, an online publication that began in 2009 and is edited by Hugh Eakin, a senior editor of the *Review*. With the same high standards of intellectual rigor that inform the paper's print edition, Hugh has made the blog an incisive and timely vehicle for topical commentary and thus has significantly extended the paper's reach to a new generation of followers. Matthew Howard, the *Review*'s director of electronic publishing, has been of enormous help in bringing my writing to that wider audience.

It is perhaps not customary for writers to thank the doctors who attend them, but in this case I consider it obligatory to mention the two men who have quite directly enabled me to complete this book. During the winter of 2009–2010, when in close succession I suffered a pulmonary embolism and a ruptured heart valve, my life was saved because of the combined efforts of my primary-care physician, the gifted and compassionate cardiologist Timothy C. Dutta, M.D., and the great cardiothoracic surgeon Leonard N. Girardi, M.D., of New York Presbyterian Weill-Cornell Medical Center in Manhattan. Together they restored me to health, my family, and my work, and have made me aware on a daily basis of John Ruskin's irrefutable admonition that "there is no wealth but life."

By my side not only throughout that ordeal but at every step along the way during the past thirty-five years has been my wife, mainstay, and inspiration, Rosemarie Haag Bletter, the love of my life. By far the soundest judge of architecture I have ever met, as well as a distinguished scholar and historian of the Modern Movement with few equals, Rosemarie has been the single most important influence on my thinking since we first met at Columbia nearly forty-five years ago. I flatter myself to think that what I have learned from her, and continue to learn from her every single day, is evident here, most obviously in my chapters on the Bauhaus and on Ernst May and Margarete Schütte-Lihotzky, which are among her areas of particular expertise. Because I was eager to have "Grete Lihotzky: Der Kompagnon von May & Co."—a 1920s satirical poem written most likely by the architect's husband, Wilhelm Schütte (see pages 68–71)— available in English, I am especially thankful to Rosemarie, my first and most valued reader, for her translation from the German of this delightful and evocative verse.

This book is dedicated to Robert Silvers, who first asked me to write for *The New York Review* in 1985 and thereby not only opened the most important chapter of my career but also, I believe, thoroughly transformed the quality of my work. As has long been noted by the many writers who have benefited from his encyclopedic knowledge in multiple disciplines, Bob's mastery of technique and diction, his impeccable taste, his keen insights into the psychology of creative motivation, his social acuity, and his unfailingly sound judgment make him the foremost literary editor of our time. His half-century of heroic public service at the *Review* has established and maintained it as the international paragon of what an intellectually, politically, socially, culturally, and morally engaged paper can be.

When I first came to New York as a Columbia freshman, in September 1966, the issue of *The New York Review* then on the newsstands included, among other offerings, a new poem by W. H. Auden, a review of Bernard Malamud's *The Fixer* by V. S. Pritchett, and a civil-rights manifesto by Stokely Carmichael titled "What We Want." This was an intoxicating mix for a teenager with one eye on the Columbia College Contemporary Civilization syllabus and another on current events. I soon noticed that the brightest of my classmates invariably had in their rooms this intriguing-looking paper, its front page emblazoned with chunky serif type (Clarendon Bold, I later discovered) like some hip Wild West wanted poster, a robust font so different from the anemic sans serif Helvetica then in vogue. Very shortly I became a devoted reader of the *Review* myself, thrilled by its early and courageously outspoken stance against the war in Vietnam, its wickedly incisive David Levine cartoons—Daumier on the hoof—and its essays by Morningside Heights neighbors, including Hannah Arendt, F.W. Dupee, and Susan Sontag, who were objects of intense fascination among my small circle of friends. Above all, the *Review* gave a biweekly demonstration of how clear, superlative writing and spirited, persuasive argument could shape the thinking of one's contemporaries and set the agenda for our more serious discussions, even amid the social unrest, political upheaval, and countercultural distractions that swirled around us.

What I never could have imagined at the time was that within two decades I would find my own work welcomed in the *Review*'s pages, and still less that upon this, the paper's golden anniversary, I would have been a contributor for more than half of its existence. This long run I owe entirely to Bob. I feel that he has consistently brought out the best in me, and though he might demur that this is no more than any good editor's job, the awe-inspiring evidence provided by the 1,049 issues he has presided over during the *Review*'s first half-century—which by any measure comprises the most formidable concentration of literary talent in our time—makes his achievement all the more prodigious and historic. Having worked for several of the supposedly legendary figures in modern American publishing, I can attest that Bob is the only one among them who deserves that much-overused designation. As an architecture critic, I have been particularly heartened by his conviction that my subject is worthy to be included in the *Review* among the other matters of high public concern that the paper regularly addresses.

The fifty-year voyage of Robert Silvers at the helm of *The New York Review of Books* has been the embodiment of a ceaseless personal quest—the upholding of excellence, the pursuit of justice, and the enlightenment of minds. To be a fellow sailor on this great journey has been the glory of my professional life, and I salute Bob with the same optimistic and ever-encouraging words he customarily uses to sign off on the editing process with his grateful writers: "And on we go!"

Martin Filler
Southampton, New York
February 1, 2013

Introduction

LIKE THE FIRST volume of *Makers of Modern Architecture* (2007), this sequel is not intended to be a thoroughgoing history of the building art since the beginnings of the Modern Movement, but rather a series of interpretive studies of some leading architectural personalities from around the turn of the last century to the present day. Three figures addressed in the first volume are revisited in these pages: Frank Lloyd Wright and Le Corbusier, whose personal histories I here discuss in greater detail than in my earlier, more general overviews. Those two masters share an unchallenged position atop the critical hierarchy, and their status seems even more justified with the passage of time and the support of seemingly inexhaustible new scholarship. Conversely, among present-day architects Renzo Piano continues to be a prolific yet puzzling designer whose uneven but sporadically superlative output illuminates the crucial role that sympathetic patronage plays in the outcome of a commission, a factor that affects all architects though seldom as clearly as in his case.

The pieces on which the following chapters are based were all initially suggested by some topical occasion, including anniversaries, awards, newly completed buildings, exhibitions, publications, deaths, or some combination thereof. These events in turn prompted a variety of responses from me: reconsideration of widely renowned architects whom I thought merited more accurate historical judgment (Stanford White, the Bauhaus group), reassessment of once-celebrated figures subsequently much less well regarded (Edward Durell Stone, James Stirling), reestimation of canonical reputations rarely called into question (R. Buckminster Fuller, Eero Saarinen), recognition of unjustly neglected masters (Margarete Schütte-Lihotzky, Carlo Scarpa), and evaluation of present-day practitioners with enough completed work to establish their relative standing (Rem Koolhaas, Bernard Tschumi).

If there is one recurrent theme that unites all these essays it is the central role that character and personality play in the creation of architecture, not altogether surprising given that this is the most public of art forms and thus inevitably indicative of the social values of its sponsors. The ways in which designers conceive, rationalize, develop, explain, execute, and promote their works are as varied as the commissions they receive, but their goal is always the same: to persuade others to have faith in their sometimes improbable visions and their ability to bring them to fruition. Even for the greatest master builders, the pursuit of their art is a never-ending series of confrontations and challenges, accommodations and compromises, imposed by the needs (or desires) of clients, financial limitations, legal requirements, and countless other factors that constrain architects to a greater extent than their counterparts in other artistic mediums. Added to those impediments, the larger, inexorable forces of politics and economics always have an enormous effect on the profession, whether or not its exponents are politically engaged (although designers who work in the public sphere should always expect that their efforts will have direct social implications and, on occasion, unpleasant repercussions).

The greatest architectural disjunction of the twentieth century was caused by the rise of Hitler, a failed painter and architectural aspirant whose hatred of Modernism in all mediums brought an abrupt end to Germany's primacy as an incubator for artistic innovation. Hitler's maniacal anti-Semitism of course most immediately affected the numerous Jewish designers and clients who were in the forefront of the new architecture. But the repressive culture of Nazism affected non-Jews as well. Among the foremost exponents of the new architecture and urbanism whose careers were destroyed, derailed, displaced, or at the very least long delayed by the Dozen-Year Reich were two gentiles: Ernst May, impresario of Frankfurt's phenomenal social-housing campaign of the 1920s and early 1930s, and one of his chief collaborators, the Viennese architect Margarete Schütte-Lihotzky.

Even before Hitler took power, the global economic depression prompted May, Schütte-Lihotzky, and many other Modernists to work for the Soviet government, one of the world's few large-scale architecture patrons during Stalin's initial Five-Year Plan of 1928–1932. This association alone disqualified the leftist May and the Communist Schütte-Lihotzky from work under the Nazis, yet they fared little better with the Soviets. Members of the "May Brigade" who stayed on in the USSR after their boss left in 1933 in some cases faced imprisonment, and their Russian colleagues were executed. May, who was publicly denounced by the Nazi propaganda minister, first found refuge in British-controlled Kenya, but during the Mau Mau uprising of the early 1950s returned to Germany where he finally resumed his role as a city planner during his homeland's massive postwar reconstruction. On the other hand, Schütte-Lihotzky, who joined the anti-Nazi resistance following the *Anschluss*, found it difficult to find work in Austria after the war because of her continued allegiance to communism in nominally neutral Austria.

Recent research has also shed a harsher light on the attitudes and activities during World War II of the Swiss-French architect Le Corbusier, who turns out to have been more avid and successful in trying to gain work from France's Nazi-puppet Vichy government than had been previously known. On the other hand, Le Corbusier's younger Brazilian contemporary and admirer Oscar Niemeyer saw his professional prospects in the United States effectively wrecked by his membership in the Communist Party, which he joined in 1945, just in time for the advent of McCarthyism and the denial of American entry visas to artists with leftist affiliations or even sympathies.

Economic shifts and downturns can displace architects just as surely as putsches, coups, revolutions, and rebellions. In fulfillment of Daniel Burnham's irrefutable exhortation "first, get the job"—rule number one in an artistic medium that demands a patron before the creative act can begin in earnest—architects have always had to go where the work is. Gian Lorenzo Bernini's arduous 1665 transalpine carriage journey from Rome to Paris was prompted by the prospect of expanding the Palais du Louvre for Louis XIV, which, despite the ample papal patronage this artistic polymath enjoyed back home, seemed to be an offer he could not refuse. Arguably the first international architectural celebrity, Bernini was greeted along the way by crowds that sporadically lined his route. But his flamboyantly Baroque project was ultimately rejected—Claude Perrault's more reserved Classical design would be executed instead—and this futile experience proved that even the greatest architects are not immune from the humiliations of the supplicant artist.

Closer to our own time, during the recession and "stagflation" of the early 1970s, out-of-work American architects flocked to Iran, where the shah sponsored vast public works schemes that came to an abrupt halt with his overthrow at the end of that decade. Similarly, the global economic meltdown of 2008, which initially left China relatively unscathed, sent countless American architects in search of the lucrative commissions that have abounded in Beijing and the ninety other Chinese cities (many of them whose names are unknown to foreigners) with populations over a million.

The first volume of *Makers of Modern Architecture* was faulted by some commentators for the relatively few women it contains— Ray Eames and Denise Scott Brown are the only female subjects among the book's seventeen chapters. This second selection will likely elicit a similar response, there being but four women discussed here in detail: Schütte-Lihotzky, Billie Tsien, Kazuyo Sejima, and Elizabeth Diller.

The only possible justification for this imbalance is that in any general study of the building art, women are still bound to be in a minority, given that female enrollment in architecture schools did not begin to approach parity with men until at least the 1970s, and only now are women practitioners receiving major commissions in any significant numbers. One review of the Spanish-language edition of *Makers of Modern Architecture* was titled "Los machos alfa de la arquitectura del siglo XX" (The Alpha Machos of Twentieth-Century Architecture), a fairly accurate characterization of the male-dominated profession in that period.

The marginalized role of women even at the Bauhaus, which was otherwise among the most forward-thinking, not to say radical, of twentieth-century educational institutions, gives some indication of the ingrained prejudices that had to be overcome, and still do. The three aforementioned female architects currently at work all have a male partner or partners (in two instances their husbands), a pattern established in earlier generations by Charles and Ray Eames, Alison and Peter Smithson, and Denise Scott Brown and Robert Venturi. That tendency has been continued more recently by such distinguished American spousal teams as Craig Hodgetts and Hsin Ming Fung, Diana Agrest and Mario Gandelsonas, Laurie Hawkinson and Henry Smith-Miller, and Marion Weiss and Michael Manfredi. In other pairings, Richard Fernau and Laura Hartman, professional partners since 1980, were once romantically involved but have long been married to others, whereas Thomas Hanrahan and Victoria Myers continue to practice together after their divorce. Deborah Berke, Winka Dubbeldam, Jeanne Gang, Zaha Hadid, Maya Lin, and Toshiko Mori are among the most notable high-style practitioners who head offices without a principal male partner.

The burgeoning presence of women in the highest echelons of architecture has hardly been the biggest change in the profession in recent decades, however. Certainly computer technology has had the greatest impact on the conception, planning, and execution of buildings since the adaptation of new industrial methods of construction during the first half of the nineteenth century. Digital techniques for drafting and rendering designs now allow for prospective depictions of projects as lifelike as photographs of completed buildings. Yet this seems a mere sleight of hand compared to the astounding new engineering and fabrication capabilities opened by unprecedented advances in architecturally applicable software. As had often occurred during earlier periods of technological breakthrough, there were fears that computers would somehow fundamentally alter, not to say pervert, the very nature of the creative act, rather than becoming just another tool in the arsenal of human artistry. Without question, the new architectural possibilities enabled by computerization have had an immense effect on the look of contemporary design, but as with all comparably epochal advances before it—printing, photography, and telecommunications, to name but a few—what emerges is only equal to the intelligence and imagination of those whose master them.

Another signal phenomenon of our times has been the cult of the celebrity architect. To be sure, more than a century ago the scandalous private lives of Stanford White and Frank Lloyd Wright—two showboating public personages who thrived on popular attention—provided ample fodder for the sensationalist press. For his sins White was gunned down at the age of fifty-two; Wright died (of natural causes) a few months shy of ninety-two, and used those four extra decades of life to transform his image from that of cheating husband, deadbeat dad, and outspoken advocate of free love by morphing into a benign dispenser of heartland American verities, a veritable Carl Sandburg of architecture. Wright's instinctive mastery of new forms of mass publicity—from newspaper interviews in the 1910s, to newsreel bits in the 1930s, to television talk- and game-show appearances in the 1950s—obliterated popular recall of his lurid past and helped burnish his image as a beloved national cultural treasure quite apart from his stupendous body of work.

There is no question that public recognition has always helped architects to win further clients, and increasingly so since the celebrity industry has metastasized in its variety and reach. However, not until the 1980s did the international celebrity architect fully emerge. This phenomenon paralleled the contemporaneous rise of the "name" fashion designer, promoted by luxury-goods conglomerates to spur sales of scent, accessories, and other ancillary items bearing the names of couturiers whose bespoke garments were far beyond the means of average people. Even though Wright, with his budget-priced Usonian houses of 1936 onward (and his earlier, wholly unsuccessful attempts at prefabrication), tried to bring his revolutionary concepts to a wider public than his costly one-off commissions, by the late twentieth century an architect-built house could be afforded by only a small economic elite. Thus the retailing of all sorts of architect-designed household goods allowed those priced out of the custom residential market to participate in the aura of high-style architecture with an Alessi teakettle by Michael Graves or a Swid Powell coffee mug by Robert Venturi.

Architect-endorsed "branding" soon extended from useful or decorative objects to buildings themselves, especially luxury developments in large urban centers where apartment buildings, hotels, and boutiques have lately been marketed as much for the designer's imprimatur as for any intrinsic aesthetic quality. Yet very few of the many high-style architects who built condominiums in New York City before the global market crash in 2008 rethought the basics of the high-density multiunit dwelling. Instead, they concentrated on clever surface effects that would set their efforts apart from the competition's. This sort of superficial decoration was little different from that pursued by Philip Johnson during his corporate skyscraper phase of the 1980s, when he freely admitted that in working with property developers who presented him with a predetermined high-rise building envelope calibrated to maximize profits, there was little he could do beyond gussying up the curtain walls in one eye-catching mode or another.

Celebrity architects also became more familiar to the general public through such rare events as the televised presentation in 2002 of the semifinalists' designs in the competition for the reconstruction of the World Trade Center site. On a more regular basis, *The Charlie Rose Show*, which was first broadcast by PBS in 1991, has offered an upper-middlebrow forum in which scores of high-profile master builders have attempted to elucidate their work to an informed general audience. Whether these designers succeeded in demystifying their creative process for laymen remains debatable. Given the strong emphasis that avant-garde practitioners have placed on theoretical concerns during the past several decades, the more pretentious among them often add to the obfuscation. Apart from a few indefatigable press-friendly performers like Wright and Fuller, the predominant twentieth-century notion of the architect was that of an aloof, hyper-rational engineer rather than that of an approachable, intuitive artist.

Before the professionalization of architecture in the nineteenth century, it was standard procedure for an aspiring mason or carpenter to begin his apprenticeship at fourteen and to become a master builder by his early twenties. But with today's protracted educational adolescence and a much longer life expectancy, architects now finish schooling in their mid- to late twenties, work for an established firm during their thirties, and then, if sufficiently talented, embark on independent practice at around forty.

Designing a house for one's parents is an almost cliché rite of passage—Le Corbusier and Robert Venturi are prime twentieth-century examples of helpful familial patronage—followed by more residential work and nondomestic renovations or additions. Only after two decades of sustained experience do big jobs generally start to arrive, although by the age of fifty typecasting also sets in. If one is fortunate enough to bring off several well-received projects, a Pritzker Prize might come during one's sixties, depending on that coveted award's shifting and often inscrutable notions of artistic excellence and geopolitical distribution. Winning the Pritzker assures a flood of work in one's seventies and eighties, commissions necessarily carried out by assistants as the demands of modern-day cultural stardom and the inevitable waning of physical capacities prevent many architects from attaining the transcendent final phase more easily achieved by artists in other mediums. Architecture is not a profession for the fainthearted, the weak-willed, or the short-lived.

The self-identification of architects as artists, which began to reassert itself in the architectural avant-garde around the mid-1970s, was intensified by the increase in the numbers of what would become the most conspicuous public building category of the late twentieth century, the art museum, which was superseded around the turn of the millennium by a comparable increase in the construction of performing arts halls. To win commissions in either format, architects found it to their advantage to posit themselves as artists, and in many cases have validated that comparison, as demonstrated most notably by Frank Gehry, of whose Guggenheim Museum Bilbao it has been said (as had earlier been claimed of Wright's original Guggenheim) that the building itself is the institution's greatest work of art, and whose Walt Disney Concert Hall in Los Angeles might be said to be a composition equal to some of the greatest of those played within its billowing walls.

Writing in the very first issue of *The New York Review of Books* in 1963, Robert Lowell wisely observed, "The arts do not progress but move along by surges and sags." This is particularly true of architecture. Although today it is more than ever a highly collaborative process, it is still driven forward by the vision of relatively few practitioners—some well-known to the public, others familiar only to specialists—whose work is closely watched by their peers and thus has a disproportionate effect on the direction of the discipline. All the same, my emphasis on personality and character ought not to be misinterpreted as an endorsement of a Great Man (or Great Woman) Theory of architecture. Rather, it reflects my belief that the human element, both individual and collective, in the creation and the habitation of the built environment is central to any understanding of the universal impulse we all share: to make ourselves a sheltering home on earth.

I

CHARLES McKIM, WILLIAM MEAD, AND STANFORD WHITE

IT MAY SEEM odd to begin a book about modern architecture with a firm now generally considered to be historical revivalists, but a strong case can be made that McKim, Mead & White was a proto-modern partnership not only in its corporate organization but also in its audacious address of new building forms engendered by the machine age. Changing attitudes toward historically inspired architecture, and Classicism in particular, have led to reassessments of buildings that were long dismissed by proponents of the Modern Movement as retrogressive but that now are widely regarded as advanced despite their outwardly traditional appearance. There is no better example of this reversal of posthumous fortune than New York City's Pennsylvania Station of 1905–1910 (see Illustration 1b), still keenly mourned as the lost masterpiece of Charles Follen McKim, one of the triumvirate—along with William Rutherford Mead and Stanford White—who gave their surnames to the most prolific and celebrated high-style American architectural practice during the half-century between the Civil War and World War I.

It had long been commonplace to emphasize McKim, Mead & White's dependence on Old World prototypes. For example, White based his Renaissance Revival New York Herald Building of 1890–1895, which fronted Herald Square, on Fra Giovanni Giocondo's Palazzo del Consiglio of 1476–1492 in Verona, and he modeled the Mozarabic tower of his Madison Square Garden of 1887–1891 (once the third-tallest structure in the city, after the Brooklyn Bridge and the Statue of Liberty) on the Giralda of 1184–1198 in Seville. Similarly, McKim's Beaux Arts–inspired Boston Public Library of 1888–1892 owes an obvious debt to Henri Labrouste's Bibliothèque Sainte-Geneviève of 1843–1851 in Paris, whereas his Pennsylvania Station followed a conjectural reconstruction of Imperial Rome's Baths of Caracalla of 212–216 AD.

Though McKim, Mead & White's historical eclecticism almost never attains the quality of its sources, and on occasion appears little more than a skillfully executed precursor of the touristic landmarks we now see replicated at Las Vegas theme hotels, the best of the firm's work, however derivative in outward expression, on occasion comes close to that of the foremost American master builder of the generation before it: H. H. Richardson, in whose employ McKim and White first met. Yet despite McKim, Mead & White's current critical esteem—considerably higher than it was half a century ago—in order to find the true muscle and sinew of advanced American architecture during the heyday of this arch-establishment partnership we must look instead to the mystically inclined but commercially aware Louis Sullivan, spiritual father of the tall office building, and to his spiritual son, Frank Lloyd Wright, the apostle of organic design derived from the native soil. Their heroic quest for an authentically American architecture set them in diametric opposition to what they saw as the deadening hand of Classicism, so powerfully wielded by McKim, Mead & White (however much Sullivan and Wright may have absorbed and subsumed historical models themselves).

The American public was rudely reawakened to the significance of

McKim, Mead & White by the demolition of Pennsylvania Station, which began in October 1963 but took nearly three years to accomplish because of the huge building's extraordinarily solid and deep construction. By the time the vast site was cleared and ready to receive the crowning indignity of Charles Luckman's ticky-tacky Madison Square Garden, completed in 1968, the historic-preservation movement had gathered to prevent comparable acts of cultural vandalism. New York's only other equivalent landmark, Grand Central Terminal of 1904–1913 (a collaboration between the firms of Reed & Stem and Warren & Wetmore), was spared a similar fate when opponents derailed a disastrous redevelopment scheme by Marcel Breuer for its site during the 1970s thanks to the shameful precedent of Penn Station (though the creation of the New York City Landmarks Preservation Commission in 1965 was too late to stop the vast, ugly Pan Am Building from going up next to the terminal).

McKim's design marked a significant departure from earlier railway depots because it was built to accommodate the newly electrified trains of the Pennsylvania Railroad, which freed him from the standard arrangement of a train shed attached to a shelter for ticket sales and passenger waiting areas, all at street level or only somewhat recessed (as was the case at the steam-driven New York Central Railroad's Grand Central Terminal). Electrified trains emit no noxious fumes, so they could run through tunnels rather than on viaducts or in open trenches and thus remain deep underground once they reached their destinations, which enabled McKim to submerge components that previously needed to be above ground.

The new possibilities provided by electrification afforded McKim the freedom to make his ground plan for Pennsylvania Station a marvel of modern efficiency. In choosing the Baths of Caracalla as his model for its exterior, the architect found an ideal scheme that allowed him to encompass the entire eight-acre site—which covered two full city blocks from West 33rd to 31st Streets and from Seventh to Eighth Avenues—in one immense but cohesive whole, united by a colossal order of granite columns that formed a monumental colonnade on its principal façade along Seventh Avenue and concealed a porte-cochere driveway that ran along its north flank on 33rd Street. This ingenious arrival sequence, which protected travelers from the elements in all seasons, was arranged so that luggage could be conveniently unloaded first and then moved to baggage cars via mechanical conveyors, before passengers were driven on to a final stop situated as close as possible to the departure gates, located below street level.

Although Penn Station's stupendously grand waiting room was decked out with all the elaborate masonry detailing of the Classical copybook, the concourse—where travelers descended to the train platforms on the level beneath it—dispensed with stone cladding and left the building's steel supports exposed. With its barrel-vaulted glass-paned ceiling and machine aesthetic, the concourse resembled Joseph Paxton and Charles Fox's Crystal Palace of 1850–1851 in London; with its strong vertical development and interplay of light and shadow it also brought to mind Giovanni Battista Piranesi's *Carceri d'invenzione* of 1745–1751, etchings of imaginary prisons in which the Venetian architect and printmaker concocted vertiginous multilayered networks of mysteriously interconnected spaces. (Rare film footage of Penn Station's concourse and porte cochere can be found in the early talkie *Applause* (1929) directed by Rouben Mamoulian.)

McKim's unexpectedly harmonious synthesis of two divergent and supposedly irreconcilable architectural approaches, the Classical and the industrial—a melding earlier perfected by Labrouste—would have been a most instructive object lesson during the architectural style wars that were to rage during the two decades following the scandalous sack of McKim's marvel. No one saw the dire implications of that insane decision more clearly than an anonymous editorial writer in *The New York Times*, who sounded, at least, like Ada Louise Huxtable, that infallible Cassandra of urbanism:

> Any city gets what it admires, will pay for, and, ultimately, deserves. Even when we had Penn Station, we couldn't afford to keep it clean. We want and deserve tin-can architecture in a tinhorn culture. And we will probably be judged not by the monuments we build but by those we have destroyed.

McKim, Mead, and White began working together in New York City in 1879 when White, now the best remembered of the partners, joined forces with his two older colleagues. Although Mead has sometimes been unfairly characterized as a glorified office manager, or at best a mediator between his two antithetical if extravagantly gifted associates, there is no question that the magnetic (and occasionally mutually repellent) poles of the consortium were McKim and White. This can be neatly summarized by juxtaposing a pair of contemporaneous, functionally identical, but tellingly different New York City schemes that exemplify the two architects' respective qualities: McKim's Low Memorial Library of 1895–1898 at his new campus for Columbia University in Manhattan's Morningside Heights, and White's Gould Memorial Library of 1897–1902 at his University Heights branch of New York University in the Bronx (which became Bronx Community College when NYU gave up the property in 1973). Each building serves as the focal point for its academic ensemble, is compact in ground plan, and has a shallow centralized dome and a columned entry portico of Roman derivation, but there the similarities end.

The Columbia library is massive, stolid, sober, devoid of ornamental frippery, and though a bit dull conveys an aura of gravitas thoroughly suited to high-minded intellectual pursuits. On the other hand, White's uptown NYU library is characteristically lighter in volume and enlivened by sprightly detailing, which suggests that a little learning can be a delightful thing. Like Richardson, McKim studied at the École des Beaux-Arts in Paris and possessed an innately more decorous temperament than White, who had almost no formal training but was such a natural-born designer and quick study that his lack of education would have been betrayed to only the most pedantic of Classical scholars. Instead, it was the far more important differences in personal character between McKim and White that held the seeds of destruction for this architectural dream team.

McKim, Mead, and White made their reputations, at first individually and then in concert, during the 1870s and 1880s with a remarkable series of large wood-frame vacation houses (see Illustration 1a) in fashionable resort communities along the Atlantic seaboard, including Elberon, New Jersey; Newport, Rhode Island; Lenox, Massachusetts; Tuxedo Park, New York; and the East End of Long Island, where from 1880 to 1883 White designed the Montauk Association—a group of seven capacious "cottages" nicknamed the Seven Sisters, along with a communal recreation building—on a bluff near the tip of the South Fork, a property laid out by Frederick Law Olmsted, landscape architect of New York's Central Park of 1857–1873.

The novel domestic format devised by the collaborators stemmed less from American precedents than from vernacular traditions in Normandy and the residential work of their older British contemporary Richard Norman Shaw, who in turn harked back to English rural forms with rambling, irregularly angled, multigabled compositions that seemed to be the accretions of many years, if not several centuries. But whereas Shaw clad his houses in half-timber or slate tiles, McKim, Mead & White used natural-colored wood shingles, a vernacular American material, which it deployed in varied interlocking textures that the architectural historian Henry-Russell Hitchcock vividly likened to birds' plumage.

The architectural historian Vincent Scully dubbed this format the Shingle Style, and in his classic study *The Shingle Style and the Stick Style: Architectural Theory and Design from Richardson to the Origins of Wright* (1955) rescued these seminal works from decades of critical oblivion and accorded them a central place in the American canon. To the untutored eye these houses—with their deep wraparound porches (or "piazzas" in the contemporary parlance), overhanging eaves, cylindrical turrets topped by conical "candlesnuffer" roofs, multiple massive chimneys, and profusion of gables and dormers—may seem indistinguishable from countless other residences of the well-to-do in every good-size town in the United States, an indication of how pervasive this format became in the decades between the American Independence Centennial and World War I.

But as Scully and Hitchcock both stressed, McKim, Mead & White's major innovation was a radical spatial reconception of the domestic interior, which gave their houses a breathtaking expansiveness quite the opposite of typically compartmentalized Victorian residences, in which every room was a veritable world unto itself. Scully, in one of his most rapturous passages, gives an even more specifically Jamesian explanation of why this kind of private exurban refuge met with such an enthusiastic reception among a sensitive segment of America's moneyed class after the Civil War:

> Civilized withdrawal from a brutalized society encouraged interminable summer vacations (the real decadence of New England here?) to Nantucket, Martha's Vineyard, and the coasts of Massachusetts and Maine, where the old houses weathered silver, floating like dreams of forever in the cool fogs off the sea.

This sense of genteel social retirement and grand self-sufficiency was most apparent in the spacious living halls the firm designed for a number of their Shingle Style schemes. As with the multifunctional ground-floor reception and sitting areas that became popular in mid-nineteenth-century Britain, McKim, Mead & White's adaptations were focused around a vast hearth (often with an adjacent seating alcove, or inglenook) that infused visitors' first impression with a welcoming warmth both figurative and literal. Though usually paneled in dark wood, the typical McKim, Mead & White living hall was well illuminated through broad expanses of multipaned windows, often on two sides of the room, which in many cases gave onto the firm's signature enveloping verandas.

But there was also a distinctly East Asian feeling, which, as Hitchcock noted, went well beyond the superficial application of Japanesque decorative motifs that became a widespread craze during the zenith of the Aesthetic Movement in the 1880s:

> The main rectangular space, of which the shape is emphasized by the ceiling beams and by the abstract geometrical pattern of the floor, seems to flow out in various directions into other rooms and into several bays and nooks; but the actual room-space is sharply defined by a continuous frieze-like member that becomes an open wooden grille above the various openings. There can be little question that the major influence here is from the Japanese interior, but the Japanese interior understood as architecture.

Credit for introducing this continuous flow of space to America is most often given to Wright, whose interest in classical Japanese architecture is well known. But McKim, Mead & White was executing these sweeping proto-modern interiors two decades before Wright went even further with that openness in his celebrated Prairie Houses of 1901 onward, with Le Corbusier and Ludwig Mies van der Rohe taking the concept to its logical culmination in their *plan libre* houses of the 1920s.

McKim, Mead & White's output was enormous, more than a thousand buildings all told, with some three hundred in New York City alone. Among the latter were the Columbia and uptown NYU campuses; the Century, Colony, Freundschaft, Harvard, Metropolitan, Players, and University clubs; high-end commercial work for such luxury-goods purveyors as Tiffany and Gorham; several banks; town houses for magnates—the Whitneys and Pulitzers—as well as fellow artists, including Louis Comfort Tiffany and Charles Dana Gibson, in addition to nearby country retreats for the plutocratic Astor, Mackay, and Oelrichs families.

Although Stanford White remains among the very few architects whose name is widely recognized among laymen in this country, his urban designs were demonstrably lightweight in comparison to McKim's. White is perhaps most accurately seen as the John Nash of American urbanism, a facile and pleasure-giving *metteur en scène* of enchanting set pieces that catch the eye but rarely provide much intellectual substance, as was also the case with the equally well-connected English architect who put his mark on Regency London as indelibly as White did on New York at the height of the Gilded Age, but who also often seems more an ingenious urban stage designer than a shaper of modern civic life.

All the same, there is no doubt that apparently without exception White's clients adored what he gave them, as indicated by one instance in which his work proved more mobile than is usual in the static art of architecture. During an 1878 study trip through France with McKim, White photographed the triple-arched portico of St.-Gilles-du-Gard, a Romanesque abbey church of circa 1125–1150 in

Provence, which he deemed the finest work of European architecture. This landmark served as his model for a portal he appended in 1900–1903 to St. Bartholomew's Church, a Lombardic-Romanesque pastiche of 1870–1872 by James Renwick Jr. (the eclectic revivalist best known for New York's Neo-Gothic St. Patrick's Cathedral and Washington's castellated Smithsonian Institution). St. Bart's parishioners grew so fond of White's limestone frontispiece that when they abandoned Renwick's building in favor of Bertram Goodhue's Byzantine Revival sanctuary of 1917–1930 on Park Avenue, they took the narthex along with them and had it incorporated into the congregation's new home. The resulting palimpsest still imparts an incongruous whiff of hybrid exoticism to an otherwise dreary corporate stretch of midtown Manhattan.

McKim's characteristic perfectionism (which contrasted with White's sometimes slapdash solutions) would never be indulged more fully than by J. Pierpont Morgan, who commissioned him to build the New York private library and gallery of 1903–1906 that in 2010 emerged, more magnificent than ever, from an exemplary interior restoration by Beyer Blinder Belle. To some extent this respectful refurbishment compensated for the affront imposed by Renzo Piano's unfortunate Morgan Library and Museum addition of 2000–2006, the most objectionable aspect of which was its repositioning of the beloved institution's main entrance from East 36th Street to a new and corporate-looking façade on Madison Avenue, a shift that reduced McKim's regal vestibule—one of the finest entry spaces in the United States—to a vestigial backdoor appendage.

Morgan's commission to McKim yielded an exceptionally restrained single-story white marble Classical pavilion, its façade centered by a graceful Palladian archway. "I want a gem," Morgan told the architect, and he got one, though not before spending a small fortune on specifications of almost manic exactitude. During a visit to the Acropolis in Athens, McKim became fascinated by the ancient *anathyrosis* technique of assembling precision-ground blocks of masonry without mortar (a refinement the Incas later independently mastered and employed in rather less regular fashion for their famous walls at Cuzco). Climatic differences would not permit an exact duplication of the Greek method of mortarless assemblage, but McKim came very close by adding a thin layer of lead between the Morgan Library's marble blocks to compensate for expansion and contraction caused by New York's more extreme temperatures. This nicety, which Morgan instantly assented to, set him back an extra $50,000 (about $1.2 million in current value).

McKim is the closest America has ever come to having a national architect, and his imprint on the city of Washington is still palpable on both the urban and the domestic scale. He was a member of the Senate-appointed panel responsible for the so-called McMillan Plan of 1901 (named for the Michigan legislator who sponsored it), which sought to restore order to the capital's original 1791 design by the French-born civil engineer and architect Pierre-Charles L'Enfant. That grandiose Baroque layout, with radial principal boulevards superimposed on an overall grid of lesser streets, had been only sketchily realized when the federal government moved to Washington from Philadelphia in 1800.

Over the next century, L'Enfant's scheme was repeatedly compromised, no more so than with the imposition of an undulating Romantic landscape devised in 1851 by Andrew Jackson Downing to surround Renwick's Neo-Gothic Smithsonian of 1846–1855. This visual non sequitur encroached onto the broad greensward L'Enfant hoped would extend westward from the Capitol building to the Potomac. The far-reaching remedial proposals set forth under McKim's supervision, which were largely but not fully implemented, reasserted the French architect's intentions, especially in the creation of the

National Mall, the strong outlines and verdant integrity of which remain intact at the precinct now considered America's sacrosanct front yard.

McKim's strong hand in reshaping the nation's capital can be seen most frequently in television broadcasts from the White House, where the main floor of the Executive Mansion—especially the East Room, scene of many presidential press conferences and ceremonies; the Cross Hall, through which the president passes to face the cameras; and the State Dining Room, where foreign heads of state are entertained—were all redesigned by him as part of a thoroughgoing renovation ordered by Theodore Roosevelt in 1902. A century after James Hoban's President's House of 1792–1800 was first occupied, the Neoclassical character of the original structure had been sadly undermined. The exterior was overburdened by a chaotic jumble of greenhouses appended to the west side of the mansion (where the McKim-designed executive office wing now stands), and Victorian interior accretions were aptly likened to the gaudy, overstuffed decor of a Mississippi riverboat.

McKim stripped away these excesses, including Louis Comfort Tiffany's Aesthetic Movement stained-glass windscreen of 1882, which shielded the Cross Hall from the drafty lobby. But rather than going back to Hoban's delicate Neoclassical interior detailing (which McKim had carefully covered over but was ripped out in the gut reconstruction of 1948–1952 decreed by Harry Truman), the architect substituted a beefier Anglo-Classical aesthetic that at the time passed for the then-popular Colonial Revival style. Here is yet another example of the inevitable tendency of Classical revivals to reflect the moment of their creation, in this case the nascent imperial ambitions of America in the days of the Great White Fleet.

Only four years after the completion of this incomparably prestigious and much-admired project, McKim, Mead & White's glory years came to an abrupt and bloody end. White had always been the most assertively, even aggressively, "artistic" of the partners. He amassed objets d'art, antique furniture, and decorative bric-a-brac as compulsively as his younger contemporary William Randolph Hearst, though lacking a tycoon's resources the architect was forced into a sideline as a sub rosa dealer to defray the crushing debts he accrued. A social animal to the bone, White never let his family—conveniently rusticated at Box Hill, the idyllic Shingle Style house on Long Island he built and constantly remodeled for them between 1884 and 1906—interfere with his frenetic social life in the city, which he rationalized as a means of getting jobs from the nabobs of finance, transportation, and industry. Never has there been a more adept architectural networker than Stanny White, who moved with intuitive ease among the various subsets of New York's economic and social elite as he made friends and garnered commissions everywhere he went.

White also had a thing for underage girls, a predilection that he hardly concealed in the louche theatrical haunts that were no less a part of his strenuous nightly rounds than Manhattan's most exclusive men's clubs or expensive restaurants. His predatory habits may not have been much different from the tactics of other stage-door Johnnys, but the forty-eight-year-old lech met his nemesis in the ravishing but snakelike sixteen-year-old chorus girl Evelyn Nesbit, who was being primed for a career as a courtesan by her conniving mother. Nesbit quickly became a favorite of "art" photographers, including Gertrude Käsebier and Arnold Genthe, and her image was widely circulated on wildly popular picture postcards during the first years of the new century.

The lurid tale of White's fatal attraction for Nesbit has been told many times, and given the unedifying nature of their relationship, trashier accounts get closer to the seamy reality than bowdlerized versions. This folie à deux was the subject of Richard Fleischer's 1955 film *The Girl in the Red Velvet Swing,* which starred Ray Milland as White and Joan Collins, who at twenty-two was already somewhat long in the tooth to portray the jailbait Nesbit. The title referred to one of the architect's favorite erotic pastimes, in which he would position himself beneath a velvet-covered trapeze apparatus in one of his several secret playrooms scattered around the Flatiron district—which he euphemized as his "studios"—in imitation of Jean-Honoré Fragonard's voyeuristic painting *Les Hasards heureux de l'escarpolette* (1767–1768), which shows a young gallant peering up the skirts of a young woman oscillating above him.

Briefly put, after having Nesbit's teeth fixed and taking her virginity, White still had no intention of getting divorced, let alone remarrying a tart, and the gold-digging girl married the rich but unhinged and sadistic Harry Thaw, who became fixated on the architect's supposed corruption of little Evelyn (whom Thaw nonetheless saw fit to horsewhip). The denouement to Thaw's mad obsession came in 1906, when he gunned down his imagined erotic rival from behind at the roof-garden theater White designed at his Madison Square Garden, as the architect watched the finale of a musical trifle called *Mamzelle Champagne.* White likely and luckily never knew what hit him. The autopsy disclosed that he had nephritis and was unlikely to have lived more than a few months anyway.

The ensuing scandal was enormous, but since White's weaknesses were well known in the bonhomous circles he frequented, little if any opprobrium attached to his partners, who were models of probity. McKim, a depressive already in failing health and further dispirited by his mercurial but beloved colleague's fate, died in 1909. Mead carried on until his death, in 1928, but the practice's output plummeted once his two partners left the stage, though the nominal McKim, Mead & White plodded on until it was absorbed by another firm in 1961. That precipitous decline is confirmed by the epigonal

CHARLES McKIM, WILLIAM MEAD, AND STANFORD WHITE

McKim, Mead & White office's drab, warehouse-like New York Racquet and Tennis Club of 1916–1919 on Park Avenue, one block but a world away from White's vivacious, peripatetic portico for St. Bartholomew's, a contrast that in a single glance explains why this unequal triangle was never again the same without its two most acute coordinates.

2

FRANK LLOYD WRIGHT

THE MOST REMARKABLE thing about the extensive literature on Frank
Lloyd Wright—new additions to which flow forth season after season, even as the stream of other architecture books dwindles—is not
its magnitude (491 titles as of 2013, according to the Library of Congress catalog, more than the 433 executed buildings in Wright's catalogue raisonné). More striking is the extreme disproportion in the
coverage of different aspects of his seven-decade career. In addition
to many lavish Wright picture albums, there is no end of publications
on individual houses by America's greatest architect. The finest of
those studies have been by the architectural historian and critic Donald Hoffmann, whose magisterial Wright series for Dover began to
appear in 1978. In particular, Hoffmann's penetrating monographic
analyses of the Robie house of 1906–1910 in Chicago and Fallingwater of 1934–1937 in Bear Run, Pennsylvania, are unrivaled and
likely to remain so. Such classic works have been vastly outnumbered
by the self-aggrandizing memoirs written by many patrons who commissioned Wright houses late in his career, whether or not the buildings they paid for were of any special quality.

Yet such is the seemingly unquenchable popular thirst for information about the Wizard of Taliesin that even books on relatively minor

aspects of his career find an eager audience. When the critic Herbert Muschamp's brief but nonetheless disorganized treatment of the master's contentious stance toward America's largest metropolis, *Man About Town: Frank Lloyd Wright in New York City,* appeared in 1983, its subtitle brought to mind the ethnic-stereotype jokes about books with only one page: *Italian War Heroes* or *Irish Teetotalers.* Although one of Manhattan's supreme architectural glories, the Solomon R. Guggenheim Museum of 1943–1959, is also Wright's last masterpiece, he built little else in the city and its environs, and never lost his country-boy misgivings about the corruptions of Gotham. Nonetheless, as an architect who had few peers as a self-promoter, Wright was inexorably drawn to New York and its influential opinion-makers in publishing, broadcasting, and the arts. With each well-publicized visit, the architect perfected his carefully crafted image of a curmudgeonly embattled genius, as he dependably supplied reporters and cameramen with pithy quotes, clever photo ops, and droll newsreel turns, like another incorrigible press hound of the period, George Bernard Shaw.

Wright adapted quickly and adeptly to new forms of mass communication as they emerged. Kinescopes and tapes preserve several of his frequent appearances on such early TV programs as *Conversations with Elder Wise Men* (in dialogue with the young Hugh Downs), *The Today Show* (with its first anchorman, Dave Garroway), and *What's My Line?* (where a blindfolded Dorothy Kilgallen, the Hearst newspaper gossip columnist, correctly guessed the mystery guest's identity). After deftly fielding several aggressive questions from the host of *The Mike Wallace Interview* in 1957, Wright twitted his chain-smoking interlocutor about "that thing you have in your mouth" and "doing commercials for the cigarette" made by the show's sponsor, Philip Morris. Not until Philip Johnson managed to silence the interruptive Charlie Rose, four decades later, would an architect so dominate a television talk-show personality.

Wright's New York base of operations was the luxurious Plaza Hotel, where he first stayed in 1909, two years after its opening, on his way to Europe with his lover, Mamah Borthwick Cheney, who left her husband for the architect after he designed a house for the couple not far from his own home in the Chicago suburb of Oak Park. In 1954 Wright leased a Plaza pied-à-terre, which he dubbed "Taliesin East," for his use during the three-year construction of the Guggenheim, thirty blocks to the north. A compulsive spendthrift who lived high on the hog even when flat broke, Wright redecorated the hotel's suite 223–225—overlooking Central Park and Fifth Avenue at the building's northeast corner—with a mélange of Asian-inspired and modern furnishings (including chairs carved with a swan's-head motif, left behind by the previous tenant, the couturier Christian Dior), and obscured the rooms' Beaux Arts detailing with panels of gold-flecked Japanese rice paper. Although the Plaza's beer-baron architectural historicism exemplified the deracinated styles he rebelled against as a young firebrand, Wright the Olympian sage took a more benign view of the hotel's forgettable architect than he did of formidable competitors like Le Corbusier and Ludwig Mies van der Rohe. "Good old Henry Hardenbergh," Wright told one client. "Of course, I wouldn't do anything like it, but it is an honest building."

However, the many redundant or pointless Wright publications only emphasize major lacunae in the master's imbalanced bibliography. For example, there is still no adequate study of his love affair with the automobile, which shaped—in fact, dominated—his approach to regional development. No other master builder has maintained a more enduring hold on the American imagination than Wright, not even Thomas Jefferson (who is considered first and foremost an architect by Neoclassical fanatics). Although Jefferson's reverence for the Vitruvian tradition was the antithesis of Wright's contempt for historical revivalism, they shared an antiurban vision of the United States as a gridwork of small farms and single-family houses, punctuated by modestly sized towns. Both men viewed big cities with instinctive suspicion. The major difference was that Wright's idea for modern exurbia—his unrealized Broadacre City scheme of 1932–1934, a low-rise, low-density Nowhere Land he hoped would encourage "lives lived in greater independence and seclusion"—depended on the private automobile as virtually the sole means of transportation. Broadacre's formula for communal dispersal and social isolation presaged the rampant sprawl that has become the ruination of our national landscape, a consequence very much at odds with the environmentalism imputed to Wright's earthy organic architecture. This conjunction in Wright's work of two quintessential American manifestations—the destructive effects of the car culture and the unchecked individualism fetishized as "freedom"— remains unexplored, but it could yield a critique of far-reaching significance and contemporary relevance.

The biggest gap on the Wright bookshelf remains a biography that begins to approach John Richardson's multivolume masterpiece *A Life of Picasso*. Retellings of Wright's life story continue to appear and just as predictably vanish. None thus far has been wholly satisfactory, although the most useful collection of facts is to be found in the uneven *Frank Lloyd Wright: His Life and His Architecture* (1979) by Robert Twombly. One can understand why any historian would shrink from the all-consuming effort needed to realize a comprehensive life-and-works of this prolific figure, who died when he was ninety-one. However, such an achievement would guarantee its author a place in the Boswellian pantheon along with Richardson, Leon Edel, Richard Ellmann, and other masters of the genre. In the absence of such a biographer, Wright's personal history lends itself all too readily to the salacious scandalmongering that makes for nonfiction best sellers.

After the two-decade eclipse precipitated by the Mamah Borthwick Cheney scandal, Wright's salvation came in the form of the Taliesin Fellowship, the school-cum-professional practice he set up in 1932 at his estate in Spring Green, Wisconsin—less out of love for pedagogy than as a survival strategy when the Great Depression exacerbated his desperation and made even erstwhile devotees see him as an irrelevant anachronism. The fellowship rescued Wright financially, spiritually, and creatively (until advanced old age began to sap his powers). He based his putatively democratic—though in fact rigidly hierarchical—brotherhood on English Arts and Crafts antecedents like the Guild of Handicraft, established in 1888 by his architect friend C. R. Ashbee. The American's enormous debt to the design theorists and social activists of the Arts and Crafts Movement, above all its presiding spirit, William Morris, is abundantly evident throughout *Modern Architecture: Being the Kahn Lectures for 1930*, the texts of six talks Wright gave at Princeton during the lowest ebb of his fortunes. The endpapers of the original edition of *Modern Architecture* are embellished with Wright aphorisms that recall the improving mottoes typically displayed in Arts and Crafts interiors: "Principle is the safe precedent," "A matter of taste is usually a matter of ignorance," "Great art is great life," and, most inarguably, "Death is a crisis of growth." (Wright incorporated such uplifting slogans in the cathedral-like main workroom of his Larkin Company Administration Building of 1902–1906 in Buffalo, headquarters of a mail-order soap company cofounded by Elbert Hubbard, America's foremost Arts and Crafts popularizer and creator of the communal Roycrofters workshop.)

To be sure, multiple influences had an impact on Wright's thought, including the "Romantic Rationalism" expounded by the architect and theorist Eugène-Emmanuel Viollet-le-Duc, whose *Dictionnaire raisonné de l'architecture française du XIe au XVIe siècle* of 1854–1856 Wright praised as "the only really sensible book on architecture in the world." However, Francophile scholars have tended to pay less attention to the arguably greater impact on Wright of the theories of Viollet's German contemporary and counterpart Gottfried Semper, or the uncharacteristically open admiration Wright showed for a member of his own generation, the Austrian architect and designer Joseph Maria Olbrich.

Socially aware critics greeted Wright's reemergence with enthusiasm, as indicated by the rave review *Modern Architecture* received in *The New Republic* from the housing specialist Catherine Bauer in 1931 (during her affair with Lewis Mumford, one of the few critics whose support of Wright never wavered). Bauer rightly praised the book as "so rich in sound observation, trenchant comment and philosophic purity that architecture itself takes on a new dignity, a fresh social importance," foretelling the consensus that it is the most eloquent summation of Wright's artistic credo. *Modern Architecture* was also the battered but unbowed architect's reminder to a forgetful world that not only did he still exist but he mattered greatly to the future of his art form. His miraculous creative resurgence began with the three brilliant schemes that clinched his unanticipated comeback: Fallingwater; the Johnson Wax Building of 1936–1939 in Racine, Wisconsin; and Taliesin West, Wright's other home and design studio, begun in 1937, in Scottsdale, Arizona—a trio outstanding within Wright's oeuvre not only for quality but for variety.

Although Wright's Prairie Houses responded with notable sensitivity to specific sites and social settings, they also shared a certain sameness. The architect of Fallingwater insisted that "the ideas involved here are in no ways changed from those of [my] early work...."

The effects you see in this house are not superficial effects." However, there is no denying that some of its details evince the then-ascendant International Style, against which Wright felt pitted in mortal combat. For example, the monolithically planar, severely unadorned balconies of this country house for the Pittsburgh department store owner Edgar Kaufmann Sr. would have been right at home in a white-stucco Le Corbusier villa. (Wright had originally wanted to surface those parapets with gold leaf, an idea rejected by Kaufmann, who was sensitive to public relations and deemed the gilding provocatively ostentatious during the Great Depression.) Fallingwater's "disappearing" corner of outward-opening casement windows was an idea employed by several European Modernists, including Gerrit Rietveld and Truus Schröder-Schräder in their Schröder house of 1924 in Utrecht, Holland. More than one critic has pointed out that Fallingwater was Wright's not-so-subtle way of proving to a new generation of foreign upstarts that he could outdo their hallmark motifs if he felt like it.

Truer to Wright's claims of consistency with his pioneering work of the century's first decade was his Johnson Wax headquarters, which, despite being an exercise in the trendy Streamline Moderne style then sweeping the country, was rooted in his Larkin building of three decades earlier. The Johnson offices' Great Workroom reiterated the basic format of the Larkin's central workspace, the Light Court, which was similarly inward-turning, high-ceilinged, and illuminated by skylights. Taliesin West evoked a more recent Wright precedent, his temporary Ocatillo Desert Camp of 1928 in Chandler, Arizona, where the architect and his devoted staff rusticated during an ill-fated series of commissions that ended abruptly with the Wall Street crash. Although Taliesin West was initially assembled from the same unfinished board-and-batten wood siding and canvas roofs as its precursor, the diagonally sloping forms of Wright's later, larger home-and-office complex were anchored by massive piers made from local boulders cast in concrete, which gave the composition a feeling of greater permanence and connection to its surroundings. Taken as a whole, these three schemes represent a more concentrated display of Wright's prodigious talents than during any equivalent period of his career.

The early days of Taliesin West—where the fellowship escaped the harsh Wisconsin winters—were indelibly captured in photographs by Wright's longtime official image-maker, Pedro E. Guerrero, a poor Mexican-American who was allowed to enroll in the fellowship without a fee in return for his services. Although Wright harbored certain biases not unusual for a man born just two years after the Civil War ended, he betrayed no prejudice when he unhesitatingly welcomed Guerrero into the Taliesin community at a time when discrimination against Latinos was rife in the American Southwest. The architect treated his protégé with immense paternal tenderness and reflexive munificence when, after Pearl Harbor, the young man enlisted in the army, to the dismay of the pacifist Wright, a stalwart of the isolationist America First movement.

In contrast to such noble episodes, the Taliesin Fellowship, isolated and hierarchical, was to a great extent a royal court, an atmosphere promoted less by Wright than by his sinister, manipulative, and voyeuristic third wife, Olgivanna—a Montenegrin divorcée and acolyte of G.I. Gurdjieff. (Mrs. Wright's flagrant advances toward Gurdjieff during his 1934 stay at Taliesin made the depth of her attraction embarrassingly clear.) The fellowship's lithe, nubile, and enticingly underdressed apprentices responded to the climate, whether homosexual, bisexual, heterosexual, or pansexual. But it is no news that college-age youths like to have a great deal of sex, and that old folks do, too (the nonagenarian Wright improbably boasted that he "fucked his wife every night"); or that design students are perhaps more likely to be gay than many other students; or that a lothario like Wright could be homophobic. For decades, the unimpeachable gatekeeper of the Taliesin archive was Bruce Brooks Pfeiffer, of immeasurable help to historians and critics during the long twilight of Olgivanna, who outlived her husband by more than a quarter-century, and whose greed and mania for control might have brought Wright studies to a complete halt were it not for Pfeiffer. This paragon of accuracy and probity astonished fellow scholars when, in one tell-all account of life at the fellowship, he recalled informing Wright that he was gay, to which the architect replied, "Bruce, why don't you cut your dinky dick off?"

Perhaps the saddest victim of that extended household was Olgivanna and Wright's only child together, Iovanna Lazovich Lloyd Wright, who renamed herself Rosa and lived in mental institutions for much of her life. The architect's seventh offspring got off to an inauspicious start: before her parents could legally marry, the newborn and her mother were hounded from the hospital by Wright's erratic and vindictive second wife, Miriam Noel. Iovanna, the architectural counterpart of the pathetic Lucia Joyce, suffered from familial dysfunctions familiar to children of the great in every field. But as was painfully apparent, Iovanna/Rosa was also psychotic, although her flashes of intelligence repeatedly raised false hopes about her prognosis, as was likewise true of the daughter of the author of *Ulysses* and *Finnegans Wake*. This heartbreaking case history provides an insistent, melancholy counterpoint to the persistent tales of sexual antics and power intrigues that swirled around the indifferent Wright, whose imperturbable nature was a mixture of Micawberish optimism and cosmic self-absorption.

Wright's blithe disregard for others and for the havoc that such obliviousness could wreak on his high professional aspirations was never clearer than in his abandonment of his first wife, Catherine

Tobin Wright, and their six children upon his elopement with Mamah Borthwick Cheney, the wife of a neighbor for whom he built his Cheney house of 1903–1904 in Oak Park, Illinois. This escapade ended with Mamah's murder in 1914, the grisly denouement to a sex-and-homicide saga that surpassed its nearest equivalent, when Stanford White was shot to death eight years earlier by the deranged husband of the roué architect's erstwhile underage plaything, Evelyn Nesbit Thaw. For five years, Wright's real-life soap opera played out in headlines that brought him to the attention of a national audience as yet unfamiliar with his work.

However, by 1906 the architect had become enough of a local celebrity to merit a picture postcard of his own Oak Park house and studio of 1889–1898 (see Illustration 2a). The caption under that image, "The House Built Around a Tree," referred to his having reconfigured the ground plan for his octagonal home-office addition of 1897–1898 to preserve a mature gingko tree (which survived until it was felled by lightning in 1992). Wright carried out a much less edifying alteration of the structure a decade after that tree-sparing gesture, when he thoughtfully remodeled it to serve as an income-producing boardinghouse run by his forsaken spouse, after he and his free-thinking, financially independent lady friend took off together.

The moral outrage that affair ignited can be deduced from the overheated press coverage. The *Chicago Tribune* deemed the brazen liaison "an affinity tangle...unparalleled even in the checkered history of soul-mating," a widely shared perception that halted the architect's thriving career in short order. Public indignation was further inflamed by the knowledge that Wright's practice had been based on residential commissions like the Cheneys'—the revolutionary series of Prairie Houses (more than fifty in all) through which he advanced his program for a new, distinctively American form of domestic habitation. In Wright's recasting of the modern home, the routines of everyday life were exalted as sacred activities, dramatized by the altar-like dining tables that became as much a hallmark of his interiors as his leaded-glass windows. More than one potential Wright client surely felt that the architect's heedless and licentious behavior desecrated the temple of the family and made a mockery of the idealistic values that he purported his designs would reinforce. Mamah Borthwick was a follower of Ellen Key, the Swedish feminist and advocate of free love, and as such saw her own belated rejection of married life and child-rearing as an act of high philosophical principle, not an insolent flouting of bourgeois hypocrisy.

After Wright and Borthwick returned from Europe, they sought refuge in the Wisconsin farming valley where he grew up, a place where they could be away from the prying eyes of Oak Park neighbors who knew both aggrieved spouses whom the transgressors had left behind. Protected within his extended family's arcadian stronghold, Wright concealed the scope of his plans for a new dream house there. He disingenuously claimed that Taliesin (see Illustration 2b), which was named after a mythic Welsh bard, would be no more than a "bungalow:" a false-modest misnomer as laughable as a Newport Gilded Age "cottage." His most inspired design decision was Taliesin's siting: not atop a hill but nestled into the crest of a hillside, in keeping with his belief that a truly organic architecture must be subservient to nature. The expansive Taliesin complex—a serene Japanesque interplay of long, low-slung wings shaded by broadly overhanging roofs and interspersed with terraced courtyards—accorded with no one's notion of a tawdry love nest.

Then, with Wright absent, at lunchtime one Saturday in August 1914—two weeks after the Great War began—a Caribbean-born servant of the couple's, Julian Carlton, set fire to the house and went berserk with an ax. By the time his rampage ended, the structure was in ruins and Borthwick, her two children, and four Wright employees lay dead. It is impossible to outdo Wright's own words on the tragedy, in the open letter he wrote to acknowledge his neighbors' condolences. Some sense of his depth of feeling can be seen in the original document; the distraught architect bore down so hard on his pen that the nib almost tore through his writing paper:

> This noble woman had a soul that belonged to her alone—that valued womanhood above wifehood or motherhood. A woman with a capacity for love and life made really by a higher ideal of truth, a finer courage, a higher more difficult ideal of the white flame of chastity than was "moral" or expedient and for which she was compelled to crucify all that society holds sacred and essential—in name!
>
> ...The "freedom" in which we joined was infinitely more difficult than any conformity with customs could have been. Few will ever venture it. It is not lives lived on this plane that menace the well-being of society. No, they can only serve to ennoble it.
>
> ... She was true as only a woman who loves knows the meaning of the word. Her soul has entered me and it shall not be lost.
>
> You wives with your certificates for loving—pray that you may love as much and be loved as well as was Mamah Borthwick!

Her heartbroken soul mate buried Mamah Borthwick in the churchyard of the Unity Chapel of 1886 in Spring Green, his first executed building, where he himself would be interred, forty-five years after the massacre. But the preternaturally jealous and endlessly conniving Olgivanna had no intention of allowing the ill-starred couple to rest in peace together for all eternity. She left instructions that upon her own death, which finally came in 1985, her husband's remains were to be dug up and cremated, his ashes commingled with hers, and immured within the walls of their Arizona home, far from the grave of his great lost love.

3

LE CORBUSIER

DESPITE THE INHERENTLY social nature of architecture and city planning, personal histories of master builders were uncommon before the last century and are still greatly outnumbered by biographies of painters and sculptors. A turning point in the public's perception of the building art came with the publication of Frank Lloyd Wright's *An Autobiography* of 1932, a picaresque narrative that captivated many who hadn't the slightest inkling of what architects actually did. Wright's sweeping self-portrait as a heroic individualist served as the prototype for Howard Roark, the architect-protagonist of Ayn Rand's 1943 best seller, *The Fountainhead*. But the novelist transmogrified Wright's entertaining egotism into Roark's suffocating megalomania, an image closer to that of another contemporary: Le Corbusier, the pseudonymous Swiss-French architect and urbanist born Charles-Édouard Jeanneret in 1887, twenty years after Wright.

Le Corbusier was one of Wright's few competitors who matched his flair for self-promotion (Buckminster Fuller was another). However, Le Corbusier's posthumous influence has outstripped that of the greatest American architect. The European's schemes were often less specific to their sites than Wright's and thus more adaptable elsewhere (and everywhere). Le Corbusier's work in South America and India won him a third-world following that Wright never attracted. And his "Five Points of a New Architecture" of 1926 became a modern "must" list that could be copied by almost anyone, anywhere. Those veritable commandments included thin *piloti* columns on which buildings could be supported; ribbon windows; open floor plans; façades freed from load-bearing structure; and roof gardens. Such formularization was also central to the steel-skeleton, glass-skin high-rise format later perfected by another contemporary, Ludwig Mies van der Rohe, but his schemata did not offer the rich recombinations possible with the "Five Points."

During Le Corbusier's lifetime, his reputation did not derive solely from his vast corpus of designs, which still astonishes in its inventiveness and boundless implications. His renown was enormously enhanced by the more than fifty books and pamphlets through which he promulgated his radical vision of a new building art for the modern age—everything from city planning to interior design. For example, to replace the tightly knit, medium-rise urban neighborhoods he deemed insalubrious and oppressive, Le Corbusier proposed residential skyscrapers widely spaced amid parks and highways. Like his closest present-day equivalent, Rem Koolhaas, he had a size fetish and made headlines during his 1935 trip to America when he complained that New York's skyscrapers were not big enough. He was also fascinated with modern ocean liners, which helped shape his conception of large-scale residential schemes, specifically the six Unité d'Habitation apartment developments he built in France and West Berlin during his final two decades. To modernize domestic interiors cluttered with ornate furnishings and cocooned in fabric, he advocated rooms as sparse and easy to clean as a tuberculosis ward. And rather than reiterating the dull gray masonry of northern European cityscapes, he favored the gleaming white stucco of Mediterranean villages, regardless of that material's climatic suitability.

Le Corbusier was electrified by the feedback he got when he expounded his controversial proposals in public, whether to general audiences, university students, or fellow practitioners. His need for attention—the source of which was finally established by Nicholas Fox Weber in *Le Corbusier: A Life* (2008), the first full-length biography of the architect—was fed by the heavy schedule of speaking engagements he kept up for decades. He also attended many of the symposia convened by supporters of modern architecture to hash out their theories and establish a unified agenda. Those meetings could be contentious, for what we now call the Modern Movement was in fact an unruly scrum of competing factions with doctrinaire positions that often divided an allegedly common cause.

Most architects give lectures primarily to advertise themselves, and Le Corbusier was no more shy than his colleagues in basing his talks on his own work. What set his public appearances apart was the way they prompted him to reexamine fundamental concepts—from the organization of metropolitan transport to the layout of the workingman's house—as much for himself as for his listeners. Whatever his announced topic, he emphasized a constant theme: his specific version of Modernism held unique promise for elevating mankind to unprecedented levels of bodily well-being and psychic stimulation.

Despite Le Corbusier's interest in theory, his discourses were anything but cerebral abstractions, and conveyed a vigorous physicality and joyous immediacy thanks to the method through which he illustrated his thoughts. His visual aids were low-tech yet high-impact. On the wall behind him, the architect would unroll and pin up a swath of yellow tracing paper as wide as a movie screen. While he spoke, he used varicolored chalks or crayons and sketched a profusion of pictograms, scrawled a welter of catchphrases, and ended up with a dense calligraphic mural, like a Cy Twombly drawing avant la lettre. Many Le Corbusier lecture backdrops survive, intact or in tatters, thanks to souvenir hunters who swooped in and claimed them the second he exited the stage.

As is true of most other avant-garde architects, Le Corbusier established his reputation through private residences commissioned by enlightened clients brave enough to support the unconventional ideas of a young and largely untested designer. Of singular importance are the houses of the architect's so-called Heroic Period, created between 1920 and 1930 in collaboration with Pierre Jeanneret, his cousin and early partner. These nineteen schemes (fifteen of them executed) for sites in or near Paris were starkly unornamented, defiantly uningratiating structures that when new reminded many of factories. Le Corbusier took this analogy as a compliment and duly dubbed his new domestic conception the *machine à habiter*—"machine for living in." Today, these houses accord with popular notions of Bauhaus architecture, even though Le Corbusier had no official or even direct connection to that German design school.

The evolution of the Heroic Period houses shows how the designers extracted a remarkable array of compositional variations from a narrow repertoire of forms (right-angled volumes, flat roofs, windows flush with wall planes) and a limited palette of materials— white-painted stucco, glass, and metal. Le Corbusier and Jeanneret were able to do so much with so little mainly because of the former's genius for reconceiving space in novel ways, a gift he came into full possession of during this determinative decade. The climax of the cousins' astonishing residential sequence was the Villa Savoye of 1928–1931 in Poissy, in my estimation, and that of many others, the ultimate twentieth-century house. Its vivifying counterpoint of geometric rigor (through the ancient proportional system known as the Golden Section) and spatial propulsion (through dynamic ramps in place of stairs) makes the structure exhilarating to move through every step of the way from front door to roof terrace. By the time this job was finished, the architects likely realized that they had pretty much exhausted their revolutionary formula and could only repeat themselves if they stuck with it.

Soon after the completion of the Villa Savoye, Le Corbusier began to move away from industrial perfectionism and toward its polar opposite in a nascent Neoprimitive style, which emerged with his introduction of rough stone walls in several country houses of the 1930s, further evidenced itself in the raw concrete and vigorous modeling of his Pavillon Suisse of 1930–1933 at the Cité Internationale Universitaire in Paris, and culminated with his gloriously antirational Ronchamp chapel two decades afterward. Though he abandoned the mechanistic approach of his Heroic Period, the Corbusian vocabulary would become so pervasive that its author's main contribution might be seen as his codification of the closest to a true lingua franca that ever emerged from the babel we call modern architecture.

Although it was one thing for Le Corbusier to collaborate with Jeanneret, it was quite another for him to collaborate with the Nazis. Years before France fell in 1940, Hitler's animus toward modern architecture had spurred a steady emigration of practitioners whose careers in Germany had collapsed. Albert Speer, Hitler's principal architect, urban planner, and wartime munitions chief, visited Paris to oversee his design for the Third Reich's pavilion at the 1937 International Exposition, a prophetic precursor of a more pervasive German presence in France three years later. After the war, the Nazi master builder acknowledged being familiar with Le Corbusier's work, which perhaps informed his megalomaniacal plans to rebuild Berlin on a scale similar to that which Le Corbusier had envisioned for Paris. But Speer's Stripped Classicism and Le Corbusier's Minimalist Modernism were far too disparate in essence to allow for any middle ground. Le Corbusier, oblivious (for once) to his international identity as a vociferous champion of the very architecture Hitler despised, somehow imagined he could find a position with Marshal Pétain's collaborationist government. The architect moved to the provisional capital of Vichy, where he assiduously lobbied for work. He was fortunate to have failed for the most part (although the French architectural historian Jean-Louis Cohen has uncovered disturbing evidence that Le Corbusier designed more for the Vichy regime than had been previously understood), which made it that much easier to hide this shameful episode after the Liberation, when he reopened his office in Paris as though the preceding four years had never happened.

During the second half of Le Corbusier's career, following World War II, he designed many fewer single-family houses than before. Most important among his later private domestic commissions were the Maisons Jaoul of 1951–1956 in the Paris suburb of Neuilly. A pair of smallish oblong villas commissioned by a father and son, the Maisons Jaoul are stylistically antithetical to the Le Corbusier–Jeanneret residences. The sleek Villa Savoye, with its main living areas lofted above the terrain on slender *pilotis*, seems barely tethered to its site; the compacted brick-and-concrete Neuilly houses feel immovably earthbound. The Savoye house, with its peripheral colonnade supporting an entablature-like piano nobile, encouraged comparisons to the Classical tradition; the fortresslike enclosure and monastic gravity of the Maisons Jaoul provoked apt references to the medieval.

The Neuilly double houses quickly became touchstones of New Brutalism, a trend among young architects in midcentury Britain. They sought to inject much-needed energy into the waning conventions of High Modernism, as represented by carbon-copy commercial hackwork that sucked the marrow out of Mies's "skin-and-bones" formula. The New Brutalists saw greater expressive potential in Le Corbusier's favorite late-career material, concrete, though the effortful crudeness of their chunky forms and rough finishes often appeared to be little more than macho posturing. Paradoxically, although their hero Le Corbusier built nothing in Britain, he became the presiding spirit among Modernist architects there, especially during the extensive postwar reconstruction, exemplified by the Alton West Estate of 1955–1959 in the Roehampton section of southwest London, a public housing development designed by the London County Council Architects Department in the Corbusian towers-in-a-park mode. Within seven years of its completion, Alton West was deemed a perfect found movie set for François Truffaut's *Fahrenheit 451* (1966), his film adaptation of Ray Bradbury's 1953 novel about a futuristic dystopia.

Polarization of critical opinion in Britain on this widely imitated but also divisive figure is evident in several classic postwar essays—including the historian Colin Rowe's hugely influential treatise "The Mathematics of the Ideal Villa: Palladio and Le Corbusier Compared" (1947) and the architect James Stirling's "Garches to Jaoul: Le Corbusier as Domestic Architect in 1927 and 1953" (1955). Interestingly enough, the 1920s Continental upstart found an unexpected early supporter in the inventive British classicist Edwin Lutyens, whose cautiously appreciative 1928 review of *Towards a New Architecture* (the English translation of Le Corbusier's most seminal text, *Vers une architecture* of 1923) pointed out a crucial flaw in the architect's perfectionist work of the Heroic Period:

Architecture, certainly, must have constituents, but lines and diagrams, in two dimensions, are not enough. Architecture is a three-dimensional art. To be a home, the house cannot be a machine. It must be passive, not active, bringing peace to the fluctuation of the human mind from generation to generation. For what charm can a house possess that can never bear a worn threshold, the charred hearth, and the rubbed corner?

In return, the fiercely competitive Le Corbusier was unusually respectful of Lutyens's consummate triumph, the Viceroy's House of 1913–1931 in New Delhi, when he visited it in 1951 as he began planning Chandigarh, his new regional capital of 1951–1964 for the Punjab—and he adopted several of the Englishman's ideas for that evolving postcolonial scheme. Indeed, Le Corbusier's eventual volteface from the crisply efficient *machine à habiter* of the Villa Savoye to the warmly embracing *foyer de famille* of his Maisons Jaoul suggests that he took Lutyens's 1928 critique very much (though perhaps only gradually) to heart.

Although Le Corbusier was determined to be well known, he was also determined not to be known well. He never added an autobiographical memoir to his extensive writings, and he disclosed so few personal details that he seemed to have no private life at all. However, one thing everyone knew about him was his relentless Protestant work ethic, befitting the son of a Calvinist watchmaker. But as Nicholas Fox Weber persuasively argues in his revelatory and absorbing *Le Corbusier: A Life*, the architect was driven by motivations more primal than compulsive Swiss industriousness. Weber gets to the heart of the matter by employing Le Corbusier's own words to document his ceaseless struggle to win the love and affirmation of his mother, Marie Charlotte Amélie Jeanneret, née Perret (no relation to the Belgianborn architects Auguste and Gustave Perret, with whom Le Corbusier apprenticed).

Mme Jeanneret, a music teacher, openly preferred her older son, Albert, a musician of middling talent and feckless temperament. Parental approval is seldom swayed by adult achievements of less-favored offspring, and nothing Le Corbusier ever did could alter that family dynamic. He was evidently much less attuned to his watchmaker father, Georges-Édouard Jeanneret-Gris, who founded a local hiking club and indulged his son to the extent that the house the young man designed for the family, the Villa Jeanneret-Perret of 1912 in La Chaux-de-Fonds (see Illustration 3a), nearly bankrupted his parents. This previously unknown factor in the architect's psychic makeup —his intense mother fixation—is a discovery of immense importance, and Weber is right to give it a prominent place in his well-paced and judiciously balanced narrative. He is also correct to avoid simplistic psychological diagnoses and let the primary evidence speak for itself. The results are so convincing that even without knowing the full contents of the architect's archive it seems safe to say that Weber did an extraordinary job of surveying the long-sequestered papers and charting a plausible map of the inner man. He was the first writer granted unrestricted access to Le Corbusier's private correspondence, preserved at the Paris foundation he created to guard his legacy. The architect's executors, who fended off prospective biographers for more than three decades, were wise to choose Weber. Though not a trained architectural historian, he unquestionably likes his subject and remains unwaveringly sympathetic, often in the face of quite unpleasant evidence.

Yet he also indicates why the Fondation Le Corbusier delayed a full biographical accounting for such a scandalously long time. The architect constructed a public persona of hyperrational control and glacial indifference, which some have seen reflected in the inhumane streak suggested by his drastic urban renewal schemes (most notoriously his Plan Voisin of 1925, which would have razed much of Paris's Right Bank) and unreciprocated Nazi sympathies. But the infantile tone of his letters to his mother—by turns fawning, petulant, wheedling, flirtatious, obsequious, demanding, hectoring, and every bit as selfish and manipulative as the ghastly matriarch herself—exposes his appalling lack of empathy for anyone but himself and the mother whom he could neither separate from nor win over.

Weber goes so far as to assert that Le Corbusier's most acclaimed postwar work—the pilgrimage church of Notre-Dame-du-Haut of 1950–1955 in Ronchamp, France (see Illustration 3b)—was less a shrine to Our Lady than his utmost tribute to his *maman*, who was also named Marie. Without question, the cavernous biomorphic interiors of this miraculous structure (reckoned the most moving religious building of modern times by many critics, including this one) do indeed echo the sensuous contours of the female anatomy. The words from the Hail Mary that the architect inscribed, in his own hand, on one of the chapel's jewel-like stained-glass windows—*bénie entre toutes les femmes* (blessed among all women)—hint at a devotion beyond any this nonobservant Protestant ever evinced for organized religion, let alone the Blessed Virgin. Even so, it would be a mistake to see Le Corbusier's transcendent hilltop sanctuary solely, or even primarily, as a womb with a view.

Despite Weber's fondness for his subject, he unsparingly condemns Le Corbusier's despicable attempts to abet the Vichy regime. The architect's previously undisclosed remarks disclose chilling attitudes deeper and more disturbing than mere vocational opportunism. Five months into the Occupation, he reported to his mother in neutral Switzerland: "The Jews are going through a very bad time. I am sometimes contrite about it. But it does seem as if their blind thirst for money had corrupted the country." He was willing to work for anyone—but so was Mies, as were many other architects throughout history. However, in this as in all else, everything was always about him. Le Corbusier saw wartime destruction not as a human tragedy but as a career opportunity. "There are great demolitions only when a great building site is about to open," he wrote his mother. And with grotesque effrontery, this expedient Pétainiste postured as if he'd taken up arms with the Maquis: "I will not and cannot leave France after this defeat," he hypocritically declared. "I must fight here where I believe it is necessary to put the world of construction on the right track."

Apart from Le Corbusier's deep-seated *manie de maman*, his most consuming personal relationship was with his wife, the beautiful but ill-starred Yvonne Gallis. Their three-decade mésalliance was so complex and dispiriting that Weber is understandably baffled by its precise pathologies. One only hopes the sex was good, at least for her. (For his part, the architect was always happy to outsource with independent contractors.) At first glance, this unlikely pairing of a Swiss-French control freak and a Monégasque free spirit appears the proverbial attraction of opposites. However, Le Corbusier was habitually drawn to two very different sorts of women. One was the self-assured, well-educated young lady of good breeding and independent means—epitomized by the American divorcée Marguerite Tjader Harris, with whom he conducted a fitful three-decade extramarital affair, until he summarily dumped her in the early 1960s, when an American commission she tried to broker on his behalf fell through. The other feminine archetype that most aroused him was the Mediterranean peasant girl—intuitive, uninhibited, sensuous, and pleasure-loving—personified by Yvonne. As Le Corbusier wrote in his *La Ville radieuse* of 1935: "I am attracted to a natural order of things.... And I have noticed that in my flight from city living I wind up in places where society is in the process of organization. I look for primitive man, not for their barbarity but for their wisdom."

In 1929, seven years after he took up with Yvonne and a year before they married, Le Corbusier had a brief but passionate romance with Josephine Baker, the African-American *chanteuse-vedette*, whom he met (along with her complaisant husband) on a trip to Buenos Aires. Superficially, these two diametrically different international stars might be one of Miguel Covarrubias's *Vanity Fair* "Impossible Interviews" (caricatures that coupled Sigmund Freud with Mae West, and Greta Garbo with Calvin Coolidge, for example). But the madly ambitious lovers somehow regarded one another as kindred spirits of childlike simplicity and were further turned on by each other's considerable renown, as the famous are known to do. The architect also saw a potential client, though talk of his designing an orphanage for La Baker in the south of France came to naught (a dream she later realized when she bought the Château des Milandes in the Dordogne in 1947, through the venture ultimately bankrupted her).

Without assigning blame, Weber follows Yvonne's steady, seemingly inexorable disintegration, physical and spiritual—through alcoholism, eating disorders, wartime malnutrition, her husband's protracted absences, and his emotional neglect—in harrowing detail made more pitiable in contrast to the vivacious young minx she had been when Le Corbusier first fell for her. Yvonne then was a *mannequin* in Monte Carlo, and like many fashion models her soignée looks were belied by her common behavior. She adored juvenile pranks, bawdy repartee, popular amusements, and anything else that tweaked bourgeois proprieties. So did her husband, his cool public pose notwithstanding. Le Corbusier ate up the naughty provocations of his "Vonvon," which further encouraged her. (She called him "Doudou," a diminutive of Édouard, as well as baby talk for *merde*.)

At architectural conferences as well as private soirées, she became his surrogate id, blurting out home truths that her careerist spouse considered too impolitic to voice personally. Weber recounts a memorable evening chez Corbu when Walter Gropius (then director of the Bauhaus) and his new wife, Ise (the much more *bürgerlich* successor to his celebrated first spouse, the high-bohemian muse Alma Mahler), came to dine. Yvonne, bored silly by the stuffy couple, suddenly asked Gropius if he'd seen it. When he inquired what "it" meant, she slapped her rump and brightly exclaimed, "*Mon cul!*"

Reports of Mme Le Corbusier's blistering candor circulated in professional circles for decades. She was as blunt with her husband as with everyone else, which seems not to have bothered him. Decades before Weber's biography, a rare, evocative personal study of the pair—albeit in miniature—appeared in Charles Jencks's *Le Corbusier and the Tragic View of Architecture* (1973), which Weber's exhaustive research shows to have been a small masterpiece of induction, as startlingly complete as a Matisse charcoal drawing of a woman's head composed of five or six bold black strokes. Jencks cites Yvonne's reaction to the glass-walled duplex Le Corbusier created for them atop his small sixteenth-arrondissement apartment house of 1933, the new home that he hoped would give them "a new life" as their marriage deteriorated while his fame soared: "'All this light is killing me, driving me crazy,' she said.... [Le Corbusier] placed a bidet, that beautifully sculptural 'object-type,' right next to their bed. She covered it with a tea cosy."

The architect treated Yvonne appallingly all along, but it is not surprising to learn that her death, in 1957, left him desolate for the eight years that remained to him. The bereft widower made a macabre talisman of one of Vonvon's vertebrae, which survived her cremation intact. Something essential went out of Le Corbusier in that final phase, when he seemed to withdraw from the world, creatively and personally. His sudden death, in 1965, from an apparent heart attack as he swam off the Côte d'Azur against cardiologist's orders, led some to wonder if it was a suicide—the architectural equivalent of Joan Crawford striding into the surf to the strains of the *Liebestod* at the climax of Jean Negulesco's *Humoresque* (1946). Le Corbusier's implacable mother had died in 1960, just months before her centenary, and he always believed he would live as long as she did. Whether his own demise, at seventy-seven, was accidental, intentional, or something in between, the departure of the two women he could neither live with nor live without had left him very much at sea well before the waves of the Mediterranean closed over him.

4

THE BAUHAUS

FEW DEVELOPMENTS CENTRAL to the history of art have been as misrepresented or misunderstood as the brief, brave, glorious, doomed life of the Bauhaus—the epochally influential German art, architecture, crafts, and design school that was founded in Goethe's sleepy hometown of Weimar in 1919. It then flourished from 1925 to 1932 in Dessau, an industrial backwater where the school's first director, Walter Gropius, built its image-making headquarters (see Illustration 4a); and it ultimately but vainly sought refuge in cosmopolitan Berlin, where it closed in 1933, when Hitler took power. But it took nearly a century after its inception and three quarters of a century after its dissolution for the Bauhaus to be explained to the museumgoing public in terms that accurately represented its actual intent and immense achievement.

In 2009, the ninetieth anniversary of the founding of the Bauhaus was celebrated with comprehensive overviews mounted in Berlin and New York, as well as with traveling exhibitions on the work of two of its major protagonists, the Russian painter Wassily Kandinsky and the Hungarian multimedia artist László Moholy-Nagy. Even though it struck some as premature to hold full-scale Bauhaus shows ten years before the legendary institution's centenary, it was certainly time for a long-overdue reassessment of this persistently stereotyped and often maligned powerhouse of modern culture. For example, one lingering popular fixation is the very notion of "Bauhaus architecture," which has become a reflexive misnomer for pared-down Modernist building design. Many of the leading figures of advanced twentieth-century architecture had nothing at all to do with the Bauhaus, including Le Corbusier, Richard Neutra, Erich Mendelsohn, and Alvar Aalto, to name only four of the German school's most conspicuous absentees.

In fact, it was not until Ludwig Mies van der Rohe became the Bauhaus's third and final director, in 1930, that the institution's curriculum tilted decisively toward architecture, at the expense of other disciplines. Another entrenched fallacy about the Bauhaus is that it was somehow responsible for the lamentable global proliferation of boring corporate Modernist architecture after World War II. Actually, the blame lies with commercial property developers who exploited Mies's easy-to-mimic but hard-to-replicate Minimalist formula for steel-framed, glass-skinned high-rise buildings because they were cheaper and more profitable to erect than prewar masonry-clad, decoratively embellished structures; but these epigones aped his schemes without a trace of Mies's proportional subtlety or technical finesse.

The timing of the 2009 international Bauhaus *Wunderjahr* was prompted by Germany's incomparable trio of Bauhaus repositories: the Classical Foundation in Weimar, the Bauhaus Foundation in Dessau, and the Bauhaus Archive in Berlin. Their officials wanted to mark the twentieth anniversary of the fall of the Berlin Wall with a coordinated endeavor impossible before German reunification. They joined forces to present "Bauhaus: A Conceptual Model," the biggest show on the subject ever, with a thousand objects that filled Berlin's Martin-Gropius-Bau (built as the Museum of Applied Arts from 1877 to 1881 to the designs of Heino Schmieden and Martin Gropius, a great-uncle of the future Bauhaus head). Not to be outdone or deemed laggard a decade later, New York's Museum of Modern Art joined the party and mounted a comprehensive overview that drew on its own significant holdings as well as many pieces exhibited in the slightly earlier Berlin extravaganza.

MoMA, the first museum of its kind, was in fact patterned after the Bauhaus in its departmental organization, and likewise incorporated mediums overlooked by other museums before its founding in 1929, especially photography and film (and, for a while, dance). From the outset, MoMA followed the Bauhaus's strict prohibition against design that even hinted at the decorative (most notably Art Deco), a prejudice that skewed the pioneering museum's view of Modernism for decades. Thus it was fortunate for MoMA that its "Bauhaus 1919–1933: Workshops for Modernity" was organized by Barry Bergdoll, its open-minded and historically astute curator of architecture and design since 2007, with Leah Dickerman, a curator of painting and sculpture.

Their show was all the more piquant because many of the misapprehensions that still surround the Bauhaus are attributable to MoMA itself, in large part because of its 1938 retrospective "Bauhaus 1919–1928," self-servingly curated by Gropius in the same year he became chairman of Harvard's architecture school, one of four crucial academic appointments that introduced Bauhaus concepts to the United States and institutionalized them in American higher education. (The others were Josef Albers, who was asked to lead the painting program at North Carolina's newly established Black Mountain College in 1933; Moholy-Nagy, named founding director of the New Bauhaus in Chicago in 1937; and Mies, designated head of the architecture department at Chicago's Armour—later Illinois— Institute of Technology in 1938.) MoMA's shamelessly Gropiocentric 1938 Bauhaus show paid only cursory attention to the school's initial years and completely ignored the period after Gropius's departure as Bauhaus director in 1928.

The corrective, indeed penitent, nature of MoMA's 2009 recapitulation was made palpably manifest in the exhibition's first gallery, an almost chapel-like setting dedicated to the lesser-known Expressionist output of the Bauhaus in the years immediately following its founding. This introductory space offered an eye-opening experience for those familiar only with the cliché of the Bauhaus as a soulless assembly line of mechanistic design. The spiritual origins and transcendental aspirations of the Bauhaus were a direct outgrowth of the universal craving for regeneration that arose after the Great War, an apocalypse of unmitigated horror. The early Bauhaus produced several artifacts of surpassing weirdness, none more bizarre than Lothar Schreyer's *Death House for a Woman* (circa 1920), a life-size, vividly colored tempera of a stylized female figure intended for a coffin lid, at the MoMA retrospective laid out horizontally like a medieval tomb relief. It is easy to see why Kandinsky, no stranger to the outlandish, termed this unsettling image "the strangest work that I have seen in years." Another arresting oddity from those early years is *Untitled (Pillar with Cosmic Visions)* (1919–1920), a wooden sculpture carved by Theobald Emil Müller-Hummel from a World War I fighter plane propeller. Closely resembling an oceanic tribal totem, this objet trouvé—taken from an engine of mass destruction and metamorphosed into a talisman of social transformation—movingly summarizes the Expressionist search for spiritual treasure amid the wreckage of industrialized warfare.

The primal image of the Bauhaus, which appeared on the front of Gropius's four-page prospectus of 1919—commonly called the Bauhaus Manifesto—was Lyonel Feininger's angular black-and-white woodcut of a crystalline church, its three spires topped not with crosses but with five-pointed stars radiating beams of light in all directions. This imaginary structure, as much lighthouse as sanctuary, was intended to evoke not specifically religious sentiments but rather the uplifting and unifying spirit of the great cathedral-building enterprises of the Middle Ages, which lasted decades, sometimes centuries, and brought a town's entire citizenry, of all ranks and occupations, together in one high communal cause. Hopes for an analogous modern equivalent were a crucial part of the early Bauhaus ethos.

Emblematic of the Weimar school's Expressionist phase is the African (or Romantic) chair of 1921, a collaboration between Marcel Breuer, who was both an architect and a furniture designer, and the weaver Gunta Stölzl. (Though much published, the object itself, long thought to be lost, suddenly resurfaced when its owner showed up unannounced with the miraculously preserved relic in the trunk of his car at Berlin's Bauhaus Archive, which acquired it in 2004 with funds from the Ernst von Siemens Art Foundation.) Breuer and Stölzl's vigorously Neoprimitive scheme—a framework of carved wood painted in striped earth tones and upholstered with boldly patterned brocade—rises to a pointed arch behind the head of the sitter. It might be a Benin royal throne, even though such high-backed forms are uncharacteristic of sub-Saharan ritual furniture. This imposingly hieratic piece appears all the more surprising when one considers that Breuer is best known for that ubiquitous standard of twentieth-century seating, his Cesca chair of 1928, with its continuous S-curve of bent metal tubing and contrasting seat and back of natural-colored caning. There could be no more telling embodiment of the fundamental stylistic transformation of the Bauhaus from Expressionism to Functionalism than Breuer and Stölzl's wildly irrational African chair set alongside his coolly industrial Cesca model.

Stölzl, the sole woman to be named master of a Bauhaus workshop but today far less well remembered than her younger weaving colleague Anni Albers, was the rare exception to the constraints imposed on the school's supposedly liberated female faculty and students. The Bauhaus at first was intended to be gender-blind. But the chauvinistic and essentially conservative Gropius became alarmed by what he saw as the excessive number of women in a student body that never numbered more than 150 matriculants at any given moment, which prompted him to steer women away from the supposedly "masculine" architecture curriculum and toward the traditionally "feminine" crafts workshops. All the same, personal relationships of all degrees of intimacy blossomed in the hothouse atmosphere of a school that self-consciously stood apart from its provincial and traditional social surroundings in both Weimar and Dessau. The Jewish Anni Albers (née Annelise Fleischmann) and her decade-older Roman Catholic husband, Josef, a student-turned-instructor associated with the Bauhaus longer than any of his contemporaries, met and married while at the school, the most famous of many such Bauhaus liaisons, both official and informal.

What made the Bauhaus such a truly revolutionary undertaking was not so much its departure from prevailing social and aesthetic norms—most notably its rejection of historical styles—but rather its systematic recasting of the way in which the fine and applied arts were taught. During the nineteenth century, the rapid emergence and proliferation of new manufacturing methods and building technologies led to the establishment of polytechnic schools that concentrated on the practicalities of engineering and construction rather than the niceties of stylistic correctness or adherence to established precedent. In the decades just before the Bauhaus was founded, there were a few piecemeal attempts to reform some of the German and Austrian crafts schools established during the age of industrialization. Typical of these breakaway groups was the Wiener Werkstätte (Viennese Workshop), founded in 1903, which emphasized the fabrication of decorative objects to be sold through its own retail outlets.

The Bauhaus's immediate precursor was the Grand-Ducal School of Arts and Crafts, established in Weimar by the state of Thuringia in 1905 under the direction of the Belgian architect Henry van de Velde. During World War I van de Velde was compelled to resign as an enemy alien but recommended as his successor Walter Gropius, who insisted on sweeping changes when he took over in 1919 and effectively created a new institution. The hallmark innovation of the Bauhaus was the *Vorkurs* (preliminary course), a required introductory class that provided intensive back-to-basics immersion in the fundamentals of color theory and composition, with an emphasis on the arrangement of tonalities to achieve specific optical effects, and on recombinations of pure geometric forms as the elemental building blocks of design. The *Vorkurs* was conceived and initially taught by Johannes Itten, the extravagantly eccentric, mystically inclined Swiss Expressionist painter whom Gropius hired as "form master" for the school's metalwork, sculpture, wall-painting, weaving, and woodworking workshops.

An oddball even for a radical art school, Itten sported medieval-style robes and sandals, shaved his head, and consumed copious quantities of garlic. That dietary habit was a precept of Mazdaznan, the esoteric philosophy Itten followed, a hodgepodge of Zoroastrian, Theosophical, and Christian beliefs, part New Age religion, part yogic health regimen. Itten, by any measure a luftmensch, was the id to the superego of Gropius, whose skills as an administrator and persona of high-bourgeois propriety were the polar opposites of his otherworldly subordinate's meditative nature and bohemian affectations. Together this ill-assorted couple expressed both sides of the Bauhaus's bifurcated nature, at once utopian and pragmatic, intuitive and scientific, highly ordered and subversively anarchic.

Encapsulating that duality is Itten's 1921 lithograph *Color Sphere in 7 Light Values and 12 Tones*. The *Bauhäusler* (as the school's faculty and students were called) adored charts and diagrams of all sorts, and Itten's construct suggests both a Buddhist mandala and the periodic table of elements. The upper three quarters of *Color Sphere* are dominated by a twelve-point, multicolor star inscribed within seven concentric circles, flattened like an orthographic projection of the globe. The bottommost portion of this two-part composition is devoted to a grid of rectangles arranged in the color order of the light spectrum, from violet at one end to red at the other. Several other Bauhaus artists produced works based on grid themes that clearly originated with concepts embodied in this visual aid, including Josef Albers's colored-glass, metal-framed *Gitterbilder* (lattice pictures) and Paul Klee's mosaic-like paintings. That congruence seems especially noteworthy since both men went on to teach the *Vorkurs* after Itten left the school in 1923 in protest over Gropius's new determination to focus on the production of commercial prototypes rather than purely theoretical design.

Gropius did possess a definite knack for spotting talents superior to his own, and he was also a veritable weathervane of shifting trends. He abandoned the machine aesthetic of his and Adolf Meyer's critically acclaimed demonstration factory and office building at the 1914 Deutscher Werkbund exhibition in Cologne to take up Expressionism when that became the new direction in the shell-shocked aftermath of the Great War. The Bauhaus was but three years old when Gropius sensed that Expressionism was in turn becoming démodé, and he was ready to change direction once again. In 1922, Kandinsky arrived from Moscow at the Bauhaus, where a year later he was joined by Moholy-Nagy, and together they exerted a tremendous impact on the school.

No *Bauhäusler* has been more underestimated than Moholy-Nagy, who, although hardly forgotten in art circles, has never received the wide recognition enjoyed by many of his lesser contemporaries.

Today he is best remembered for his experimental photographs of the 1920s. Since the inception of photography, artists had been attempting to use this archetypically modern medium to achieve effects that would validate it as the equal of painting, a quest epitomized by Edward Steichen's heavily handworked and painterly Imagist landscape photos of the early 1900s. Conversely, Moholy-Nagy rejected prevalent pictorial conventions in photography and began to use the as yet underexploited mechanical potential of the medium to "paint" abstractions directly on film instead of trying to capture nature through a lens at a distance. In doing so he extended the nineteenth-century practice of photographing objects on flat surfaces, as William Henry Fox Talbot did with pieces of lace and Anna Atkins with botanical specimens, a camera-less method in which objects were placed on light-sensitive paper and exposed in silhouette.

Moholy-Nagy's most innovative efforts, which he called photograms (a term he did not invent but gave currency to), were often printed in the white-on-black tones of a negative and thus evinced the ghostly aura and scientific exactitude of the X-ray, which had been perfected by the German physicist Wilhelm Röntgen in 1895 with his famous skeletal study of his wife's hand. Along with a great many silhouetted everyday objects, both instantly recognizable and puzzlingly abstract, human hands figure in several of Moholy-Nagy's photograms. But rather than summoning up medical associations they strike an atavistic note not unlike handprints in prehistoric cave paintings. Expressive manipulation of photographic imagery—including the composite pictures called photomontages—entered a brave new world thanks to Moholy-Nagy, who was also a provocateur in other mediums. His dazzling kinetic sculpture *Light Prop for an Electric Stage* (1930), a perforated-metal rotating device of ambiguous, almost Duchampian symbolism, was photographed by its maker in countless sequential variations. The kaleidoscopic array of illuminations and shadows that *Light Prop* splashes onto every surface of the space in which it is displayed demonstrates how Moholy-Nagy extended the potential of sculpture in ways no less audacious than those he deployed in his deeply penetrating photograms.

The Bauhaus was preternaturally modern in its grasp of the power of publicity, both visual and textual. Ludwig Mies van der Rohe, the last of the school's three directors, took a competitive jab at the first when he asserted that "the best thing Gropius has done was to invent the name Bauhaus." Mies was right about the extraordinary resonance of that inspired coinage, which conjoined the monosyllabic root of the German verb *bauen* ("to build") with the noun *Haus*, homophone of cognates in both English and Dutch, which gave the neologism a snappy assonance as well as intimations of universality. The term also harked back to *Bauhütte* ("building hut"), the mason's lodge from which the raising of medieval cathedrals was overseen. However, the very word "Bauhaus" became a red flag to the National Socialists, and within months of Hitler becoming chancellor in 1933 acquiescent local authorities shut the school as a suspected hotbed of *Kulturbolschewismus* (cultural Bolshevism). Mies, an expert of compliant realpolitik, went as a supplicant to Alfred Rosenberg, the noxious Nazi ideologue, and begged that the Bauhaus be reopened. Rosenberg exasperatedly remonstrated, "Why didn't you change the name, for heaven's sake?"

The second-best thing Gropius did was to design the Bauhaus building of 1925–1926 in Dessau (see Illustration 4b). Although not quite a great work of architecture, it nonetheless was a first-rate advertising tool. Following the lead of Le Corbusier's Purist designs of the early 1920s, Gropius reverted to his former industrial aesthetic and gave the Bauhaus headquarters a sleek, stripped-for-action look that melded the efficiency of a factory with the cleanliness of a laboratory, neither quality associated with traditional art schools.

Gropius's scheme flaunted two bravura effects—the diaphanous glass-curtain wall of the workshop block and the two-story, ribbon-windowed bridge that spanned a roadway to link two wings—but the design was nowhere nearly as striking as Le Corbusier's alchemies of volume and space. This pair of dramatic gestures aside, Gropius's Dessau building seemed to anticipate the no-nonsense sobriety that would infuse the Bauhaus under his successor, the Swiss architect Hannes Meyer, whom Gropius engaged to head the school's architecture program in 1927, and who assumed the top job a year later.

A committed Communist with close ties to architects in the Soviet Union—where the exuberant experimentation of the early Russian Constructivists was waning, soon to be superseded by the Classicizing conformity of ascendant Stalinist neoconservatives—Meyer faced growing opposition from the increasingly right-wing government of Dessau, which funded the Bauhaus. He was forced to resign in 1930, but not before he inculcated some decidedly Soviet notions into the Bauhaus ethos, most notably the *Existenzminimum*, or minimum means for existence, which had a decisive influence on social-housing design in Germany and elsewhere. It is thus important to remember that it was only under Meyer's two-year directorship that this extreme utilitarian functionalism (a concept he took from 1920s Soviet housing and planning) prevailed at the Bauhaus, a brief, joyless interlude that has loomed larger in historical hindsight than it ought to.

A more life-affirming presence at the Bauhaus was Kandinsky, a master who exerted a powerful influence on his fellow *Bauhäusler*, and who in turn absorbed the equally potent influence of other giants among them, most notably Klee. A 2009 Kandinsky survey at New York's Guggenheim Museum offered the additional thrill of experiencing Frank Lloyd Wright's last masterpiece abrim with precisely the kind of art for which this institution—originally named the Museum of Non-Objective Painting—was created. As one stood at the low parapet that edges the museum's helical ramp and looked across Wright's monumental rotunda, the pulsating colors and hyperactive forms of Kandinsky's canvases seemed to ricochet all around a void that had never seemed more alive. The Guggenheim possesses one of the three greatest Kandinsky collections, rivaled only by those of the Lenbachhaus in Munich and the Pompidou Center in Paris. With its approximately 250 Kandinskys, the Guggenheim could have readily mounted a full-scale retrospective without borrowing a single item. One loan in the 2009 show, from the Beyeler Foundation in Switzerland, was unusually poignant: Kandinsky's lyrical oil-on-canvas abstraction *Fugue* (1914), back in New York nineteen years after the Guggenheim sold it for $20.9 million, to help pay for its acquisition of the Panza di Biumo collection of Minimalist and Conceptual art, a trade-off that rightly provoked howls of protest.

Kandinsky is often deemed the father of abstraction—art that is nonrepresentational and evokes a mood or state of mind rather than actual objects. This transformation was announced by his *Untitled (First Abstract Watercolor)* of 1910, now in the Pompidou Center. This pivotal work—a buoyant overall pattern of multicolored splotches and calligraphic squiggles—was made three years after Picasso's seminal *Demoiselles d'Avignon*. The basic difference between these respective breakthroughs was that Picasso's oil painting remained essentially representational no matter how stylized or distorted his means of depiction, whereas Kandinsky never returned to the overt folkloric subjects and landscapes that he had once favored—his alpine views, cavorting peasants, and riders on horseback deliquesced into the electrifying ether of his mature pictures (although the art historian Rose-Carol Washton Long has pointed out Kandinsky's "veiling" of thematic subject matter that may seem abstract on the surface). Around the time that Kandinsky began teaching in Weimar, his paintings became more geometrically precise and formally calculated in ways that often seem at odds with the breathtaking fluency of his early abstractions, a tightened organizational tendency that only increased during his Bauhaus years. Several Kandinskys from that period indicate the magnetic pull of Klee on his Russian colleague, especially several works on paper in which the latter incorporated mosaic-like checkerboard patterns often employed in Klee's work. Kandinsky's 1929 oil-on-Masonite *Levels (Etagen)*—now in the Guggenheim collection—is likewise reminiscent of Klee in its juxtaposition of a white rectilinear armature that suggests the splayed arms of a high-tension power pole, interspersed with playful geometric pictograms against a solid Prussian-blue background.

One of the most insightful considerations of Kandinsky was presented by the art historian John Golding in a 1997 lecture, "Kandinsky and the Sound of Colour," later collected in his magisterial *Paths to the Absolute* (2000). As Golding writes:

Kandinsky had originally sensed the potential of a purely abstract art through his belief in the "musicalization" of painting, although he had insisted from the start that he had no desire to paint musical pictures. He had soon come to feel that the achievements of painting could surpass those of music....In doing so he was bringing to fruition a long line of enquiry going back more than a century.

This conviction echoed the obsession of early Modernists in all fields who sought to break down the barriers between mediums through synesthesia—"hearing" color or "seeing" sound—in order to create a *Gesamtkunstwerk*, or total work of art. That endeavor was at the very heart of the Bauhaus project, which attempted to integrate the entire spectrum of arts into one life-enhancing whole.

It is generally held that Modernism celebrates fragmentation and opposes the continuity implicit in the Classical tradition. But despite the frequent antics of the Bauhaus's youthful adherents—the costume parties, the cabaret evenings, the Charleston contests, the jazz sessions, the kite festivals—these high-spirited college kids were anything but lords (and ladies) of misrule. During the politically precarious but creatively fertile years of the Weimar Republic, the *Bauhäusler* gathered under one roof to learn, practice, and teach arts as ancient as weaving and as novel as photography with utter seriousness and optimistic conviction. By viewing all mediums with fresh eyes, they made the old new again, and the new timeless as never before, proven by the myriad works that can still astound us almost a century after the Bauhaus set the arts in perpetual motion.

5

ERNST MAY AND
MARGARETE SCHÜTTE-LIHOTZKY

THERE IS NO sadder tale in the annals of architecture than the virtual disappearance in recent decades of the defining architectural form of the early Modern Movement—publicly sponsored housing. The provision of decent dwellings for all people was a cardinal tenet of the reform movements that arose throughout the industrialized world during the late nineteenth century, when new building materials and construction techniques seemed to put that ideal within the grasp of reality. Particularly after the cataclysm of World War I and the resultant rise of social democratic governments in Europe, large-scale housing programs were undertaken as a means of establishing political stability, promoting equality, and nurturing a productive workforce.

That dream has effectively vanished both abroad, where several European nations have lately faced insolvency and have drastically cut government spending on social services, and in the United States, where public housing has long been demonized as a breeding ground for a vicious cycle of dependence, indolence, poverty, and crime. The inspiring careers and enduringly livable designs of two towering but still insufficiently recognized figures in modern architecture—the German architect and city planner Ernst May and one of his chief collaborators, the Austrian architect and interior designer Margarete

Schütte-Lihotzky—represent the zenith of socially responsible housing in the twentieth century. For five decades, from the 1920s until his death in 1970, May's architecture had a strong influence in Germany, the Soviet Union, East Africa, and then Germany again, the three locales of a career shaped—some would say distorted—by three of the twentieth century's major political forces: communism, fascism, and colonialism.

May was born in Frankfurt am Main in 1886 (the same year as Ludwig Mies van der Rohe). The son of a prosperous Protestant factory owner and a Jewish mother, he received his architectural training at the Technische Hochschule in Munich. During a summer break he worked for the British architect and town planner Raymond Unwin, who was then constructing Letchworth Garden City in Hertfordshire, the first development of its kind, founded in 1903 by Ebenezer Howard, father of the Garden City Movement, which aimed to supplant congested, overgrown metropolises with far smaller, self-sufficient communities that brought their inhabitants closer to their workplaces and nature through environmentally aware site planning that emphasized open green spaces. At Letchworth May was steeped in that housing-reform group's ethos of urban decentralization, ecological conservation, communal land ownership, and humane scale. Though Germany had its own vigorous offshoot of the Garden City Movement—exemplified by such New Towns as Theodor Fischer, Hermann Muthesius, Richard Riemerschmid, and Heinrich Tessenow's Hellerau near Dresden and Bruno Taut's Falkenberg near Berlin—May's formative English experience is evident in the intelligent layouts and sensitive landscaping of his mature work.

He was conscripted into the German army during World War I, designed military cemeteries in Romania and France, and during the last year of the conflict joined the Deutscher Werkbund (German Work Federation), the progressive design group founded in 1907 to promote closer cooperation between designers and industry. In 1919, under the Weimar Republic, May was named the technical director of the Schlesische Heimstätte (Silesian Homesteads), a government home-building agency in the eastern German state of Silesia, where he oversaw construction of housing in a more conservative architectural style than would soon be his practice. In 1924 he joined Walter Gropius, Martin Wagner, and Taut in forming a *Kopfgemeinschaft* (think tank) to address innovative housing solutions. A year later he was called to Frankfurt, where his accomplishments were historic.

Between 1925 and 1930, May, as the director of the city's housing department, constructed twenty-three Frankfurt-region *Siedlungen* (settlements) that provided some 15,000 dwelling units, a logistically astounding accomplishment. His closest rival in the quantity and quality of that output was Taut, who during the Weimar years built about 10,000 units in and around Berlin. Although these housing estates were financed by a variety of sponsors that included local municipalities, labor unions, and private building societies, they were substantially underwritten by the national government following the enactment in 1924 of the *Hauszinssteuer* (house mortgage-interest tax) applied to private residential structures built before World War I as a means of equitably subsidizing desperately needed new housing. This considerable income stimulated a huge increase in public residential projects until the international market crash hit economically shaky Germany with particular force at the end of that decade. In her classic survey *Modern Housing* (1932), the American urbanist Catherine Bauer estimated that one in ten German families benefited from this nationwide initiative, among the proudest attainments of the often beleaguered and much maligned Weimar Republic, which has frequently been caricatured as a cesspool of moral laxity and hedonistic decadence. According to Bauer, who was at the center of similarly motivated but much less thoroughgoing initiatives in the

United States at that time, this was "the most fruitful epoch of modern housing which the world has yet to know." In contrast to such widely published contemporaneous showpieces as Gropius's Bauhaus of 1925–1926 in Dessau and Mies van der Rohe's German Pavilion of 1928–1929 at the Barcelona International Exposition, May's diffuse Frankfurt ensembles could not be summarized in single photographic images and were best comprehended through aerial views. That elevated perspective is especially useful in appreciating the most admired of his housing projects, Römerstadt, in the suburb of Heddernheim, which like others in this homesteading program was sited to plug gaps in the periphery of Frankfurt's urban sprawl. Römerstadt combines long, whiplash-like rows of three-to-five-story apartment blocks with semidetached and terraced private houses, all interspersed with playgrounds, sports fields, a primary school, and shops. That graceful organic layout feels notably different from the geometric handling of the central feature at May's Bruchfeldstrasse Siedlung of 1926–1927—the so-called *Zickzackhausen*, with imposing flanks of flats set at serrated ninety-degree angles—or the rigid ranks of parallel rectangular residential structures, called *Zeilenbau* (linear blocks), that predominate in some of his other Frankfurt developments, including Praunheim of 1926–1929 and Westhausen of 1929–1931.

The ground plan of Römerstadt follows and emphasizes the undulating contours of the shallow Nidda River basin in which it is sited. To echo that flowing quality, both ends of the two main residential blocks terminate in rounded bays (see Illustration 5a), a streamlined treatment that recalls the favorite motif of May's contemporary Erich Mendelsohn, whose curvilinear tendencies stand in marked contrast to the strict rectangularity of much early Modernist architecture. A series of four rampart-like raised terraces overlooking the river valley are similarly sinuous, and mediate between the housing units above and a fan-shaped field of narrow allotment gardens below, in which residents could grow their own vegetables and flowers, a participatory interaction with nature prized in Garden City communities. Further softening the somewhat severe appearance of May's unornamented architecture, the stucco façades at Römerstadt were painted in harmonious earth tones, from a delicate rose-beige to a deep terra-cotta. The cumulative effect was quite different from the all-white exteriors that many now erroneously think were mandatory for Modernist workers' housing, a coloristic freedom that was taken to even greater heights of expression by May's *Kopfgemeinschaft* colleague Taut, whose work in Magdeburg and Berlin exhibited the most inventive use of architectural pigmentation during the interwar period.

But no matter how they were configured, May's housing projects invariably were oriented to optimize southern exposure. Following traditional Garden City planning principles, they were laid out to free large internal portions of the site for shared open space. And the problem that bedeviled the few Garden Cities ventured in the US— what to do with the cars?—was moot in a setting where automobile ownership was rare and tram lines provided cheap and convenient transportation from these new outlying communities to jobs in the city center. Residents who had grown up in the cramped, dark, un-hygienic quarters of Frankfurt's medieval core found the idyllically landscaped new *Siedlungen*—spacious, sun-washed, sanitary, and salubrious—to be nothing less than a revelation. More than eight decades later they remain well-kept, attractive places to live.

To drum up broad support for his grand enterprise, May became an adept publicist. He put out a strikingly designed magazine, *Das Neue Frankfurt*, to chronicle his *Siedlungen* in particular and spread the gospel of Modernism in general. He lectured extensively, encouraged the publication of enticing picture-postcard series, set up popular home-outfitting exhibitions to demonstrate and promote new building materials and labor-saving appliances, and used the emergent medium of radio broadcasting to reach an even wider audience. More important, the charismatic May's extraordinary administrative skills, political acumen, and dauntless willpower enabled him to achieve much in little time at Frankfurt. He was furthermore physically imposing: he stood nearly six foot three and was feared by bureaucrats and his assistants alike for his intimidating gaze.

"May the Magician" (as one awestruck employee dubbed him) stayed well informed about rising talents in the international planning community. One of his smartest moves was to hire Margarete Lihotzky, a young Austrian who was the first woman to receive an architecture degree from Vienna's School of Applied Arts and had been working for the pioneering Minimalist architect Adolf Loos for the city of Vienna, which under its social democratic government from 1918 to 1934 carried out a public housing program comparable to Frankfurt's in its ambitiousness and excellence. Later known as Grete Schütte-Lihotzky, after she married another of May's architects, Wilhelm Schütte (who designed schools for his boss's *Siedlungen*), she was born in 1897 in Vienna. Her father was a liberal-minded civil servant with pacifist sympathies, and her mother a homemaker who joined the Red Cross during the Great War, which broke out when Grete was seventeen.

Schütte-Lihotzky's most famous design, for the pathbreaking ready-made all-in-one unit known as the Frankfurt Kitchen (1926–1927; see Illustration 5b), was informed not only by recent advances in standardization, prefabrication, and mass production—interconnected concepts through which reformers believed that good design could be made affordable for everyone—but also by time-motion studies, sociological tracts on domestic economy, and above all a conviction that more efficient food preparation would free women from a central aspect of oppressive household chores that fell disproportionately to them, at a time when even in the most progressive German households cooking was still deemed to be *eine weibliche Pflicht* (a wifely duty). Dimensionally, the Frankfurt Kitchen—which measured approximately thirteen feet long by seven feet wide by nine feet high (proportions that varied slightly from one *Siedlung* to the next)—is a marvel of what German theorists (who took their cues from Soviet contemporaries) called the *Existenzminimum* (minimum means for existence). This was clear when a rare intact example of one such unit, removed from an unrenovated apartment in May's Höhenblick housing estate in Ginnheim (where he himself lived in a cubic single-family villa of his own design), was acquired by New York's Museum of Modern Art in 2009 and displayed there two years later. For New Yorkers resigned to even smaller, often windowless galley kitchens, Schütte-Lihotzky's light-filled, shipshape design seemed anything but minimal. MoMA's example of the Frankfurt Kitchen is the smallest of three variations devised by Schütte-Lihotzky for different residential developments. However, some more affluent urban dwellers might be caught short less by its size than by the kitchen's battleship-gray cupboards and drab linoleum-covered work surfaces, unfathomably austere for present-day America, where a disproportionate amount of our gross national product goes toward granite countertops and cherrywood kitchen cabinets. (In 2005 the Victoria & Albert Museum salvaged another intact exemplar from the same Höhenblick estate, but the London unit is painted a more pleasing blue-green color than New York's soberly utilitarian version.)

Schütte-Lihotzky's close reading of home-management texts by such pioneering feminists as the American Christine Frederick, along with her own careful observations about the order in which women prepare, cook, serve, and clean up after meals, prompted her very specific positioning of elements in the Frankfurt Kitchen to make each task as labor-conserving as possible. Following the time-motion studies of Frederick Winslow Taylor, she positioned the gas range, industrial-style metal sink, and fitted glass-fronted cabinets in optimal relation to each other, arranging them to coincide with the general order of tasks through which meals are made and cleaned up after. Among her labor-saving devices was a built-in grid of eighteen drawer-like aluminum containers for sugar, flour, rice, coffee, and other dry foodstuffs. Each neatly labeled, removable scoop-like aluminum compartment came complete with a handle and spout that allowed it to be lifted out and the contents poured. When the designer was told that inquisitive toddlers were prone to wreak havoc when they tried to use these easy-to-remove components as playthings, she prudently elevated the enticing handles beyond their reach in further refinements of her scheme. Other simple but ingenious labor-saving devices in the Frankfurt Kitchen included a slatted wooden dish-drying rack that was set into a shelf over the sink, which let water drip directly down into the drain. And a hinged upright ironing board, like a Murphy bed, pivoted horizontally next to the window to take advantage of daylight. The ensemble was so intelligently organized that it could only have come from the mind of a woman who had personally experienced firsthand the illogic, drudgery, and waste of traditional kitchens.

To maximize the efficiency of every square centimeter of space, Schütte-Lihotzky emulated fitted-kitchen models from early modern transportation—steamboats, railroad cars, and lunch wagons—which employed prefabricated components to achieve ultimate efficiency. By operating within industrial guidelines of interchangeable parts, Schütte-Lihotzky could mass-produce her Frankfurt Kitchen at low cost for all the new *Siedlungen*. As Susan R. Henderson noted in her 1996 essay "A Revolution in the Woman's Sphere: Grete Lihotzky and the Frankfurt Kitchen":

Lihotzky's points of reference were far removed from the woman's sphere: ship galleys, the railroad dining car kitchen, and the lunch wagon.... With Lihotzky, the kitchen came to full maturity as a piece of highly specialized equipment—a work station where all implements were a simple extension of the operator's hand.

Yet for all the designer's emphasis on modern innovation—notably her application of assembly-line techniques perfected by Henry Ford—this kitchen-in-a-box was a low-tech affair, not only because of strict budgetary restrictions (the local government limited the cost of each kitchen to one-and-a-half times an average worker's monthly salary, an amount amortized through rental fees) but because labor-saving electrical appliances were not yet generally available. For example, Schütte-Lihotzky specified no refrigerator, which was considered a superfluous extravagance at a time when people shopped for fresh food daily and in a place where it rarely got very hot in summer.

May and Schütte-Lihotzky did not agree on every feature of the Frankfurt Kitchen. She wanted an eat-in kitchen, but size and budget constraints made this impossible, whereas he was somewhat overly concerned about the hygienic separation of cooking and dining. Schütte-Lihotzky, who considered the subject from an empathetic female perspective, tried to bring the woman of the house into closer contact with other family members as she went about her chores (which would later be encouraged by kitchen pass-throughs in postwar American subdivisions), whereas May held to a more conventional, bourgeois male point of view about women's subservient place in the home. The Frankfurt Kitchen could be constructed so successfully because May had the purchasing power to make its manufacture economical within the limited budgets set by the city government. Prefabrication never became the panacea many thought it could be because industrially produced components seldom were ordered in numbers large enough to be dramatically cost-effective. But the unprecedented scope of the Frankfurt housing experiment gave May the ability to specify customized elements—especially precast concrete wall panels, for the production of which he established a factory—in sufficient quantity to actualize new concepts that remained mere theories to others.

Schütte-Lihotzky's revolutionary role as a woman in this allegedly "masculine" profession was alluded to in a delightful *Spottgedicht* (satirical poem) from the 1920s that was likely written by her future husband Wilhelm Schütte, but which captured the spell that she cast on her other male coworkers as well:

Grete Lihotzky
Der Kompagnon von May & Co.

O Grete! Als ich sah dein lieblich Bild
In einer Zeitung, hab ich mich gewandelt,—
Ich war ein Nörgler, war fuchsteufelswild,—
Nun weiss ich wohl, dass ich nicht recht gehandelt.

Mir hat es angetan dein Bubischopf
Und deine schnippisch-kecke Nasenspitze;
Du kommst mir Tag und Nacht nicht aus dem Kopf
Und bringst mein kühles Blut zur Siedehitze.

Die Wohnungsnot liegt mir im Magen schwer;
Vor May, dem Zaubermann, es oft mir graute;
Hab ihn verwünscht, weil in die Fluren er
Voll Wollust seine Plattenhütten baute.

Jetzt denk ich anders! Nett muss es doch sein
In solchem winzig kleinen Heim zu weilen:
Denn für das Glück ist wohl kein Raum zu klein—
Doch müßtest du mit mir die Bude teilen!

Was braucht ich mehr? Die Küche ist komplett,
Ein Tischlein geht zur Not in's "Herrenzimmer."
Das Kämmerlein hat Raum für's Himmelbett,—
Ach Grete komm! Mach glücklich mich für immer!

Denn wenn am Gasherd du das Szepter führst
Und mit den zarten und so flinken Händen
Voll Unmut die Kartoffelsuppe rührst,
Fühlt man sich wohl auch zwischen kahlen Wänden.

Bescheiden würde ich aufs Bügelbrett
Mich kauern und dich liebevoll umschmeicheln
Und hin und wieder—wäre das nicht nett?—
Dir deinen schlauen Bubischädel streicheln.

Dann würde ich, vom Größenmahn befreit,
Mich künftig nie mehr mit Problemen quälen
Und dir zu Füßen, allzeit hilfsbereit,
Gemüse putzen und Kartoffeln schälen.

Dein neuer "Lebenstil." –das geb ich zu,—
Die Krätscher und die Zweifler leicht bekehret
Besonders wenn solch süßes Kind wie du
Mit milden, weise Worten sie belehret.— — —

Grete Lihotzky
The Associate of May & Co.

Oh Grete! When I saw your lovely picture
In a newspaper, I was transformed,—
I was a fault-finder, was as wild as a devilish fox,—
Now I know well that I did not act correctly.

I was smitten by your boyish cropped hairdo
And the saucy-bold tip of your nose;
Day and night I can't get you out of my head
And you bring my cool blood to a boil.

The housing shortage lies heavily in my stomach;
I'd often dreaded May, the magician,
I'd cursed him while in the meadows he
Enthusiastically built his slab huts.

Now I think otherwise! It must certainly be nice
To linger in such a tiny little home;
Because no room is too small for happiness—
But you would have to share the digs with me!

What more do I need? The kitchen is complete,
A little table can fit if need be into the study.
The little chamber has space for the four-poster bed,—
Oh Grete come! Make me happy forever!

For when you are reigning at the gas range
And with tender and swift hands

Full of ill-humor you stir the potato soup,
One even feels well between barren walls.

I'd humbly cower on the ironing board
and flatter you lovingly
and every now and then—wouldn't that be nice?—
I'd caress your smart boyish hairdo.

Then, freed from delusions of grandeur,
I'd never again be bothered by problems in the future,
And at your feet, always ready to help,
I'd clean vegetables and peel potatoes.

Your new "lifestyle"—I confess it—
Easily converts the skeptics and critics
Especially when such a sweet child as you
Enlightens them with gentle words of wisdom.— — —

—Translation by Rosemarie Haag Bletter

Thanks to feminist historians, since the 1970s a growing awareness of women's contributions to the modern building art has revived
the reputations of other such neglected innovators as Eileen Gray,
Lilly Reich, and Charlotte Perriand, who like Schütte-Lihotzky overcame prejudice against the involvement of women in anything architectural beyond decorative embellishment. Unlike those other
women, however, Schütte-Lihotzky's career prospects were further
circumscribed by her deep political engagement. She joined the Austrian Resistance in 1940, which led to her imprisonment by the Nazis
for almost five years, and her adherence to her Communist beliefs

after the war worked to her detriment in officially neutral Austria, where Soviet troops remained until 1955. Yet she finally received the historical recognition she so richly deserves, signified by a major exhibition at Vienna's Museum for Applied Arts in 1993. When she died in 2000, days before her 103rd birthday, she was justly hailed as an exemplary feminist pioneer and the last survivor of a singularly uplifting episode of the Modern Movement.

The second annual meeting of the Congrès International d'Architecture Moderne—the Modern Movement's main policymaking and agenda-setting organization, of which Ernst May was a founder— was held in 1929 in Frankfurt at his behest. There he organized visits to his *Siedlungen* for conference attendees, and they came away duly impressed with his remarkable achievement. Many of them would apply ideas they were exposed to for the first time in Frankfurt in their own work back home. The following year, when the USSR was in the midst of its initial Five-Year Plan, Soviet officials invited May, whose renown had spread internationally, to deliver a series of lectures on housing and town planning. His hosts were so won over that they asked him to become chief architect of the country's extensive building endeavors. He accepted with alacrity, not only because of the dire effect the worldwide depression was having on Germany's already ravaged economy but also because the Soviets allowed him to bring a contingent of nearly two dozen longtime associates (including Schütte-Lihotzky and her husband). The May Brigade, as they were called in a Communist double entendre, would become the core of an office of eight hundred charged with realizing twenty major projects throughout the country.

May's three-year stint in the Workers' Paradise followed the all-too-predictable path of other European Modernists enticed there by promises of large-scale construction freed from capitalism's compromising profit motive (see front endpapers). The May Brigade's leader termed the hero's welcome they received a *Kaviargewöhnungskur* (getting-used-to-caviar cure), and his wife wrote to a friend in Germany that they "have never lived as magnificently anywhere." His subordinates, however, were less than ecstatic about their living conditions, since they were compelled to board in collective dwellings and eat in communal kitchens, Communist requirements from which their demanding and fastidious boss had carefully exempted himself and his family. The group's workload was overwhelming and their supervisory visits to far-flung construction sites for new industrial cities were exhausting, but May and his loyal cohort were sustained at the outset by their certainty that they were engaged in a noble cause. Instinctive political animal that he was, however, May rightly sensed, as the first Five-Year Plan wound down to its end in 1932, that his days in the USSR were numbered.

He was demoted and placed under the thumb of commissars; his budget, salary, and authority were reduced; and his team's herculean efforts had deeply disappointing results, especially when their Master Plan for Greater Moscow of 1932 was shelved. Photos of the May Brigade's surviving housing blocks and schools in such dismal Siberian outposts as Magnitogorsk and Novokuzneck indicate that even when brand new these drab structures were but dim reflections of what May and his team had brilliantly accomplished just a few years earlier in Germany. Though May's unhappy departure from the USSR was papered over by Stalinist officials as a triumphant exit, one of his closest associates who stayed on, Werner Hebebrand, was jailed for a year before being deported in 1938. According to the German politician and cultural historian Thomas Flierl, May eventually learned that "all the Soviet protagonists of a modern town-planning policy who had close links to him had been liquidated," a denouement all too typical of Stalin's xenophobic paranoia.

There was no question of May's returning to Germany after Hitler took power in early 1933. The architect was doubly damned by the Nazis: his mother was Jewish, and his Marxist politics and Soviet sojourn caused him to be denounced by Goebbels in a radio rant. May decided to emigrate not to the US (because he was repelled by American commercialism) but instead to East Africa. This startled those closest to him, who didn't suspect that he had apparently gathered a highly romanticized view of the Dark Continent from a popular book, *Fremde Vögel über Afrika* (Strange Birds over Africa), by Ernst Udet, a World War I flying ace who later helped build the Nazi Luftwaffe. The architect and his family first settled in what is present-day Tanzania on a coffee plantation he bought with his substantial Soviet earnings. But after three years he grew bored and relocated to neighboring Kenya, where he opened an architectural office in Nairobi. There he built Kenwood House of 1937, a delightful five-story residential and commercial complex with a streamlined exterior of semicircular concrete bays shaded by continuous visor-like sunscreens that projected from each floor. His small but thriving practice was interrupted during World War II, when he was jailed for two years by Kenya's British colonial government as an enemy alien.

After his release, May and the architect George Blowers invented the Hook-on-Slab system of 1945, an ingenious construction technique whereby flanged panels of precast reinforced concrete could be slotted into one another to create slightly curving load-bearing exterior walls. May used this as the basis for a housing prototype modeled on traditional East African grass houses, which in his more solid rendering resembled Quonset huts with their pronounced parabolic profile. As the historian Philipp Sturm has dryly noted, "The Africans were impressed by the technology of this building, but stated that they would prefer to live in European-type houses." Despite May's leftist leanings and commitment to social justice, his fortunately unexecuted Urban Expansion Plan of 1945–1952 for Kampala, the capital of Uganda, then a British protectorate, would have abetted racial segregation through its demarcation of strictly separated residential enclaves for Europeans, Africans, and Asians if it had been implemented. Perhaps the architect simply reflected attitudes of the colonial government that commissioned him, but his implicit acceptance of such pernicious social engineering tarnished his long-standing reputation as a progressive and has led some leftist critics to scorn him as a white supremacist.

After two decades in Africa, May had become deeply disillusioned about the untapped potential he once imagined its peoples possessed and was alarmed by the Mau Mau uprising. With large-scale postwar urban reconstruction underway in Germany, he returned to his homeland in 1953 at the outset of the *Wirtschaftswunder* (economic miracle). During this final phase of his career he served as chief planner for several cities, including Hamburg, Mainz, and Wiesbaden. Nothing May subsequently did ever approached the coup he carried off during his brief but astonishingly productive Frankfurt heyday. By comparison, Franklin Roosevelt's fitful greenbelt New Town schemes never approached their earlier Weimar Republic counterparts either in comprehensive scale or design distinction, and America's subsequent government-sponsored housing programs retained a degrading class stigma that deepened with each passing decade.

After Lyndon Johnson's Great Society, the belief in decent public housing as a political right or social obligation was supplanted in the US by the notion that suitable shelter should be an act of charity rather than governmental policy. Thus in the absence of taxpayer-sponsored initiatives there have been volunteer construction programs such as Habitat for Humanity, Homes for Heroes, Make It Right, and Rural Studio—honorable in intent but pitifully limited in scope, and focused on erecting single-family dwellings rather than creating cohesive multiunit housing communities. In view of America's

75

postmillennial political and social direction, it seems quite unlikely that we will soon see anything approaching the miracle of late-1920s Frankfurt in America. But for as long as dreams of equality advanced through architecture persist, the surpassingly humane work of Ernst May and Margarete Schütte-Lihotzky will continue to show irresolute idealists just how much principled pragmatists can achieve in a very imperfect world.

6

OSCAR NIEMEYER

WHEN OSCAR NIEMEYER died on December 5, 2012, ten days before his 105th birthday, he was universally regarded as the very last of the twentieth century's major architectural masters, an astonishing survivor whose most famous accomplishment, Brasília, was the climactic episode of utopian High Modern urbanism. That logistical miracle and social adventure took just three and a half years from conception to completion, yet fell far short of its transformative intentions. This was the most audacious planning scheme in a century that saw the creation of several other start-from-scratch capital cities that signified the waning of colonialism and the ascent of nationalism, including Walter Burley Griffin's Canberra in Australia (1912–1920), Edwin Lutyens and Herbert Baker's administrative nexus of the British Raj at New Delhi (1913–1931), and Le Corbusier's regional seat for the Indian Punjab at Chandigarh (1951–1964).

Brasília, laid out by Niemeyer's mentor Lúcio Costa in 1957 and built principally by Niemeyer from 1958 to 1960, would have been enough to secure the architect's place in history. Yet posthumous recapitulations of his epochal career remind us that during the two decades that preceded this colossal undertaking—especially the early

1940s, when South America remained free from involvement in World War II and thus was able to build with abandon—Niemeyer stood at the very peak of architectural innovation and invention. In those dark times he almost single-handedly upheld life-affirming values counter to the industrialized mayhem being visited on so much of mankind. Niemeyer's work has rightly been likened to Brazilian music: the swaying lines and swelling contours of his biomorphic 1940s designs evoke the samba, the sensuous and insinuating dance that encapsulates that country's vibrant multiracial mix and easygoing sexuality. The cooler syncopations of bossa nova were echoed in the measured visual rhythms of the architect's more self-consciously elegant Brasília phase of the late 1950s and early 1960s. His work was then contemporaneous with the emergence of the "new beat" that caused a global sensation just as fantastic images of his dream-come-true city were splashed across the international press.

Oscar Ribeiro de Almeida Niemeyer Soares Filho was born in Rio de Janeiro in 1907 into a prominent upper-middle-class family of German descent; his father was a typographer and one grandfather was a supreme court justice. In 1929 he entered the National School of Fine Arts in Rio and studied architecture under Costa, who, along with his partner, the Russian émigré Gregori Warchavchik, was a founding father of Brazilian Modernism. Upon receiving his architecture degree in 1934, Niemeyer joined the Costa firm. Two years later Costa won the commission for a new Ministry of Education and Health headquarters in Rio and invited Le Corbusier, who had lectured to great acclaim in the city in 1929, to serve as design adviser. Forward-thinking Brazilian architects eagerly embraced Le Corbusier's precepts, particularly his use of reinforced concrete, which is cheaper, more adaptable to tropical settings, and offers greater sculptural plasticity than conventional steel-frame construction.

During his first visit to Brazil, Le Corbusier urged his young coprofessionals to take freely from his work, but when Niemeyer showed that he was a bit too adept at improving on those prototypes, the Swiss-French master, ever wary of potential rivals, lashed out. One big problem in adapting Le Corbusier's slab-like tower schemes to warmer regions was providing climate control at a time when mechanical air-conditioning was still in its infancy. In his unbuilt Plan Obus of 1933 for Algiers, Le Corbusier specified louver-like *brises-soleils*—sun-breakers—for the scheme's exposed façades, but he had still not executed any by the time Niemeyer beat him to the punch at the Rio ministry. The young architect also raised the slab's ground-level *piloti* columns to a more monumental height of thirty feet, which resulted in a widely admired work that by common consent out-Corbusiered Le Corbusier.

From the outset Niemeyer favored a design element found only occasionally in his idol's pre-1930 oeuvre: the curve. As he wrote:

I am not attracted to [right] angles or to the straight line, hard and inflexible, created by man. I am attracted to free-flowing, sensual curves. The curves that I find in the mountains of my country, in the sinuousness of its rivers, in the waves of the ocean, and on the body of the beloved woman. Curves make up the entire Universe, the curved Universe of Einstein.

Niemeyer found his ideal horticultural counterpart in the two-years-younger landscape architect Roberto Burle Marx, who created strong biomorphic ground patterns in large monochromatic beds of plants (analogous to the free-form compositions of Jean Arp, Alexander Calder, Joan Miró, and other Surrealist artists of the 1930s). A gifted botanist, Burle Marx domesticated many native plant species, more than thirty of which now bear his name. He fully integrated the natural and the man-made with indoor-outdoor water features and other illusionistic devices. Thanks to Burle Marx's work, Niemeyer's buildings achieved an aura of Edenic wonder unmatched in Modernism. Costa and Niemeyer collaborated on the Brazilian Pavilion at the 1939 New York World's Fair, the indisputable architectural hit of the exposition (which also featured Alvar Aalto's now legendary Finnish Pavilion). This exotic Modernist efflorescence dazzled visitors with its languorously attenuated ramps, delightfully ambiguous transitions between exterior and interior, and a pond designed by Burle Marx to display the gigantic Amazonian water lily *Victoria regia* (which had inspired the structure of Joseph Paxton's ridged glazing at London's Crystal Palace of 1850–1851). Niemeyer's remarkable early designs were likewise highlights of the Museum of Modern Art's avidly received 1943 survey "Brazil Builds," an upbeat escapist interlude during America's architecturally deprived war years that tied into the Roosevelt administration's Good Neighbor Policy, aimed at improving relations with Latin American nations through political nonintervention, economic cooperation, and cultural exchange.

The commission that fully displayed Niemeyer's individual genius for the first time was his stunning complex of small buildings at Pampulha, a prosperous new suburb of Belo Horizonte, capital of Brazil's mineral-rich Minas Gerais state. Here in 1940 Juscelino Kubitschek de Oliveira, a physician-turned-leftist-politician known as the city's "hurricane mayor" because of his whirlwind initiatives, began his two decades as Niemeyer's greatest champion. Kubitschek's urge to build big—which he continued as governor of Minas Gerais (1950–1955) and finally as president of Brazil (1956–1961)—makes French President François Mitterrand's *grands projets* of 1981–1998 seem somewhat underreaching. In hiring Niemeyer to design a series of recreational public buildings around a new man-made lake at Pampulha, Kubitschek caught the architect at the very peak of his powers. Positioned at spacious intervals around the amoeba-like shoreline are the Casino, House of Dance, Yacht Club, Golf Club, and Church of Saint Francis of Assisi. In particular, the Casino of 1940–1943 (converted into an art gallery when Brazil outlawed gambling in 1946) is a spatial marvel. Set on a gently sloping waterside bank, this two-story structure comprises a square ground-floor entry defined by an equilateral grid of thin *pilotis* (much like those in Corbusier's Villa Savoye of 1928–1931 in Poissy, France) with window walls that dematerialize the concrete-framed exterior. Atop this simple plinth is a second rectangular level containing the gaming room and, within an ovoid appendage that expands out toward the lake, a restaurant tiered with multiple concentric levels to maximize seeing and being seen.

To increase the efficiency of the Casino's several leisure functions —dining, dancing, and gambling—Niemeyer devised an ingenious tripartite circulation system with separate stairways, ramps, and catwalks so that patrons, entertainers, and service staff could pursue their activities without colliding. We are now aware that the interiors of early Modernist buildings were considerably less austere and colorless than has been imagined, but the Pampulha Casino was more hedonistic than most European pleasure domes of the interwar period. Here, amid brightly hued, alluringly fragrant gardens laid out by Burle Marx, Niemeyer combined walls paneled in onyx, exotic native woods, and rose-tinted mirrors; floors of parquet and polished travertine; slender stainless-steel-clad columns; hangings and upholstery of organza, satin, taffeta, and tulle; and a circular, translucent etched-glass dance floor lit from below—all of which together conjured what Cole Porter memorably called "a night of tropical splendor."

As if to give habitués of this nocturnal adult playground remission from its many occasions of sin, Niemeyer's Church of Saint Francis of Assisi of 1940–1942 (see Illustration 6a) stood nearby to offer absolution—or would have, had not conservative Catholic prelates, offended by the chapel's freewheeling form and frank sensuality, refused to consecrate it until 1959, by which time the globally celebrated architect had become a national culture hero. His church features a lateral line-up of four parabolic arches formed from thin concrete shells (faced with a blue-and-white azulejo tile mural of scenes from the life of the saint by Cândido Portinari); the gracefully rhythmic arches suggest the rolling contours of a mountain range, or perhaps a recumbent female nude. The similarly vaulted nave, which telescopes into the arch of the high altar like the stem of the letter T, reiterates the traditional format of Baroque churches in Minas Gerais, as does this little gem's extravagant sculptural quality.

In 1946, a year after the United Nations was founded, the philanthropist John D. Rockefeller Jr. donated $8 million for the purchase of a sixteen-acre parcel bordering the East River in midtown Manhattan as the new organization's permanent home. The honor of designing the headquarters was deemed too great for any one member nation to bear, so an international Board of Design, which included Le Corbusier and Niemeyer, was established under the direction of Wallace K. Harrison, the Rockefeller family's longtime architectural factotum. This complicated saga is revealed in illuminating behind-the-scenes detail in *A Workshop for Peace: Designing the United Nations Headquarters* (1994) by George A. Dudley, a young architectural assistant of Harrison's charged with documenting the proceedings, which now seem like a veritable master class in the pitfalls of design by committee.

Though the forty-year-old Niemeyer was the most junior among the design team, his schematic outline—essentially the UN complex as we now know it, dominated by the slender high-rise slab of the

Secretariat Building set parallel to the river—caused a sensation among his collaborators. As Dudley recorded:

> It literally took our breath away to see the simple plane of the site kept wide open from First Avenue to the [East] River, only three structures on it, standing free, a fourth lying low behind them along the river's edge. . . .
>
> The comparison between Le Corbusier's heavy block and Niemeyer's startling, elegantly articulated composition seemed to me to be in everyone's mind. As different as night and day, the heaviness of the block seemed to close the whole site, while in Niemeyer's refreshing scheme the site was open, a grand space with a clean base for the modest masses standing in it.

Le Corbusier disagreed: in his notebook he labeled a thumbnail sketch of his own proposal "*beau*" and Niemeyer's "*médiôcre*" [*sic*], though in fact it was quite the reverse. As the oldest, most eminent member of the panel, Le Corbusier pulled rank and at one meeting, according to Dudley, "blew his top and shouted, 'He's just a young man; that scheme isn't from a mature architect.'" Though Le Corbusier could not get his own proposal accepted, he cowed the twenty-years-younger Niemeyer into altering his configuration, eliminating the open areas between buildings the Brazilian called for, and thereby grievously diminished the ensemble's spatial qualities. The execution of the project was handed over to Harrison and his partner, Max Abramovitz, whose lackluster detailing further diluted Niemeyer's exhilarating initial vision. Though the participants had agreed that the UN Headquarters would be credited as a group effort, Le Corbusier tried to claim sole authorship, and evidently altered and backdated his sketches to support that fraudulent impression. Yet even in its compromised final state, this eloquent and hopeful midcentury landmark remains most identifiably the conceptual work of Niemeyer.

Though the idea of relocating Brazil's government from the old Portuguese colonial capital of Rio on the Atlantic coast to a virgin site deep within the hinterlands arose several centuries ago, Brasília's origin myth—a miraculous tale disseminated by Kubitschek to spur popular support for his quixotic $40 billion endeavor—is of more recent vintage. According to this mystical account, in 1883 an Italian missionary priest, Giovanni Bosco (later canonized as Saint John Bosco and now the patron saint of Brasília, popularly known as Don Bosco), had a dream in which he traveled by train through the Andes to Rio accompanied by an angelic companion. As Bosco recalled his vision:

> Between the fifteenth and twentieth degrees of latitude, there was a long and wide stretch of land which arose at a point where a lake was forming. Then a voice said repeatedly:... there will appear in this place the Promised Land, flowing with milk and honey.

Niemeyer, a Communist and lifelong atheist, framed the argument for the move to the prophesied latitude of 15° 45' in more political terms:

> Rio is a lavish show-window which hides from public view the poor, backward, and forgotten....The seat of government must be established in the heart of Brazil's vast territory, so that it surveys the whole national panorama, so that it will be within reach of all the classes and all the regions.

Yet Brasília turned out to be anything but egalitarian, and Niemeyer eventually confessed that this putative everyman's utopia "was a city constructed as a showcase of capitalism—everything for a few on a world stage."

The rapid and relatively economical construction of the new capital was aided by a disastrous drought in northeastern Brazil that in early 1958 propelled ten thousand out-of-work laborers to the building site. The refugees created instant favelas—Rio-style shantytowns that Brasília was meant to eradicate—that grew into the ring of impoverished satellite communities that still encircle the capital, an island of bureaucratic privilege within a sea of squalor. (Only in 1985 did Costa finally add a group of low-cost residential units on the edge of Brasília.) Kubitschek insisted that an international jury preside over a competition for the master plan, which infuriated Le Corbusier, who deeply coveted the job and denounced such unseemly auditioning as "democratic cowardice." He persuaded French President Charles de Gaulle to intervene on his behalf with the Brazilian president, but to no avail.

As many commentators have noted, Costa's airplane-shaped *plano piloto* (pilot plan)—with a 3.75-mile-long monumental axis that comprises the "fuselage" and a perpendicular 8-mile-long residential axis that forms the curving "wings"—is a distorted version of Le Corbusier's Ville Radieuse (Radiant City) of 1924, his radical vision of an ideal metropolis dominated by skyscrapers widely spaced amid sweeping greenswards and serviced by broad automobile thoroughfares. According to Costa's wife, he came up with the idea for his plan not during an air flight but on a sea voyage between New York and Rio, "in the middle of the Atlantic Ocean with the same 360° stretch of horizon as the Central Plain." Incredibly, after an initial site visit in 1957, Costa did not return to Brasília until 1974, for a conference on the city's urban problems. The capital's planner avowed that he could never leave Rio to live in his most famous creation: "I'm too *comodista*, addicted to the comforts here."

Flanking Costa's monumental axis are Niemeyer's two rows of identical ten-story horizontal-slab governmental ministry buildings —ten on one side, seven on the other—ranged in eerily monotonous ranks like the German architect Ludwig Hilberseimer's unexecuted Hochhausstadt (High-Rise City) project of 1924. In these buildings, there is no hint of the "free-flowing, sensual curves" Niemeyer had earlier celebrated. Furthermore, the structures were environmentally disastrous. Lacking *brises-soleils* and air-conditioning, they became so unbearably hot that at least one government minister kept offices on opposite exposures and moved between them at noon.

At the very "nose" of this virtual aircraft stands the triangular Plaza of the Three Powers (see Illustration 6b), an architectural embodiment of the executive, judicial, and legislative triad. The two legislative bodies are signified by paired, shallow domes that surmount a long rectangular base: the cupola of the Senate and the Chamber of Deputies' bowl-like reversal of that form. Centered behind them rise the twin towers of the Congressional Secretariat, two parallel twenty-eight-story slabs linked midway by a flying bridge that completes the outline of a mammoth capital H. The adjacent presidential office block and Supreme Court building are similar glass-walled boxes, each with two elevations enlivened by flaring, finlike marble colonnades.

The loveliest of Brasília's structures is the presidential residence, the poetically named Palácio da Alvorada (Palace of the Dawn) of 1956–1958, a transparent, rectilinear Miesian pavilion with screen-like curvilinear embellishments on its long sides. (It was decorated in the high International Style manner, like a number of the architect's other works, by his only child, the interior designer Anna Maria Niemeyer, who died at eighty-two, six months before her father.) The building's white-marble colonnades of swooping, bladelike forms bring to mind an upside-down sequence of arches and were instantly dubbed "Oscar's cardiogram." Yet despite many crude and debasing knockoffs, this wholly convincing attempt to recast an essential Classical motif in modern form has endured the test of time thanks to its creator's brilliant sense of fluid line and precise proportion.

Brasília's most distinctive architectural presence is Niemeyer's Metropolitan Cathedral of Our Lady of Aparecida (1958–1971), a dramatic circular arrangement of eighteen boomerang-shaped concrete columns that are joined by clear- and stained-glass panels and flare upward like a chalice, a crown of thorns, or, more irreverently, a crown roast of lamb—though perhaps the best analogy is a bound sheaf of wheat, a motif associated since ancient times with the Eucharist and salvation. Set to one side of the monumental axis, the church is entered through a subterranean tunnel that intensifies a sensation of soaring, light-flooded uplift as one emerges into the dome-like sanctuary.

In 1945, Niemeyer joined the newly founded Brazilian Communist Party after giving shelter to opponents of Getúlio Vargas's dictatorship in his house, which he soon turned over to the Party. His formal Communist affiliation (contemporaneous with that of Pablo Picasso and Pablo Neruda, who were among several notable artists and intellectuals to become Party members at the end of World War II) did not debar him from coming to the US to work on the UN scheme—representatives of the organization's Communist member states enjoyed diplomatic immunity—but it did cost him other work in the States. Invited to teach at Yale in 1946, he was denied an entry visa, and when he was offered the deanship of Harvard's Graduate School of Design in 1953 he had to decline on similar grounds, as happened yet again in 1967 when he was asked to design a business center near Miami. His only built American work apart from the UN is the Strick house of 1963 in Santa Monica, California, a breezy, low-slung pavilion commissioned by a Hollywood movie director with leftist sympathies and supervised by the architect in absentia. Another California project, a Montecito retreat for the renowned contemporary art collectors Burton and Emily Tremaine, came to naught. Several years after the 1964 coup by the right-wing general Humberto de Alencar Castelo Branco installed a military dictatorship, Niemeyer went into exile for seventeen years. Offered a French passport by de Gaulle in 1967, he resettled in Paris, where he opened an office on the Champs-Élysées and produced large-scale schemes for international clients, including headquarters for the publisher Mondadori in Segrate, Italy (1968–1975), and the University of Constantine of Algeria (1969–1972). His abiding political allegiance was demonstrated by his French Communist Party headquarters of 1967–1980 in Paris—an undulating mid-rise slab that adjoins a shallow concrete dome atop a below-street-level conference hall rather like the UN General Assembly Chamber.

Niemeyer's extraordinary longevity allowed him to witness the cyclical ups and downs of artistic reputation come full circle within his own lifetime. The ecstatic reception that greeted Brasília's inauguration on April 21, 1960, soon gave way to well-deserved dissections of its serious failings as socially imaginative planning. No critique has been more incisive than James Holston's *The Modernist City: An Anthropological Critique of Brasília* (1989), which skewers the scheme's humanitarian aspirations toward creating a classless society while in fact it has abetted further division between rich and poor. For a Communist, Niemeyer had an oddly passive, cynical, or at the very least fatalistic attitude about architecture's ability to effect social improvement. In 2005 he noted that although Le Corbusier "thought...that architecture can change life...I don't agree at all with that view. I believe exactly the opposite is true. It is life that influences architecture." He had used that laissez-faire attitude to jus-

7

EDWARD DURELL STONE

LIVES OF ARCHITECTS written by their sons are a tradition at least as old as *Parentalia* (1750), an account by the namesake child of Christopher Wren. Closer to our own day is John Lloyd Wright's *My Father Who Is on Earth* (1946), whose subject—the all-controlling but parentally vagrant Frank Lloyd Wright, who abandoned his long-suffering first wife and their six offspring to elope with a client's spouse—tried to quash that filial memoir. "Of all that I don't need and dread is more exploitation," the architect wrote plaintively to the author. "Can't you drop it?" More recently we have had Nathaniel Kahn's Oscar-nominated movie *My Architect: A Son's Journey* (2003), which concerns the filmmaker's emotional ties to his brilliant but absentee father, Louis Kahn, who sired three children by three women (one of them his wife, another of them Nathaniel's mother). In 2013, James Venturi, the only child of Robert Venturi and Denise Scott Brown, was at work on a long-awaited film about his parents, *Learning from Bob and Denise*, while Rem Koolhaas's son, Tomas, was preparing a documentary on his father.

Hicks Stone, a son of Edward Durell Stone—the architect who was lionized during the 1950s and 1960s, died in 1978 at the age of seventy-six, but today is almost unknown to a younger generation—

circulation route (the *marche*), and the tripartite handling of exteriors in the Classical division of base, column, and capital, all of which remain evident in his mature work.

After working as an assistant on Schultze & Weaver's Waldorf-Astoria Hotel of 1929–1931 in New York City (where he designed the Starlight Roof restaurant, with its grilled, retractable ceiling, and the still-intact ballroom), Stone got his big break in 1931 when he was hired by Associated Architects, the huge architectural consortium assembled to execute Rockefeller Center. That mixed-use office, retail, and entertainment complex in midtown Manhattan was America's biggest urban development scheme during the Great Depression, when a quarter of the country's architects were unemployed. For that complex Stone designed the Moderne interiors of the Center (originally New RKO Roxy) Theater of 1931–1932 (demolished in 1954), and his contributions to the nearby Radio City Music Hall of 1931–1932 included the theater's monumental proscenium of four concentric golden arcs, often likened to a sunrise or sunset over the ocean. Stone's soaring Grand Foyer at the Music Hall, one of New York's most uplifting indoor public spaces, remains an unrivaled populist masterpiece with a monumental staircase promenade that provided a democratic equivalent of Charles Garnier's *escalier d'honneur* at his Paris Opéra of 1861–1875.

Associated Architects was overseen by Wallace K. Harrison, a Rockefeller family in-law and the dynasty's accommodating architectural majordomo for half a century. He recommended Stone as codesigner for another Rockefeller-sponsored project, the recently established Museum of Modern Art's first purpose-built home several blocks north of Rockefeller Center. Although MoMA's founding director, Alfred F. Barr Jr., composed an excellent short list for the new structure—Le Corbusier, Walter Gropius, Ludwig Mies van der Rohe, J.J.P. Oud, and Frank Lloyd Wright—his recommendations

Westchester County, and the National Geographic Society in Washington, D.C.; the Kennedy Center for the Performing Arts, also in the nation's capital; and the structure that rocketed him to international renown, the circular US Pavilion at the 1958 Brussels World's Fair, which set off a brief worldwide vogue for that uncommon building shape (see Illustration 7). Whether or not one likes Stone's work, there is no denying that he was one of the most representative architects of America at the height of its postwar prosperity and power.

Edward Durell Stone was born in Fayetteville, Arkansas, in 1902 (a year after Louis Kahn and four years before Philip Johnson, respectively the most gifted and the most celebrated American architects of their generation). Although his father was a successful drygoods merchant and his hometown is the seat of the state university, Stone always considered himself somewhat of a country bumpkin, a lingering insecurity reflected in his choice of socially adept wives and appetite for lavish living. He never took a degree in architecture, but his apprenticeship in a Boston architectural firm was an educational alternative no different at the time from an aspiring attorney's clerking in a legal office instead of going to law school. Stone's impressive drafting skills were recognized when in 1927 he won the Boston Architectural Club's coveted Rotch Traveling Fellowship, a two-year stipend for a European Grand Tour that included a sojourn at the American Academy in Rome.

From his early study of Beaux Arts drawing techniques and of Classical monuments, Stone absorbed traditional architectural values that he retained throughout his career, as was also true of his great contemporary Kahn, an even more talented draftsman as well as a far more original and convincing reinterpreter of Classicism in a modern mode. Though Stone picked up the new aesthetic of Modernism easily enough during the 1930s, he never lost respect for the cardinal Beaux Arts principles of symmetry, a strongly defined central in 2011 became the latest child of a master builder to commemorate his father in print. Memoirs by scions of celebrities are instantly suspect of being either hagiographies or hatchet jobs. Yet *Edward Durell Stone: A Son's Untold Story of a Legendary Architect* provides a judiciously balanced and often unsparing assessment of the author's parents: the affable alcoholic designer and his ambitious second wife (the writer's mother), an Italian-American bombshell aptly called Maria Elena Torch—a shameless publicity-seeker who persuaded her once-lackadaisical husband to go on the wagon, use his euphonious full name, and become a global celebrity. The disparity between Stone's fame during his lifetime and his veritable disappearance from the canon after his death is as if the general public in 2050 were to have no idea who Renzo Piano was. (In fact, that Italian architect's shoebox-shaped, colonnaded structures occasionally bear more than a passing resemblance to Stone's, as seen in Piano's California Academy of Sciences building of 2000–2008 in San Francisco.)

This posthumous reversal of fortune seems even stranger given the extraordinary range of Stone's numerous, far-flung, and prestigious commissions. His still-astonishing job roster includes the state capitol in Florida and state legislative building in North Carolina; the American embassy in New Delhi; skyscrapers for Standard Oil in Chicago, General Motors in New York, and the International Trade Mart in New Orleans; houses for Vincent Astor in Bermuda, Clare Boothe and Henry Luce in South Carolina, and Victor Borge in Connecticut; campuses for Harvey Mudd College in California, Windham College in Vermont, and the State University of New York at Albany; the Museo de Arte de Ponce in Puerto Rico, the Stuhr Museum of the Prairie Pioneer in Nebraska, and the Huntington Hartford Gallery of Modern Art in New York City; the Stanford University Medical Center and the Eisenhower Medical Center, both in California; corporate headquarters for Tupperware in Florida, Pepsico in

7

EDWARD DURELL STONE

LIVES OF ARCHITECTS written by their sons are a tradition at least as old as *Parentalia* (1750), an account by the namesake child of Christopher Wren. Closer to our own day is John Lloyd Wright's *My Father Who Is on Earth* (1946), whose subject—the all-controlling but parentally vagrant Frank Lloyd Wright, who abandoned his long-suffering first wife and their six offspring to elope with a client's spouse—tried to quash that filial memoir. "Of all that I don't need and dread is more exploitation," the architect wrote plaintively to the author. "Can't you drop it?" More recently we have had Nathaniel Kahn's Oscar-nominated movie *My Architect: A Son's Journey* (2003), which concerns the filmmaker's emotional ties to his brilliant but absentee father, Louis Kahn, who sired three children by three women (one of them his wife, another of them Nathaniel's mother). In 2013, James Venturi, the only child of Robert Venturi and Denise Scott Brown, was at work on a long-awaited film about his parents, *Learning from Bob and Denise*, while Rem Koolhaas's son, Tomas, was preparing a documentary on his father.

Hicks Stone, a son of Edward Durell Stone—the architect who was lionized during the 1950s and 1960s, died in 1978 at the age of seventy-six, but today is almost unknown to a younger generation—

tify his primarily aesthetic approach in very similar terms five years earlier:

> I do not know why I have always designed large public buildings. But because these buildings do not always serve the functions of social justice, I try to make them beautiful and spectacular so that the poor can stop to look at them, and be touched and enthused. As an architect that is all I can do.

Yet Niemeyer might well have looked to the impressive accomplishments in public housing by leftist German architects of the Social Democratic Weimar Republic like Bruno Taut and Ernst May during the 1920s for ample evidence to the contrary. One of the most trenchant critiques of this glaring oversight—Niemeyer's most obvious blind spot—came from a fellow Communist, the Italian émigré Brazilian architect Lina Bo Bardi. In her 1958 essay "Architecture or *Architecture*," published in the *Diário de Notícias*, Bo Bardi already observed a disturbing departure from the humane quality of his earlier work at Pampulha:

> But what is architecture if not the most efficient means of combating, through its example, that same social injustice, the very status quo that pained Niemeyer but that he nonetheless felt obliged to contribute to and perpetuate (given his popularity and influence over the young). Is the modern architect—as a builder of cities, neighborhoods, and public housing—not an active combatant in the field of social justice? What is it that instills moral doubts, an awareness of injustice, in a strong, confident mind, if not a keen sense of collective responsibility and, with this, a willingness to fight for a positive, moral goal?

As Postmodernist design began its brief ascendance in the 1970s, Brasília's Space Age aesthetic was derided by neotraditionalists and its Corbusian grandiosity denounced by proponents of the neoconservative New Urbanism Movement. But as attitudes shifted yet again, the 1988 Pritzker Prize was given jointly to Niemeyer and Gordon Bunshaft—the first dual conferral of that award—in what was widely interpreted as a rebuke to Postmodernism after its adherents James Stirling and Hans Hollein had been thus honored. Accolades continued to mount as Niemeyer grew older and older; in 2003 he was asked to design that summer's temporary pavilion at London's Serpentine Gallery in Hyde Park, a sure index of contemporary architectural hipness. (And also an index of the taste of Peter Palumbo, chairman of both the Pulitzer Prize since 2004 and the Serpentine Gallery since 1995. Of the thirteen Serpentine Pavilion architects until 2012, all but two of them—Daniel Libeskind and Snøhetta—had won the coveted award.)

Niemeyer's last works are far from his best, but that has not affected their popularity. His white disk-shaped Niterói Contemporary Art Museum of 1991–1996, perched atop a rocky promontory overlooking Guanabara Bay and Rio de Janeiro to the west, has been a runaway success as a tourist attraction. But the Niterói's curves are not nearly as felicitous as those of the architect's earlier designs, and one could well imagine that this awkward flying saucer was denied landing permission at Brasília and forced to alight here instead.

Niemeyer led an eight-decade-long samba through the building art, a joyous journey that gave the world some of its liveliest modern landmarks. Samba—which attains its annual climax during the pre-Lenten bacchanal of carnival—is deeply subversive yet also an essential expression of Brazil's inner nature. Fittingly enough, the architect designed what is now the focal point of the Rio carnival, his Passarela do Samba of 1984, popularly known as the Sambódromo, or samba stadium. Intended to remove the annual procession from congested city streets and increase the celebration's visibility for the maximum number of spectators, this open-air amphitheater closely resembles a conventional football arena surrounded by high bleachers. The fifteen-foot-high, 2,300-foot-long U-shaped runway culminates in a raised proscenium fancifully named Apotheosis Square, where competing *sambistas* break loose beneath an open tripartite canopy of three slender, conjoined concrete parabolic arches, the facility's most distinctive architectural flourish.

A cardinal trait of carnival is its inversion of societal norms, a once-a-year world-turned-upside-down when paupers can be princes, saints can be sinners, and the upright can be lowdown. Inversion is also a recurrent theme in Niemeyer's architecture, as seen in his juxtaposition of a casino and a church at Pampulha; the topsy-turvy pyramid of his unbuilt Caracas Museum of Modern Art of 1955; the paired up-and-down domes at Brasília; and above all his undulating line—a "carnivalization" provocatively analyzed in Styliane Philippou's richly detailed *Oscar Niemeyer: Curves of Irreverence* (2008), the finest study yet of this subtly anarchic figure.

Though Niemeyer is often characterized as a maverick whose preference for the curve instead of the straight line and right angle set him in diametric opposition to the restrictive orthodoxies of Modernism, he in fact asserted not so much a contrarian as a parallel, liberating alternative. During his early prime, Niemeyer commanded creative gifts that were the tropical equivalent of his Nordic contemporary Aalto, who also asserted that sensuousness and delight have as much a place in modern architecture as technical ingenuity, rational simplicity, and intellectual rigor. As Charles Jencks has observed: "In many respects the personality and work of Aalto are the inverse of Le Corbusier's: relaxed and flowing rather than violent and tempestuous and patient rather than outspoken."

The same might be said of Niemeyer vis-à-vis Le Corbusier. The irascible elder architect's late-career biomorphic redirection derived in no small part from lessons he obviously learned from his more laid-back younger colleague, as can be seen from the erstwhile machine Modernist's more voluptuous handling of architectural mass in his postwar work (even though curves began to appear in his buildings with increasing frequency from about 1930 onward). Would we have had Le Corbusier's Ronchamp chapel without Niemeyer's unabashedly erotic *formação de curvas?* Whether Le Corbusier was merely being polite or sincere when he looked out over the newly completed Brasília in 1962 and told Niemeyer "Bravo, Oscar, bravo!" we will never know. Unquestionably, though, Oscar Niemeyer excelled in his rare fusion of graphic clarity, formal purity, pleasing spatial proportion, sensuous dynamism, and visceral immediacy, a mixture unique among his peers during the decades immediately before and after 1950. His meridian moment of optimistic Modernism is likely to be looked back upon with well-merited fondness for many years to come.

were set aside by the museum's board, which handed that plum assignment to their fellow trustee Philip L. Goodwin, a *routinier* Beaux Arts architect whose main qualification, as the museum's first architecture curator, Philip Johnson, later candidly recalled, was "money, money, money." Stone was given the tricky task of steering the design away from Goodwin's conservative proclivities and toward the Modernist aesthetic the young institution was promoting. It is to Stone's credit that the mismatched partners' Museum of Modern Art of 1936–1939 emerged as a thoroughly respectable if not quite thrilling specimen of the International Style, with neutrally detailed, domestically scaled galleries that became the influential new standard for exhibiting twentieth-century painting, sculpture, and design.

During World War II, Stone served as a major in the US Army, and while stationed in Washington, D.C., he designed airfields and military bases. When peace came the architect applied his newly acquired organizational abilities to large-scale projects that included resort hotels in Panama and Lebanon, as well as colleges across the United States as higher education boomed (in large part thanks to the Servicemen's Readjustment Act of 1944, commonly known as the G.I. Bill). His workload grew to an enviable degree, and he found a paradoxical admirer in Wright, whose revolutionary reputation stemmed from breaking out of precisely the kind of static boxlike configurations that Stone resorted to time and again during his postwar period, as opposed to the often dynamic layouts of his prewar houses.

Wright blamed his brush with oblivion in the 1920s on the strict reductivism espoused by Le Corbusier, Gropius, Mies, Oud, and other European modernists who abjured all applied ornament and pattern. After his triumphant comeback in the 1930s, Wright embraced increasingly florid decorative schemes to set his work apart from that of his nemeses who championed the pared-down International Style. This is where America's greatest architect and the profession's latest sensation found common ground. In Stone's Stanford and Harvey Mudd ensembles he paid Wright the compliment of using geometrically patterned precast concrete components clearly derived from the old master's pre-Columbian-inspired "textile block" concrete construction system of 1922–1923. Wright in turn said that he admired Stone's widely praised US Embassy of 1954–1958 in New Delhi, and went so far as to claim it was more beautiful than the Taj Mahal, proof that he had never laid eyes on either.

Wright's ferocious third wife, Olgivanna, always attuned to the main chance, encouraged a friendship between the two architects as Stone's star began its meteoric rise. The Montenegrin-born Olgivanna, an acolyte of the spiritualist G. I. Gurdjieff, thrived on intrigue and loved to meddle in the sex lives of the Taliesin Fellowship, Wright's architecture school–cum–professional office–cum–imperial court. After his death in 1959 there was an understandably sharp drop-off in commissions, and the widow Wright hatched a byzantine plot to draw the Stones deeper into the Taliesin circle in order to profit from his connections. As Hicks Stone writes of his mother and her new best friend, "They confided in each other about the details of their marriages, the sexual behavior of their husbands, and the role a wife can play in her husband's architectural practice." Convinced that if Ed Stone were made jealous enough he'd spend more time at Taliesin West in Arizona, the sinister Mrs. Wright successfully masterminded an affair between Maria and a neurosurgeon she had tutored in Gurdjieff's beliefs. But that dalliance wrecked the Stones' already stormy marriage, and the wicked old schemer, who belatedly feared a scandal, banished the hapless adulterers from her desert court.

Much as Francis Bacon bitchily referred to his macho fellow painter Jackson Pollock—best known for his airy, looping skeins of pigment—as "the lacemaker," that sobriquet also could have been applied to Stone once he began repetitively wrapping decorative white filigreed screens around his buildings in the early 1950s. Johnson, a much better critic than designer, delivered the sharpest one-sentence verdict on Stone when he observed that "architecture is more than putting drapes in front of a house to hide it." One of the more egregious applications of that idea was the lacy white façade Stone tacked onto his own Victorian town house on Manhattan's Upper East Side, which sticks out from its row of stolid brownstones like an enormous antimacassar. Easily and cheaply mimicked in precast concrete and other composite materials, knockoffs of his pierced screens quickly became ubiquitous architectural clichés throughout the Sunbelt, where countless breezeways and carports bear silent witness to the false dawn of a new Stone Age.

Even fellow architects who saw certain good qualities beneath the froufrou surface of Stone's postwar work were exasperated by his constant reiteration of patterned screens. Eero Saarinen, his principal rival for high-profile corporate commissions and another darling of the mainstream press in the 1950s (both appeared on the cover of *Time* magazine, a big deal back then), averred that "the best thing that could happen to Ed Stone would be for someone to take his grilles away from him." By the 1960s that opinion became so widespread among Stone's critics and potential clients that his office managers curtailed and eventually banned his hallmark motif, more as a marketing strategy than as an artistic principle. Alas, what lay behind the screens was not particularly interesting, and without those seductive peekaboo veils it became all too obvious that the exposed volumes of his unadorned work lacked either the raw power of Brutalism or the understated rigor of Minimalism, the two dominant architectural trends of the 1960s and 1970s. Stone's simpler late-career structures, almost always clad in white masonry deployed in vertical stripes, exude the denuded and forlorn air of freshly shorn sheep.

Vincent Scully, the oracular architectural historian who made the critical reputations of both Kahn and Venturi, was exceptional during the postwar period for being wholly receptive to new expressions of the Classical tradition, as exemplified by his support for both Kahn's majestic Roman-inspired forms and the playful Mannerist and vernacular conceits of Venturi and Scott Brown. But Scully could not stomach what he saw as the debased sub-Classical values of Stone and his closest contemporary counterpart, the Japanese-American architect Minoru Yamasaki (whose most famous work, the twin-towered World Trade Center of 1966–1977 in New York City, conformed closely to Stone's white-clad, vertical-striped, flat-topped high-rise format). As Scully wrote in 1969 of that shared aesthetic:

> It is superficial classicism; and it is, literally, superficial design, where the volume, into which the functions are more or less fitted, is fundamentally Miesian, symmetrical, and not overly studied, but the surface is as crumpled and laced up as the trade can afford.

Stone's rigid tendencies were most apparent, and deleterious, in his comprehensive planning schemes, never more so than in his Uptown Campus of 1954–1958 for the State University of New York at Albany. Its obsessively symmetrical layout—centered by a vast colonnaded oblong of interconnected mirror-image pavilions and roofless courtyards—is bounded beyond its outer corners by four identical freestanding high-rises surrounded at the base by deep arcades. The quadrangle has been a defining element of collegiate design since the Middle Ages, when such inward-facing spaces grew incrementally and organically out of defensive monastic prototypes and reflected the functional relationships of the buildings that surrounded them. In contrast to the logical evolution and essential intimacy of medieval university ensembles, the superscale, unitary nature of Stone's Albany campus is decidedly arbitrary, not to say Procrustean. For example, the handling of the four principal atriums is so similar that it is hard (at least for the occasional visitor) to tell exactly where within the complex one is. Likewise the indistinguishable appearance of the identical outlying towers makes it difficult to read those vertical elements as accurate reference points.

Another deficiency of this scheme—and of Stone's oeuvre in general—is a basic disregard for climatic conditions, as seen at Albany in his fetishistic fondness for open plazas and porous peripheries, particularly unsuitable for that city's frigid winters. But in that respect Stone was no different from his old boss Harrison, whose brutally exposed and windswept Empire State Plaza of 1959–1976, also in Albany, would likewise be more appropriate in Brasília than the northern Hudson River valley. Although Stone's perforated outer walls may have made good environmental sense in tropical settings—particularly the New Delhi embassy, where his openwork panels updated the traditional *jali* that shaded and ventilated classical Mughal architecture—he applied that idea so indiscriminately everywhere in the world that rather than seeming an outgrowth of well-considered design it became a mere styling gimmick. Yet even in warm locales where this formula might have made more ecological sense, Stone's contradictory combination of International Style generality, Classical rigidity, and Romantic theatricality resulted in some rather strange proposals.

One such scheme was his vast campus for the University of Islamabad (now Quaid-i-Azam University) of 1966–1985 in Pakistan, one of fifteen late-career commissions in that country, which also included the Presidential Palace of 1966–circa 1980 in Islamabad and the Pakistan Institute of Nuclear Science and Technology of 1965–1974 in Nilore. The university ensemble multiplies the SUNY Albany format to an almost manic degree, with a proliferation of identically scaled, atrium-centered buildings in a checkerboard pattern that makes the New York State campus look positively Minimalist.

Changing attitudes toward Stone's work were evident by the turn of the millennium, when one of the most misjudged preservation battles in recent decades attracted a disproportionate amount of attention given the historical insignificance of the building involved: his Gallery of Modern Art of 1964–1965 in New York City. Commissioned by the eccentric A&P supermarket heir Huntington Hartford, this privately endowed institution was conceived as a contrarian riposte to the Museum of Modern Art and what Hartford—whose taste in painting ran to the then deeply unfashionable Pre-Raphaelites and the later work of Salvador Dalí—saw as the overly restrictive view of Modernism advanced by MoMA. It was therefore no coincidence that he turned to one of that institution's original architects for his rival gallery, although the results were strikingly different from Stone's textbook exercise in International Style orthodoxy for MoMA three decades earlier.

The highly visible, easily accessible, but tightly restricted site that Hartford chose for his quixotic project occupied a small traffic island at the southern end of Manhattan's chronically ill-defined Columbus Circle. Stone maximized the small rectangular ground plan by extending the structure to a height of ten stories, and created an illusion of greater depth at street level by pushing the building envelope out to its permissible maximum on all four sides and then encircling the base with an arcade of oddly stylized columns that Ada Louise Huxtable, writing in *The New York Times*, indelibly likened to giant lollipops. Above them, the building's white marble facing was trimmed with eyelet-like holes around the edges, rather than the architect's more typical all-over perforation pattern. Stone, never very imaginative with spatial solutions, was unable to create any satisfying interiors within the structure's constricted carapace, and the

Hartford's attenuated, awkwardly proportioned display rooms felt oppressively claustrophobic. The enterprise was a financial bust for the profligate playboy patron, and after he closed the gallery in 1969 the building was taken over by the city and used as offices for its Department of Cultural Affairs.

A leading voice in favor of the old Hartford's preservation was the *Times*'s erratic and self-dramatizing architecture critic from 1992 to 2004, the late Herbert Muschamp, who in 2006 wrote a rambling 5,600-word polemic, "The Secret History of 2 Columbus Circle," which urged that the endangered structure be saved not as a meritorious landmark of design, but rather as an important locus of metropolitan gay culture. That retroactive designation came as news to many homosexual museumgoers old enough to remember the gallery in its prime, as it would doubtless have to the building's rampantly heterosexual begetters, Hartford and Stone. However, unless one necessarily synonymizes camp with a gay sensibility, it is hard to buy Muschamp's proposition, which seemed very much a matter of personal projection, a characteristic of his indulgently self-referential criticism as a whole. In any event, the Hartford's vague resemblance to a Venetian palazzo as it might have been reimagined by RKO's art director Van Nest Polglase for the Fred Astaire–Ginger Rogers musical *Top Hat* (1935) puts this urban curiosity more firmly in the realm of kitsch rather than camp.

In the end, the former Hartford was stripped down to its steel skeleton and reconfigured by Brad Cloepfil of Allied Works Architecture as the new home of the Museum of Arts and Design (formerly called the American Craft Museum), which opened in 2008. As silly as the original building may have been, it was certainly preferable to the deadening makeover it received from Cloepfil, who reclad the exterior in white and gray tiles that impart all the charm of a subway pissoir. Only in comparative terms can the effacement of Stone's fanciful exterior be seen as a loss, and regrets for its passing as anything more than misdirected sentimentality. Thus despite Hicks Stone's valiant efforts to secure a higher place for his father in architectural history (paralleled by similar attempts by other recent apologists—including the architectural historian Mary Anne Hunting, author of the unpersuasively argued *Edward Durell Stone: Modernism's Populist Architect* (2012)—he still seems no more than a middling (if also exceptionally lucky and prolific) product of his times, though personally more interesting than one had imagined.

As the younger Stone's life-and-works inadvertently indicates, this now-faded star was an opportunistic artist on a par with the painter Adolph Gottlieb, a year-younger contemporary who likewise hit upon a readily marketable Modernist formula and then cranked out increasingly weaker variants of it until the work devolved into sad self-parody. All the same, during the deeply unsettled postmillennial period, when melodramatic midcentury-themed cinematic pieces such as Todd Haynes's *Far from Heaven* (2002), Matthew Weiner's *Mad Men* (2007–), Sam Mendes's *Revolutionary Road* (2008), and Terrence Malick's *The Tree of Life* (2011) enthralled audiences with their wistful backward glances toward an ascendant (if hardly untroubled) America, it would be a mistake to discount the nostalgic spell that Edward Durell Stone's peculiar brand of modern romanticism can still exert on suggestible escapists.

8

EERO SAARINEN

THE PREMATURE DEATH of a major artist inevitably raises an unanswerable question: What might have been? But when an exceptionally promising architect such as Eero Saarinen dies at an early age the loss seems especially tragic, because the slow pace of the building process has always made architecture anything but a young man's game. A number of renowned architects throughout history have reached a great age. Christopher Wren died at ninety, an eighteenth-century Methuselah. In our own time, Frank Lloyd Wright reached ninety-one, Philip Johnson ninety-eight, and Oscar Niemeyer a prodigious one hundred and four. But Wright would still be considered a genius even if he had died at forty, having already demonstrated his most important concepts. Conversely, one of the most influential early Modernists was the Italian visionary Antonio Sant'Elia, who was killed in action in World War I at twenty-eight. Although Sant'Elia never erected a single building, his *Città Nuova* scheme of 1914—a fantasy skyscraper metropolis as psychologically fascinating and structurally implausible as Piranesi's *Carceri d'invenzione*—has inspired urban provocateurs from Le Corbusier to Rem Koolhaas. However, unlike poètes maudits and Hollywood sex symbols, it is generally a bad career move for architects to die young, or even in early middle age.

Saarinen was cut down in his prime when he succumbed to a brain tumor in 1961, a mere fifty-one years old. In his all-too-brief heyday, during the expansive Eisenhower years, he was one of America's most lionized architects, a pet of the popular and the professional press. Yet more than half a century later, there is still no critical consensus about what his precise historical place should be, mainly because this stylistic flaneur has remained so difficult to position among his more readily classifiable High Modernist peers. Saarinen's head cheerleader was his devoted and well-connected second wife, Aline, a best-selling arts journalist, *New York Times* editor, and ubiquitous cultural broadcaster during the golden age of television. As she confided to her mentor Bernard Berenson in 1958, "Now I observe myself ardently promulgating the Eero-myth."

But academic critics were not nearly as enthusiastic about Saarinen as his wife was. The Yale architectural historian Vincent Scully detected in the architect's more exuberant designs an oppressive triumphalism—epitomized by the flamboyantly engineered, whalelike David S. Ingalls Hockey Rink of 1956–1958 at Yale—and found his buildings symptomatic of "a good deal that was wrong with American architecture in the mid-1950s: exhibitionism, structural pretension, self-defeating urbanistic arrogance." Others thought Saarinen was prone to cloying scenographic effects. After the British critic Reyner Banham visited the architect's Morse and Ezra Stiles Colleges of 1958–1962 at Yale (see rear endpapers)—a village-like dormitory complex that brings to mind an opera buffa stage set or, worse, a Tuscan-themed Las Vegas resort—he wrote that it "disgusted me at sight, and it still disgusts me." And the Marxist Italian architectural historian Manfredo Tafuri denounced Saarinen's highly conspicuous schemes for some of America's biggest companies—which included Bell Telephone, General Motors, CBS, IBM, and TWA—as an insidious form of "corporate advertising." (This was hardly a novel critique, however, as the promotional nature of the tall office building had been openly acknowledged decades earlier by publicity-conscious businessman patrons like Frederick Bourne of the Singer Manufacturing Company, the dime-store magnate Frank Winfield Woolworth, and the automobile manufacturer Walter P. Chrysler, all of whom commissioned attention-getting corporate towers.)

The prestige value of a skyscraper by a name-brand architect was also not lost on William Paley, the culturally (and socially) ambitious TV mogul who hired Saarinen to design the CBS Building of 1960–1965 in New York. But the finished product, completed four years after the architect's death, failed to fulfill Paley's dream of outdoing the uncouth whiskey tycoon Samuel Bronfman, who sponsored Ludwig Mies van der Rohe and Philip Johnson's acclaimed Seagram Building of 1954–1958, three blocks east of the CBS site. The control-freak Paley micromanaged countless design details, including the stippled matte finish of the dark gray granite cladding that earned his network's headquarters the sobriquet "Black Rock." Alas, he did not reckon what a miscalculation it was for Saarinen to sink the monolithic tower's entry court two feet below street level on Manhattan's Avenue of the Americas. This deflating arrival sequence down a peripheral bank of steps is the antithesis of the uplifting approach to the sublime Seagram Building via Mies's majestic plaza elevated atop a plinth.

All artists go through distinct developmental periods, but the look of Saarinen's buildings could vary wildly, and without apparent logic, from project to project. At times he would let fly with a swooping extravagance not witnessed since the swan song of Art Nouveau half a century earlier, and exemplified by his voluptuously sculptural TWA Terminal of 1956–1962 at New York's Idlewild (later JFK) Airport (see Illustration 8), which vaguely suggests spread wings. For other schemes he would be all business, as demonstrated by the crisp modularity of his IBM Research Center of 1957–1961 in Yorktown Heights, New York.

Saarinen's Deere and Company Administrative Center of 1957–1963 in Moline, Illinois, was the finest of his corporate headquarters because it so satisfyingly mediated his bipolar aesthetic and proved how the seemingly exhausted Miesian mode could still yield far more volumetric interest than the routine, flat-walled International Style box. For this lush-budget job on a well-manicured rural site, Saarinen wrapped the eight-story glass-skinned office building in a scaffold-like exoskeleton of the newly introduced Cor-Ten steel (later to become the sculptor Richard Serra's preferred material). This beautifully proportioned grid of rust-colored columns and railings acts as a sunscreen, but more important, it dematerializes the structure's bulk and imparts to it an ethereal floating quality much like that of Kobori Enshu's Katsura Imperial Villa of 1620–1645 in Kyoto, the summit of classical Japanese architecture, which captivated Saarinen when he visited the city in 1958. Although his Deere project was already well underway, he was so taken by the exquisitely assembled, deceptively understated villa and its lyrical garden—revered by early Modernists, including Bruno Taut and Walter Gropius, who through this example reawakened the Eurocentric post–Meiji period Japanese to their own glorious architectural heritage—that upon his return he drastically reworked the plans, and reported to his client that the improved version showed "real promise of achieving...the same quality as Katsura."

Was Saarinen the Dr. Jekyll and Mr. Hyde of twentieth-century architecture, morphing with alarming suddenness from one diametrically opposed persona to another? Was he the Janus of midcentury Modernism, a pivotal figure who looked back toward the machine aesthetic of the early International Style and ahead toward the Expressionistic animation of Frank Gehry and Santiago Calatrava? Or was he little more than a straight Philip Johnson, a dab hand at tossing off instantly arresting but ultimately vacuous trophy architecture for the captains of corporate America?

One might have thought that any lingering unease over his bifurcated vision would have been allayed after the demise of Modernist orthodoxy and the rise of today's more permissive attitudes in architecture. But opinion on Saarinen has remained sharply divided, as was confirmed by the two very different points of view set forth at a Saarinen symposium held at the Yale School of Architecture in 2005. Most of the panelists—all alumni of his office, including Kevin Roche (who took over the firm after his boss died) and Cesar Pelli—spoke in the laudatory tones expected on such occasions. The keenest insights, unsurprisingly, came from Robert Venturi, a leading protagonist in the downfall of Modernist hegemony and an on-and-off Saarinen employee from 1950 to 1953. Venturi's pioneering advocacy of an inclusive, high/low, either-or approach to architecture might seem to dispose him favorably toward Saarinen's wayward design ethos. But as Venturi persuasively maintained at Yale, the trouble with Saarinen isn't that his work is too diverse but rather that it isn't complex and contradictory enough:

> There can be many ways of expression that can connect with different cultures: there is not one universal culture anymore. But I don't think this is what Eero's eclectic expressionism was about. . . . You could not call it multiculturalism because it was/ is a little like every building being in a different costume . . . at a costume ball where someone goes as one thing and another person goes as another thing. . . . The expressionistic variety was not derived from what we would call multiculturalism now, but from a kind of arbitrary, stylistic, fashionable approach.

Venturi declared his favorite scheme of Saarinen's to be the Gateway Arch at the Jefferson National Expansion Memorial of 1947–1965 in St. Louis, the 630-foot-tall stainless-steel catenary that he praised for its "modern structure, monumental scale, and appropriate symbolism!" However, with his extensive historical knowledge, he cannot have been unaware of its extraordinary resemblance to the unbuilt arch Adalberto Libera designed in 1939 for Mussolini's aborted Esposizione Universale Roma of 1942. (That unpleasant fact made headlines in 1948, when Saarinen presented his proposal. The hubbub subsided after he indignantly denied having copied the Fascist prototype, and the National Park Service proceeded with his scheme nonetheless.) I suspect that Venturi actually chose the St. Louis monument because of its subliminal Pop implications: the arch brings to mind a superscale Oldenburgian wicket awaiting a croquet ball as big and as white as the Perisphere at the 1939 New York World's Fair.

For all his populist impulses, Venturi was never an indiscriminate eclecticist but a thoroughgoing theorist with strongly held philosophical positions. Conversely, if Saarinen had articulated a systematic rationale for his extreme stylistic shifts, he might not have been stigmatized as a mercurial opportunist who abetted a culture of planned obsolescence through the architectural equivalent of novel consumer goods. Yet looking back at the 1950s boom years of the American automobile industry, its annual introduction of new car models with increasingly swollen protuberances and exaggerated fins had more than a little in common with the sexy, futuristic schemes being spun out at the same time by Saarinen's firm in the Detroit suburb of Bloomfield Hills. Perhaps because of his facile design skills, aptitude for public relations, and heady professional ascent, he felt no need to justify artistic license through theoretical argument.

By the time Saarinen's career shifted into high gear after World War II, the fundamental precepts of the Modern Movement had been so widely accepted that manifestos seemed redundant and remained so until 1966, when Venturi's self-proclaimed "gentle manifesto," *Complexity and Contradiction in Architecture*, undid what remained of his erstwhile employer's dwindling legacy. Scholars were long thwarted in their attempts to put Saarinen into proper perspective because exclusive access to the architect's drawings and papers had been monopolized by a writer whose perpetually awaited, authorized life-and-works never materialized. This Godot-like stasis ended in 2002, when Roche donated the Saarinen office archives to Yale, which broke the embargo, but the damage had been done. The protracted hiatus in Saarinen studies allowed specious claims to go unchallenged, primarily the persistent Eero-myth that he was the missing link in modern architecture's apostolic succession.

Saarinen stood apart from his peers in no small part because of the charismatically photogenic quality of his built work. The dynamic color images made by one of his foremost visual chroniclers, Balthazar Korab, practically leap off the page. The Michigan-based Korab and his two major competitors—Ezra Stoller of New York and Julius Shulman of Los Angeles—were to the photography of midcentury Modern architecture what their contemporaries Ansel Adams and Yousuf Karsh were to the western landscape and celebrity portraiture, respectively: unapologetic showmen who played to popular notions of the heroic in order to ennoble their subjects. Both Stoller and Shulman were adept (if formulaic) technicians with foolproof commercial instincts, though seemingly incapable of the sly insights that give the images of their lesser-known but prolific contemporary Pedro E. Guerrero (who began his career as Frank Lloyd Wright's official photographer) a critical edge that their work generally lacks.

Stoller's 1962 black-and-white photo essay on the TWA Terminal remains unsurpassed in conveying the essence of an unconventional architectural masterpiece. But neither he nor Shulman (whose virtuosic ability to bring out a thousand shades of gray was akin to that of 1930s cinematographers) commanded Korab's gift for high-keyed color. Like all but a few of his High Modernist colleagues, Saarinen had little interest in the expressive potential of architectural color. But the sensuously modeled contours of his strongest buildings never looked more alive than when Korab shot them against the ravishing tints of dawn or twilight. He captured the buoyant optimism of his favorite subject to perfection, the visual equivalent of Frank Sinatra's infectiously upbeat 1958 LP *Come Fly with Me*, the ideal soundtrack for Saarinen's aerodynamic structures, which seem ready to lift into orbit.

No modern architect derived greater benefit from family connections than Eero Saarinen, who was born in Finland in 1910, on the thirty-seventh birthday of his father, Eliel, their homeland's preeminent architect during the first third of the twentieth century (until Alvar Aalto, half a generation between the two Saarinens and much more significant than either). The elder Saarinen (along with his two partners, Herman Gesellius and Armas Lindgren) had started the new century with a bang thanks to their critically acclaimed Finnish Pavilion at the Universal Exposition of 1900 in Paris, which displayed an invigorating folkloristic strength that stood out from the overcomplicated *baroquerie* around it. Eero was raised at Hvitträsk, the communal country house and studio of 1902 near Helsinki created by his father and his two colleagues in the style that took its name from the Arts and Crafts–oriented National Romantic Movement, which asserted Finnish independence after centuries of domination by Sweden and Russia, a dream that finally became a reality in 1917, two months after the October Revolution.

Although the richly embellished Hvitträsk ensemble was influenced to some extent by the other new free styles that erupted around the turn of the twentieth century, the utopian young Finns who cre-

ated it were more politically motivated than their Art Nouveau counterparts. As was true with exponents of the widespread fin-de-siècle phenomenon of the *Gesamtkunstwerk* ("total work of art"), Finland's National Romanticists placed great emphasis on the complete coordination of all aspects of design, from the grandest environmental concepts to the tiniest decorative grace notes, the same unified approach then being pursued in America by Wright under his rubric of "organic architecture."

Eliel Saarinen attracted further international attention with his second-place entry in the Chicago Tribune Building competition of 1922. Many thought it superior to the prizewinning scheme, by John Mead Howell and Raymond Hood, which was fussed up with incongruous Neo-Gothic ornament. Saarinen's powerfully massed, clean-lined proposal, free of anachronistic historical details, made an immediate impact on American skyscraper design (as seen in the rapid adaptation of his principal ideas by Ralph Walker for his look-alike New York Telephone Building of 1923–1926 in lower Manhattan). Rarely has losing a competition been such a boon to an architect's career. Favorable publicity about Saarinen caught the eye of the Detroit newspaper magnate George Booth, who wanted to establish an American design school based on Arts and Crafts principles. He asked the recent émigré not only to design the Cranbrook Academy of Art, built on Booth's estate in suburban Detroit, but also to head the school and shape its curriculum, whereupon the elder Saarinen resettled with his family on the nascent campus.

Eero's formidable mother, Loja (herself the child of an eminent architect, Eliel's partner and Hvittrāsk collaborator Gesellius), was an accomplished textile designer and sculptor who ensured that her boy's precocious talents were not merely encouraged but given ample opportunity for application. He began working in his father's architectural office at fifteen, creating decorative elements and furnishings for Cranbrook. (Such early employment was a throwback to craft apprenticeships, which traditionally began after religious confirmation at age fourteen.) Although the younger Saarinen's mature work adhered to the High Modernist proscription against the applied ornament and vivid pattern so integral to his father's Arts and Crafts credo, he never abandoned his great concern for the sympathetic furnishing and landscaping of his buildings with the "organic" unity espoused by the designers of the Arts and Crafts Movement.

Saarinen *fils* had a gift for furniture design, which was rewarded when he and a close Cranbrook contemporary, Charles Eames, won two first prizes for chairs they collaborated on for the Museum of Modern Art's Organic Design in Home Furnishings competition of 1940. Eames and his wife, Ray, went on to become the supreme furniture designers of the twentieth century. Eero Saarinen was not nearly as important in that sphere, but he did create two icons of modern seating: the spindly-legged but warmly enveloping Womb chair of 1946–1948 (a wool-upholstered reinterpretation of the traditional high-backed club chair) and the sleekly reductive Tulip or Pedestal chair of 1954–1957 (a continuous linear flow of white-painted aluminum with a fiberglass seat supported by a single, centered column flaring upward from a circular base). These classics are still produced by Knoll, the high-style furniture manufacturer whose longtime presiding spirit, Florence Schust Knoll, studied at Cranbrook during the 1930s and was welcomed into the Saarinen family circle (although she did not marry Eero, as his mother wished).

By the time large-scale civilian construction resumed after World War II, young Saarinen—a partner in Eliel's practice since 1937—was better positioned than any other architect of his generation to land the big new jobs that poured forth following years of pent-up demand. The backing of his father's long-established office lent weight to the thirty-seven-year-old's winning entry in the St. Louis memorial competition. Two years before Eliel's death in 1950, Eero assumed full creative control of the firm, which saw the last of his father's somewhat stuffy Stripped Classicism—the farthest the essentially conservative Eliel was prepared to go on the road to High Modernism. The younger Saarinen, always a quick study, grasped how avidly the postwar American business establishment was taking to the cost-efficient, easily adaptable International Style. In his nononsense, meticulously Miesian design for the General Motors Technical Center in Warren, Michigan, begun in 1948, we can see the exact moment when the mantle passed from father to son.

On his own, Eero quickly became more famous than Eliel ever had been. Saarinen's output as a whole divides quite easily between the building categories he excelled at (corporate offices and airports) and others he never seemed to master (embassies and dormitories). In 1954, the State Department began a commendable (if ultimately disappointing) program to improve the quality of its foreign service architecture, reflecting America's new position as an international superpower. Although several of the country's (and the century's) most lauded architects were enlisted—Gropius, Marcel Breuer, Paul Rudolph, and I. M. Pei among them—none delivered his best work, perhaps inhibited by notions of official decorum or daunted by how to represent the nation abroad in architectural form.

Saarinen's skyrocketing professional status was confirmed by his receiving three of these coveted commissions: an addition to the American Embassy in his homeland's capital, Helsinki (1952–1953, but never executed), and the US Chancellery buildings in Oslo (1955–1959) and London (1955–1960). The London legation offices were accorded a prestigious site on Grosvenor Square in Mayfair. The architect's early sketches document his struggle with a landmark urban setting worlds away from the spacious corporate arcadias and idyllic campuses he was used to. He finally gave up his updated Classicist attempts and defaulted to a variant of his Modernist Oslo solution: a long, relatively low, flat-roofed structure, its façade paneled with stone-framed, upright rectangular windows. Ten years after V-E Day, debate still raged over whether bombed-out London ought to be reconstructed in a historical or contemporary manner. Saarinen somehow thought his buff-colored, New Brutalist scheme was sympathetic to its redbrick Georgian surroundings. Few British critics, traditionalist or Modernist, agreed, and they stirred up the biggest controversy of Saarinen's career. The embattled architect was not helped when he asked the Polish-American sculptor Theodore Roszak to fashion an enormous eagle to adorn the Grosvenor Square façade. This garish gilded-aluminum mascot, with the wingspan of a small plane and a predatory mien, handed the project's opponents a made-to-order caricature of Ugly American hubris at a time of mounting British resentment over the role reversal between the two imperial powers—ours waxing, theirs waning.

The unprecedented growth of American higher education after World War II demanded new student housing to keep up with ballooning enrollment. A year before victory, Saarinen was asked to prepare a master plan for Antioch College in Yellow Springs, Ohio, one of many institutions bracing for the influx of demobilized soldiers eager to complete their education thanks to the G.I. Bill. In the typical pattern of architectural patronage, one commission begat a similar one, then another and another, but more often than not Saarinen's academic schemes were as lackluster as his State Department designs. Oddly for an architect who grew up on a campus designed by his own father, he had little apparent feeling for the social aspects of student life, and his dorm layouts often failed to encourage personal interaction.

For example, his Hill College House of 1958–1960, a women's dormitory at the University of Pennsylvania in Philadelphia, is entered via a walkway conceived as a virtual drawbridge to symboli-cally protect the inhabitants from male visitors. In that respect Saarinen was no different from Louis Kahn, whose Erdman Hall Dormitories of 1960–1965 at Bryn Mawr College in Pennsylvania likewise resembled a medieval fortress, a defensive posture that in hindsight seems even more anachronistic in light of the upheavals set in motion by the feminist movement within only a few years of these buildings' completion. Just as tellingly, the Hill College House living quarters that face the inward-turning structure's central atrium are screened by louvers that suggest a zenana, the female precinct of Is-lamic domestic architecture. One noteworthy exception to Saarinen's social myopia was the visitors' lounge at Vassar's Emma Hartman Noyes House of 1954–1958. This secluded seating area, which the architect recessed below floor level, encouraged intimacies unantici-pated by the bemused client but seized upon by grateful residents and their suitors, who dubbed Saarinen's popular innovation "the pas-sion pit." However, none of his many dormitory designs approached the brilliance of his countryman Alvar Aalto's Baker House of 1946–1949 at MIT. Aalto's audacious, serpentine ground plan emerged from his desire to minimize the dehumanizing effect of long residence-hall corridors, rather than to maximize an eye-catching exterior, all too often Saarinen's seeming motivation.

Saarinen's desire to make modern architecture more emotionally expressive, at a time when the late International Style seemed to be running on empty, won his office a particular following for its churches, a growth industry during the suburbanization of 1950s America. But his attempts to convey spirituality through a new vo-cabulary of forms were only sporadically successful. Unlike Aalto, who used indirect natural light to define sacred space with a power matched in modern architecture only by Le Corbusier and Kahn, Saarinen relied for the most part on new iterations of familiar religious motifs. For example, the needlelike, 192-foot-high spire of his North Christian Church of 1959–1964 in Columbus, Indiana (commissioned by his most frequent patron, the industrialist J. Irwin Miller, who turned his small hometown into a Modernist architectural wonderland), updated the imagery of medieval spires and proved that the flèche is not weak if the spirit is willing. His most moving work of religious architecture was his nondenominational Kresge Chapel of 1950–1955 at MIT, the form and materials of which owe a great deal to Aalto's Baker House, a few hundred feet away. The rough-finished brick that Saarinen chose for both the circular exterior and undulating interior walls of this small but monumental cylinder is so similar to the cladding of the undulating Baker House that direct inspiration seems certain. The chapel's windowless sanctuary is illuminated by an oculus directly above the Minimalist white marble altar, behind which is suspended a see-through, floor-to-ceiling metal screen of gilded oblongs by the sculptor Harry Bertoia. Only cynics will interpret Bertoia's glittering reredos as a rain of golden banknotes fluttering down from a beneficent and munificent deity.

Saarinen came closest to expressing the zeitgeist of the incipient Space Age in his three superb aviation terminals: TWA; Dulles International Airport of 1958–1963 in Chantilly, Virginia; and Ellinikon International Airport of 1960–1969 in Athens. It is hard enough for an architect to rethink conventional attitudes toward familiar functional problems. It is an even greater challenge for an architect to invent a structure that can accommodate a function for which there is little or no precedent. The latter was often required during the nineteenth century, when the proliferation of new technologies prompted innovative architectural solutions that could mesh modern functions with the existing urban fabric. The train station is the prime example of this phenomenon: a building unknown before the Industrial Revolution but essential to all cities after the advent of railways.

Commercial air travel was no longer a novelty by the time Saarinen was hired by Trans World Airlines in 1956, but the air transport industry was about to embark on a vast expansion made possible by the new generation of large-scale jet aircraft, which would transform a privilege for the elite into a commonplace for the masses. The idea of transcontinental and foreign air travel needed to be marketed to an inexperienced public skeptical or even afraid of flying, at a time when high-fatality passenger plane crashes often made headlines. All three of Saarinen's airport schemes were intended to make getting onto a plane an exciting but above all a reassuring experience. While the TWA Terminal's soaring lines suggest the common perception of it as a bird in flight, the architect disclaimed any intentional resemblance and other analogies make equal sense. The womb-like, cavernous interiors flow from one into another with an organic inevitability reminiscent of various biological morphologies or geological formations. (The terminal was given a long-overdue renovation by its new owner, JetBlue, which in 2008 returned the run-down landmark to something like its original state.)

Saarinen's denial that he was making representational references at TWA (not surprising given High Modernism's emphasis on abstraction) was the opposite of Santiago Calatrava's latter-day avowal of avian symbolism in his flock of air and rail terminals. Although Saarinen has been accused of some of the same tendencies now held against Calatrava—particularly a fondness for ostentatious engineering displays when simpler solutions would suffice—Saarinen, even at his shallowest, had far more depth than Calatrava. Nonetheless, despite the best efforts of Saarinen's valiant partisans, their rehabilitation campaign forces the unfortunate conclusion that his body of work simply cannot bear the sustained scrutiny merited by the oeuvre of a true underappreciated genius of Modernism like Aalto (whose lifespan overlapped Saarinen's and exceeded it by a decade at each end). The disproportionate interest in Saarinen in recent years shows how historical perspective can be skewed by contemporary fixations, and how immediate concerns can make us believe that we best see the past not through a clarifying lens but reflected in a mirror. As Venturi mused at Yale:

> Is it not ironical that the neo-modernism characteristic of today's architecture, which is spectacularly expressionistic via its forms rather than richly iconographic via its symbolism, can be said to represent a kind of Saarinen revival—or survival?

1a. McKim, Mead & White, Isaac Bell house,
Newport, Rhode Island, 1881–1883.
Stately Shingle Style country houses such as this "cottage" by Stanford
White established his New York–based firm's national reputation.

1b. McKim, Mead & White, Pennsylvania Station, New York, 1905–1910.
Charles McKim modeled the stone exterior of his masterwork on ancient
Rome's Baths of Caracalla, but the depot's steel-and-glass concourse
owed more to the French protomodernist Henri Labrouste.

2a. Frank Lloyd Wright, Wright house and studio,
Oak Park, Illinois, 1889–1898/1909.
When Wright eloped with a client's wife, he reconfigured
his own home so his estranged wife could take in boarders.

2b. Frank Lloyd Wright, Taliesin, Spring Green, Wisconsin, 1911–1959.
The architect envisioned his sprawling hillside home and office in the
farming valley settled by his Welsh forebears as a refuge for him and his
lover, Mamah Borthwick Cheney, who would be slain there in 1914.

3a. Le Corbusier, Villa Jeanneret-Perret,
La Chaux-de-Fonds, Switzerland, 1912.
Built for the architect's parents, this early work already exhibits the bold
geometric simplification that would soon become his hallmark.

3b. Le Corbusier, Notre-Dame-du-Haut, Ronchamp, France, 1950–1955.
The master's much-admired pilgrimage chapel in northeastern France is
dedicated to the Virgin Mary, but its biomorphic contours seem to
celebrate all women, including his mother, named Marie.

4a. Walter Gropius, Bauhaus, Dessau, Germany, 1925–1926.
The pinwheel layout of the most renowned modern design school
(with offices at center, dormitories at bottom left, and workshops at top)
was clearest through the then-new medium of aerial photography.

4b. Walter Gropius, Bauhaus, Dessau, Germany, 1925–1926.
With its flat roofs, straight lines, and lack of applied ornament and
pattern, the Bauhaus building perfectly embodied the innovative
architectural principles taught there by Gropius, Mies, and others.

5a. Ernst May, Rundhaus, Römerstadt Housing Estate,
Frankfurt-Heddernheim, Germany, 1926–1927.
Head of Frankfurt's public housing program during the Weimar Republic,
May built 15,000 dwellings, mainly apartments, on twenty-three estates.

5b. Margarete Schütte-Lihotzky, Frankfurt Kitchen,
Höhenblick Housing Estate, Frankfurt-Ginnheim, Germany, 1926–1927.
The prefab kitchen unit devised for May's social-housing projects was a
revolutionary concept informed by domestic work-efficiency studies.

6a. Oscar Niemeyer, Church of Saint Francis of Assisi,
Pampulha, Brazil, 1941–1943.
The frank sensuality of this design prompted conservative
prelates to prevent its consecration until 1959.

6b. Oscar Niemeyer, Plaza of the Three Powers, Brasília, 1956–1960.
Niemeyer's new capital city for Brazil, his monumental masterwork,
was the most ambitious fulfillment of start-from-scratch
urbanism in the twentieth century.

7. Edward Durell Stone, United States Pavilion,
Universal and International Exposition, Brussels, 1957–1958.
The round plan of this temporary exhibition hall was a rare
departure from Stone's grille-wrapped shoebox formula.

8. Eero Saarinen, Trans World Airlines Terminal, Idlewild (now John F.
Kennedy International) Airport, Queens, New York, 1958–1962.
By evoking the organic grace of a bird in flight, this lyrical design
conferred a still-unsurpassed glamour on mass air travel.

9. R. Buckminster Fuller, United States Pavilion,
Expo 67, Montreal, 1964–1967.
Fuller applied the engineering techniques of his self-supporting
geodesic dome to this transparent globe for a world's fair exhibit.

10. Carlo Scarpa, Brion Tomb, San Vito d'Altivole, Italy, 1969–1978.
Scarpa conceived this private family necropolis as a metaphoric journey
from birth to death. He himself is immured within a wall of
his timeless masterpiece of modern funerary design.

11a. James Stirling and James Gowan, Engineering Building,
Leicester University, Leicester, England, 1959–1963.
This landmark of Britain's postwar welfare state melds ideas ranging from
the Victorian industrial vernacular to Russian Constructivism.

11b. James Stirling and Michael Wilford,
Neue Staatsgalerie, Stuttgart, 1977–1984.
At the heart of this large museum addition, a vast open-roofed stone-clad
rotunda forms one of the grandest public spaces in postwar Europe.

12a. Renzo Piano, The Shard, London, 2000–2013.
Resembling a colossal glass stalagmite, this ninety-five-story mixed-use
tower on the South Bank of the Thames is the architect's most
sophisticated essay in high-rise design and by far his tallest.

12b. Renzo Piano, Astrup Fearnley Museum of Modern Art,
Oslo, 2009–2012.
Piano departed from his familiar colonnaded-pavilion format to dynamic
effect in this waterfront gallery with a vast sail-like roof canopy.

13a. Rem Koolhaas and Joshua Prince-Ramus/
Office for Metropolitan Architecture, Seattle Central Library, 1999–2004.
Occupying an entire city block, this dazzlingly crystalline structure
signifies that the activities pursued within it are of high civic import.

13b. Rem Koolhaas and Ole Scheeren/Office for Metropolitan Architecture,
China Central Television Headquarters, Beijing, 2004–2012.
The home of China's state broadcasting agency, engineered by Arup,
glamorizes the might of the repressive regime that built it.

14a. Bernard Tschumi, Parc de la Villette, Paris, 1982–1987.
The redevelopment of an abattoir district in northeast Paris, this 125-acre
park is enlivened by thirty-five red-painted follies that allude to the
"heroic" modernism of the Russian Constructivists.

14b. Bernard Tschumi, Acropolis Museum, Athens, 2001–2009.
Conceived to impel the return of the Elgin Marbles to Greece, this
showcase looking up to the Acropolis mirrors the layout of the Parthenon,
sculptures from which are shown in the rooftop gallery.

15a. Tod Williams and Billie Tsien,
Barnes Foundation Gallery, Philadelphia, 2004–2012.
Although they retained the interior layout of this collection's first home,
the architects nonetheless created a new setting of notable originality.

15b and 15c. Tod Williams and Billie Tsien, American Folk Art Museum,
New York City, 1997–2001 (left), and Reva and David Logan Center for
the Arts, University of Chicago, 2007–2012 (right), which display the
architects' virtuosity in cultural design.

16a. Kazuyo Seijima and Ryue Nishizawa/SANAA, 21st Century
Museum of Contemporary Art, Kanazawa, Japan, 1999–2004.
In a provincial town unfamiliar with museums, this transparent-walled
gallery was conceived as a welcoming community center.

16b. Kazuyo Seijima and Ryue Nishizawa/SANAA,
New Museum, New York, 2003–2007.
Towering over a tight mid-block site, this elegant metal-mesh-clad
Minimalist structure reflects delicate shifts in light and weather.

17a. Diller Scofidio + Renfro, Alice Tully Hall and
Juilliard School of Music renovation, New York, 2003–2010.
This transformation of Pietro Belluschi's 1969 Brutalist structure
imparts an enlivening transparency but respects the spirit of the original.

17b. Diller Scofidio + Renfro (with James Corner Field Operations),
High Line renovation, New York, 2003–2013.
The extraordinary success of this "park in the sky" derives from its
architects' acute sense of how people like to interact in today's cities.

18. Snøhetta, Norwegian National Opera and Ballet, Oslo, 2002–2008. Spectacularly sited on the Norwegian capital city's harborfront, this performing arts center is as noteworthy for its creation of a grand and hugely popular public space as for the architecture itself.

19. Michael Arad and Peter Walker, National September 11 Memorial, New York, 2003–2011. The winning design for the Ground Zero site reestablished the square footprints of the fallen Twin Towers with a pair of thirty-foot-deep pools.

9

R. BUCKMINSTER FULLER

ONE OF THE most persistent yet elusive dreams of the Modern Movement in architecture has been prefabrication: industrially made structures that can be assembled at a building site. Although prefabrication has a long history—the ancient Romans shipped precut stone columns, pediments, and other architectural elements to their colonies in North Africa, where the numbered parts were reassembled into temples—the idea took on a new impetus with the technological advances of the Industrial Revolution. Nineteenth- and early-twentieth-century exponents of prefabrication were certain it would supplant age-old traditions of individualized design and handcrafted construction. The building art would be revolutionized by freeing designers and construction workers from repetitive tasks, and democratized by making high-style architecture more affordable to everyone.

However, in the century and a half after the first comprehensive masterpiece of modern architectural prefabrication—the Crystal Palace of 1850–1851, which combined modular planning, interchangeable parts, and fast construction—entirely ready-made buildings were scarce at best, although some prefabricated components are now used in virtually all construction. The major impediment has been a matter of economics. The financial benefits of prefabrication have never been as large as its advocates predicted, for although some labor costs can be reduced by machine manufacturing, on-site assembly of any building still depends to a significant extent on the handwork of skilled craftsmen. The human element that can never be entirely eliminated from the construction process was addressed by Buster Keaton in his two-reel film *One Week* (1920), a prescient satire on prefabrication that must have bemused as well as amused audiences at a time when growing numbers of Americans were buying factory-made houses from mail-order catalogs such as the ubiquitous Sears, Roebuck "dream book." Rather than celebrating this modern innovation, Keaton—the peerless master of intricately choreographed and perfectly timed sight gags—imagined practically every catastrophe that could occur after the pieces for a ready-to-assemble dream house were delivered. It says a great deal about the overestimated potential and unfulfilled promise of prefabrication that so many of these schemes were never carried out.

But lack of success in bringing such schemes to reality, and even more so to widespread currency, does not necessarily condemn a designer to obscurity, and in fact quite the opposite was the good fortune of R. Buckminster Fuller, whose best-remembered conception, the geodesic dome, was far outnumbered by his many schemes for mass-produced and prefabricated designs that never progressed far beyond the drawing board or a few prototypes. Yet that did not deter this relentlessly ambitious and quintessentially American character from carving out a distinctive role for himself as a kind of national guru of futuristic technology for more than half a century. Evanescent visions of the future such as Fuller nurtured throughout his quixotic career are symptomatic of troubled times like the postmillennium period, and they also were common during the politically and socially volatile 1960s, when many felt that modern architecture had subsided into rote academic convention.

In 1960, the Museum of Modern Art's "Visionary Architecture" show, curated by Arthur Drexler, caused a sensation by displaying works like Fuller and Shoji Sadao's *Dome over Manhattan* project of 1960, a two-mile-wide transparent canopy that would have enclosed the island's midsection and made skyscrapers look like taxidermy specimens under a bell jar. In a review of that startling MoMA survey, *Time* magazine reassured its readers that such proposals "are not the work of crackpots but of reputable men." Ulrich Conrads and Hans-G. Sperlich's *Phantastische Architektur* of 1960 abounded with illustrations of built, unbuilt, and unbuildable schemes by a host of nineteenth- and twentieth-century visionaries outside the mainstream Modernist canon, including Fuller, whose geodesic domes were depicted. The revolutionary fervor that fueled the early Modern Movement had cooled by the early 1960s. But new, alternative versions of Modernism found a plausible prehistory in *Visionary Architects: Boullée, Ledoux, Lequeu* of 1968, the catalog for an eye-opening exhibition of little-known eighteenth-century French renderings of hypothetical monuments that was on view at the Metropolitan Museum of Art just as *les événements de mai* played out on the streets of Paris.

Visionary schemes produced during the 1960s (many of which involved prefabrication, or employed engineering techniques devised or championed by Fuller) have in recent years been reevaluated by architectural historians, including Larry Busbea, whose superb study *Topologies: The Urban Utopia in France, 1960–1970* (2007) was the first book-length investigation of a time and place when technologically innovative design proposals flourished on architects' drawing boards but languished in the corridors of power. The most characteristic manifestation of France's postwar architectural avant-garde was the multifunctional megastructure, idealized by leftist theorists and practitioners as a catalyst for social transformation. Exemplified by the Hungarian-born architect Yona Friedman's several unbuilt Spatial City schemes of the late 1950s and early 1960s for Paris and Tunis, these sprawling mixed-use agglomerations resembled vast jungle gyms connected by lengthy public concourses and interspersed with modular enclosures. Friedman considered his designs the building blocks for an "extendable city" in which easily reconfigurable lightweight frameworks would supersede socially oppressive urban patterns, epitomized by Haussmann's Paris city plan of the mid-nineteenth century. Busbea focuses on the theoretical issues that shaped architectural thought during the initial decade of the French Fifth Republic, and places those concerns within the larger intellectual setting of the Prospectivists, a forward-thinking coterie that included politicians such as Pierre Mendès France and the journalists Jean-Jacques Servan-Schreiber and Françoise Giroud, who shared a conviction that their country's restoration to its prewar international prominence could be achieved through a concerted program of scientific and technological progress.

With the election in 1958 of the culturally conservative President Charles de Gaulle—who built very little for a French chief of state, and contented himself with cleaning soot-blackened *monuments historiques*—officials increasingly viewed the avant-garde's new urban vision as too disruptive, ambitious, and unpredictable in political impact to risk their sponsorship. The exception was Renzo Piano and Richard Rogers's Georges Pompidou Center of 1971–1977 in Paris (though it derived from an English source: the unbuilt Fun Palace of 1961–1964, a performing and visual arts complex conceived by the architect Cedric Price and the dramaturge Joan Littlewood). Several designs by French architects and engineers adapted ideas closely associated with Fuller, such as Günther Günschel's Project for a Dome Composed of Hyperbolic Paraboloids of 1957, a variant of the geodesic dome, and an undated structure by David Georges Emmerich, based on the principle called "tensegrity," which Fuller picked up from the sculptor Kenneth Snelson at Black Mountain College. Snelson realized that the powerful forces needed for high-performance engineering could be held in dynamic tension with minimal structural apparatus. Fuller applied that finding to his compositions of weblike scaffoldings, both rectilinear and curved, which supported themselves with astonishing efficiency.

During the 1960s, the American counterculture found a most unlikely idol in Fuller, who was over seventy and had worked for the military, but nonetheless achieved the status of a rock star. In countless public lectures at colleges, conferences, and festivals throughout the hectic final decades of his life, this born salesman and indefatigable self-promoter mesmerized audiences with his epic lectures, which went on for as long as sixteen hours. As the ever-observant Philip Johnson enviously reminisced, "No one had the kids eating out of his hand like he did." Films of Fuller in action make it difficult to fathom why so many were so excited by his personal appearances, except perhaps as feats of extreme endurance. He was unusually short and so shortsighted that thick eyeglass lenses magnified his gaze to disconcerting immensity—a combination of traits that brought to mind the cartoon character Mr. Magoo. Fuller's clipped New England monotone was no match for Robert Frost's adorable twang, but he was nonetheless clearly charismatic and exerted a hypnotic effect that belied his unprepossessing appearance, as he spun out homilies on how easy it would be to right all the world's wrongs if only we followed his simple instructions.

It was hard to disagree with much of what he said—the unconscionable inequities in the global distribution of wealth ought to be redressed; no one anywhere should be allowed to live in hunger, disease, or poverty; science and technology must be harnessed for peaceful purposes rather than war. However, Fuller seldom got around to

MAKERS OF MODERN ARCHITECTURE, VOLUME II

specifying the exact means by which these much-needed but undoubtedly utopian reforms could be instituted. His rambling discourses, far less comprehensible on the printed page than they seemed when he delivered them in person, provide ample proof of a fertile but scattered mind and help to explain his obsession with inventing new systems and with wordplay, which he perhaps hoped would organize his hazy and disconnected ideas. (Fuller's *World Game* of 1969, meant to teach the public about international resource allocation, has won him an avid constituency among linguistic theorists.)

His spellbinding delivery of fuzzy prose brings to mind his greatest architectural contemporary, Louis Kahn, similarly verbose and vague. However, Kahn was no charlatan, which cannot be said with absolute certainty of Fuller, a talented structural engineer but a most unreliable social engineer who abandoned more than one of his almost-finished projects, it would seem, because the results might have disproved his overreaching claims or shown his theories to have been faulty, if not downright fallacious. His most fantastic invention was not the geodesic dome—in retrospect the fool's gold of mid-twentieth-century architecture—but rather the fictionalized life story he fed to credulous biographers. Fuller's self-serving and auto-mythologizing version of things remained unchallenged until Stanford University acquired the engineer's archive in 1999 (sixteen years after his death) and finally opened his copious papers to the full scrutiny of scholars.

As with Richard Nixon and his White House tapes, Fuller was the agent of his own historical undoing by meticulously recording in private the very activities he lied about with such impunity in public. He called his omnium-gatherum of 847 life-and-works scrapbooks the *Dymaxion Chronofile*, but a better name might have been *Witness for the Prosecution* because of all the damning evidence they contain. To be sure, Frank Lloyd Wright was less than wholly truthful in *An Autobiography*, but unlike Fuller he was unashamed to admit professional or personal setbacks, and there was often an essential veracity even in the great architect's lies. Among the first scholars to make use of this revealing trove was the late Loretta Lorance, whose *Becoming Bucky Fuller* (2009) cites dozens of instances in which he distorted or falsified significant facts about his career, claiming, for example, that he was unfairly forced out as president of a prefab building materials and construction company because of a corporate restructuring, when in fact he was let go because of his own incompetence and mismanagement.

Richard Buckminster Fuller was born in 1895 to a distinguished Massachusetts family that arrived from England six years before the founding of Harvard, which he attended for two years until he was expelled. As he recalled, "I cut classes and went out quite deliberately to get into trouble, and so naturally I got kicked out." In 1917 he married the long-suffering Anne Hewlett, of the Long Island Hewletts, but he did not give up carousing until a string of personal and professional disasters led him to the brink of suicide ten years later. In his autobiography, Fuller related that just as he was about to throw himself into Lake Michigan and end it all, he was suddenly encased within a "sparkling sphere of light" that levitated and hovered in midair, while a disembodied voice admonished him, "You do not have the right to eliminate yourself, you do not belong to you. You belong to the universe." That transparent celestial orb and those words of cosmic consolation evoke the peculiar blend of Emersonian egocentrism and pantheistic mysticism that typified the American Transcendentalists, one of whose more prominent members was Fuller's redoubtable great-aunt, the pioneering editor, journalist, and feminist Margaret Fuller. No wonder he became such a hit with the hippies, whose mantra of "We Are All One" was practically in the old man's genes.

Fuller's reputation rests principally on his invention, in 1947, of the geodesic dome, a demispherical shelter that requires no inner columns because its continuous surface network of rods, arranged in repetitive diagonal patterns of triangles, carries the structural load. He claimed to have made his biggest discovery in kindergarten, when his extreme myopia forced him to rely on touch during an arts-and-crafts project with toothpicks and dried peas, which he assembled into the configuration that half a century later would make him famous. It was a foundation myth Wright would have been proud of. More than once Fuller was saved by his knack for lucky timing; the urgent need for new construction of all kinds after World War II encouraged him to promote the geodesic dome as a panacea for everything from the housing shortage to industry's shift from military to civilian production. Deemed more economical, portable, adaptable, and reusable than conventional shelters, the geodesic dome also looked futuristic in a benevolent way that appealed to the optimistic mood of a victorious America, and it became the first unqualified success of his career.

It took some time for the drawbacks of Fuller's beguiling invention to become apparent. Those deficiencies included the large amount of unusable interior space around the circumference of a structure that curved down to the ground; the persistent leaks caused by the geodesic dome's multifaceted surface, with its plethora of joints and seams; and the difficulty of controlling temperature and ventilation inside what is essentially a greenhouse. (Indeed, geodesic domes have been most successfully used as conservatories, including the Climatron of 1960 at the Missouri Botanical Garden in St. Louis, by the firm of Murphy and Mackey.)

Fuller at last achieved the official recognition he yearned for when he was asked to design the American exhibition for Expo '67, the Montreal world's fair. Measuring 250 feet in diameter and as tall as a twenty-story building, his United States Pavilion of 1965–1967—

which he called the Skybreak Bubble—was the largest and most fully spherical of his executed geodesic domes (see Illustration 9). It was also the closest he came in his built work to memorializing the otherworldly see-through orb that he said had enveloped him at the transformative moment of his life, forty years earlier. In 1995, nine years after fire destroyed the structure's transparent acrylic covering, the restored former pavilion reopened as the Biosphere, an environmental exhibition on permanent display in a set of buildings constructed inside the original steel skeleton. (The outer skin, which had made the interior so costly to cool and heat, was not replaced.)

Notwithstanding that obtuseness about climate control, Fuller gained a wholly unmerited reputation for ecological awareness. None of his schemes refutes that notion more effectively than his and Sadao's *Dome over Manhattan*. This much-reproduced photomontage depicts a gigantic transparent cupola encircling and covering midtown Manhattan from river to river. Characteristically, Fuller never sufficiently explained how this Brobdingnagian blister would be entered and exited, cleaned and maintained, how it would be built, or why it was needed. It is also a prime example of Fuller's influence on others who went on to accomplish more interesting things with his ideas than he did. *Dome over Manhattan* foreshadowed megascale conceptual images, including Claes Oldenburg's drawing series *Proposals for Monuments and Buildings* of 1965–1969; Hans Hollein's photomontage *Aircraft Carrier City in Landscape* of 1964; and Gian Piero Frassinelli's *The Monument Continuous* of 1969, an altered photograph by a member of the visionary Superstudio collective.

Fuller's direct effect on the 1960s avant-garde was not solely pictorial, however, and his concepts were also applied with notable imagination by experimental architects, including Peter Cook and Ron Herron of England's Archigram group, and the Metabolists in Japan, including Kisho Kurokawa and Fumihiko Maki. The diametrical opposite of those high-tech professionals was the American hippie commune the Droppers, whose self-built Drop City of 1966 in Trinidad, Colorado, found favor with Fuller. Rosemarie Haag Bletter has pointed out the contradictions of this odd hybrid,

> loosely inspired by Fuller's geodesic domes, but…covered with old car parts, the detritus of the official car culture. Drop City won the Buckminster Fuller Dymaxion Award. The experiment of twenty people living as a commune was described by Peter Rabbit in *Drop City* (1971) as a group of "total revolutionaries; we are free men living equally with free creatures in a free universe. The story of Drop City will never end. It's the story of man on the road to be free." What freedom meant was not explained, but the group spent a great deal of time driving around in cars going to…junkyards to buy automobile parts for their domes.

It seems inevitable that the self-actualizing Fuller was drawn to automotive design, as realized in his most famous vehicular scheme, the Dymaxion "2" 4D Transport of 1934, the prototype for a zeppelin-shaped, three-wheeled car with which he planned to revolutionize the automobile industry. The eleven-passenger Dymaxion car was twenty feet long, but Fuller cleverly engineered it to make a full turn within the radius of its own length, a neat trick that caused mob scenes whenever the streamlined wonder was taken out for a spin. Alas, a headline-making crash of an earlier model at the 1933 Century of Progress International Exposition in Chicago killed the Dymaxion's driver. Investors withdrew their financing and the enterprise collapsed. (The word "Dymaxion"—a fusion of "dynamic," "maximum," and "ion"—was coined by the marketing-conscious inventor's PR man. Fuller also used the term for various versions of his metal-clad Dymaxion House, including a hexagonal model that was raised above the ground and suspended from a central mast—patented as the 4D House in 1928—and the circular, yurt-like Dymaxion Deployment Unit of 1941.)

Beyond the many unresolved questions of Fuller's highly publicized but only fitfully credible career, there remains the larger question of why prefabricated construction, and prefabricated housing in particular, has been received with much more enthusiasm in Japan and Scandinavia than in this country. It is always said that the American public simply does not like modern design (a canard lately kept alive by adherents of the neotraditional New Urbanism Movement). However, that was not at all the case immediately after World War II, when contemporary versions of the California ranch house were widely accepted nationwide. Well before that, populist forms of prefabrication like the Sears Catalogue Homes of 1908–1940—a likely source for Keaton's architectural slapstick *One Week*—found a wide and appreciative middle-class audience. These reasonably priced, ready-to-erect dwellings were offered by the Chicago-based mail-order retailer in an encyclopedic array of 447 models, from Craftsman bungalows and Cape Cod saltboxes to Tudor cottages and Spanish haciendas—stylistic promiscuity enough to give Alfred Barr, the Museum of Modern Art's puritanical founding director, the vapors.

Among those distinguished innovators who attempted prefab designs is a roll call of architectural deities—Frank Lloyd Wright, Le Corbusier, Walter Gropius, Marcel Breuer, Charles and Ray Eames, Jean Prouvé, and Fuller—all of whom tried, with usually less success than Sears, to harness new production techniques that could make their designs more accessible to the many—a central goal of the Modern Movement. Whether one reckons Fuller ludicrously overrated or insufficiently revered, his curious career and achievements seem in hindsight unequal to the extraordinary adulation showered upon him late in his life. Yet there is no denying Fuller's place in twentieth-century culture or his profound effect on the many admirers who saw him, correctly or not, as a creative genius and spiritual guide.

10

CARLO SCARPA

CARLO SCARPA WAS the greatest Venetian architect since Andrea Palladio, and he remains the foremost architect of the twentieth century still unknown to the general public. When he died, in 1978 at the age of seventy-two, he left a remarkable though quite small body of work that included very few buildings that were freestanding or of any appreciable size. They were principally museum conversions and renovations, country villas, and tombs—homes for art, the living, and the dead. Attempts to widen his renown seem doomed to failure, if the exemplary retrospective mounted in 1999 by the Canadian Center for Architecture (CCA) in Montreal was any indication. Yet his relevance to the most important values of architecture seems stronger with each passing year. Rarely has modern architecture been as powerful, as poetic, or as cryptic as his.

Scarpa was much influenced by Frank Lloyd Wright's theory of organic architecture, which proposed that all elements of a scheme be conceived as inseparable parts of a unified whole. But the Italian also had equally close affinities with his five-year-older contemporary Louis Kahn. Both men were late bloomers whose professional development was delayed by the Great Depression and World War II; both were transfixed by history and were transformed by it in middle age, during the postwar years when modern architecture was at its most amnesiac. By 1950 these two introspective and artistically ambitious men had become repelled by the spiritual emptiness and generic sameness of International Style architecture in its later, corporate phase. To redress what they saw as the loss of physical and emotional substance in modern building, they looked back at the architecture of the past, not in an attempt to imitate or revive it but instead to extract its vital essence and reinterpret it for their own time in new and pertinent ways.

"I have always had an immense desire to belong to tradition," Scarpa once said, "but without having capitals and columns." He would not use history as a grab bag of styling tricks, and would have been appalled by the ignorant and heavy-handed invocation of the past by the Postmodern phase in architecture that was just getting underway at the time of his death. Scarpa demonstrated how a contemporary architect could eloquently summon up the grandeur of the ancients by using primal geometry expressed in the reductivist vocabulary of the Moderns in his Veritti Tomb of 1951 at the Cemetery of San Vito in Udine (designed with Angelo Masieri), a veritable cube composed of thin slabs of stone, with a huge round aperture cut into the center of the façade. A Wrightian bronze entry gate screens the lower third of the circle, with a hemispherical Prairie School–style planter set asymmetrically to one side. Scarpa emphasizes the inner void of the cube—the burial chamber itself—by piercing the side and back walls with smaller geometric openings. The roof of the mausoleum is a disk as large as the frontal opening, suspended above the graves and held free from the ceiling's vacant corners; this negative-positive form is underscored by the perception that the overhead circle was removed from the façade.

Despite the heroic regenerative project that Scarpa and Kahn shared, and its vast implications for reconfiguring the commercially dominated public realm of mid-twentieth-century architecture, both men are now often regarded as architects' architects, self-absorbed specialists whose fellow designers are most likely to empathize with their sometimes uningratiating forms, unrelenting geometries, and what can seem like an obsessive focus on overly finicky details. It is certainly true that Scarpa, to a much greater extent than Kahn, lavished intense attention on what the general public would consider the little things of architecture—such subsidiary elements as door handles and hinges, wall surfaces, paving textures, stair rails, and the like. Yet he was no solipsist, and understood that it is precisely on that level of tactile material intimacy and direct physical engagement that most people experience a building.

For his 1961–1963 reworking of the ground floor and courtyard of the Palazzo Querini Stampalia in Venice, a sixteenth-century landmark that now houses an art collection and research library, Scarpa took enormous pains in designing a small but intricately detailed and perfectly proportioned footbridge of wood, metal, and stone that leads across a narrow canal to the building's main entrance. The pleasingly gentle arc of the bridge's steel double span, the resilient feel of the perfectly scaled wooden treads, and especially the wood-and-brass handrail that is startlingly sensuous to the touch offer an intriguing preview of his work inside the palazzo. Scarpa's many sheets of densely reworked preparatory sketches for the little Venice bridge—"I can see an image only if I draw it," he said—illustrate the patience and care that he invested in an element of a project that most other architects of the time would have breezed through by adopting a straightforward technological solution, or would have passed on to an underling. Appropriate local materials were also central to Scarpa's thinking wherever he worked, but above all in his native city. For an entrance plaque inscribed with the name of the Querini Stampalia Foundation he specified Istrian stone, the Adriatic limestone long used throughout the Venetian archipelago because its surface builds up a protective patina against the corrosive salt air of the lagoon.

No commission was too mundane for him to treat with anything but the utmost seriousness. In a world in which museums now sometimes seem more like shopping malls than temples of art, it is sobering to look back on a time not so long ago when Scarpa made a shop seem like a museum (and not of the MoMA white-cube sort). His Olivetti showroom of 1957–1958 on St. Mark's Square in Venice was a natural extension of the pioneering business-machine firm's identification with and patronage of high-style design. Occupying two bays of a retail arcade that in turn opens onto "the drawing room of Europe" (as Napoleon is said to have dubbed the incomparable piazza), this small but imposing *bottega* possesses a distinctly Venetian mixture of dignity and theatricality. As the American architect George Ranalli, whose own work has been deeply informed by Scarpa's ethos, wrote in the catalog for the 1999 CCA exhibition:

> Without either sacrificing his creativity or holding back on his architectural agenda, Scarpa developed a way of connecting an avant-garde design to the sensibility of the work that for centuries had been produced in this quarter. One of his strategies was to use the same artisanal techniques of construction that had formed the historic city in order to evolve new forms.

The Olivetti showroom's shimmering floor of pale gold and deep red Murano glass tesserae irregularly set in cement seems to draw visitors inward like a flood tide (a not-unintentional metaphor for the *acqua alta* that immerses the city with increasing frequency) and suffuses the long, narrow rooms with a warm reflected glow. Smooth, natural-colored stucco walls are outlined with simple strips of dark-stained wood, near rough concrete walls inset with narrow bands of brass. The company's products could be discreetly but effectively displayed on low tables and pedestals designed by the architect, making the merchandise seem like congenial analogues to the setting rather than objects of consumer worship, an unusual distinction these days. In one corner, a low, rectangular marble fountain is incised with geometric motifs that simultaneously recall classical Japanese design as well as an Islamic water garden in miniature. In another corner of the ground floor, a majestic stairway of invisibly supported marble slabs rises weightlessly to offices on the mezzanine level. This ranks as one of the most extraordinary interiors of any epoch in Venice.

The weight of the past bore heavily on Scarpa, who was born in Venice in 1906 and grew up there and in Vicenza, the nearby capital of the Veneto region, both cities with their wealth of landmarks by Palladio. Paradoxically, Scarpa's birthplace may be rich in architectural splendor, but in modern times it has been virtually devoid of opportunities for construction beyond the preservation of the old. Well aware of that fact, he studied architecture at the city's Academy of Fine Arts, earning a diploma in architectural drawing and the right to style himself *professore*. But because he refused to take the qualifying examination for architects required by the Italian government after World War II, Scarpa could never call himself an architect, and therefore was legally compelled to work with a properly credentialed collaborator on all his projects. Incredibly, in 1956, just when his building career was beginning to soar, the invidious Venice Association of Architects sued him for practicing without a license— though to the lasting honor of his hometown he was acquitted of the trumped-up charges.

Scarpa's first major project, the internal restructuring of the Gothic Ca' Foscari on the Grand Canal for the University of Venice in 1935–1937, demonstrated his sure hand at inserting strong but sympathetic modern elements into a historical framework. Returning to traditional Venetian materials, including terrazzo and scagliola (a plaster-like composite that mimics marble), he employed skilled artisans to install them using age-old techniques but in unmistakably modern configurations. In this way he endowed the interiors with a formal purity that enhanced their low-key richness, much like Ludwig Mies van der Rohe, who combined rare wood or stone to great effect in large but unadorned expanses. Such projects were rare during the worldwide Great Depression, and like most other Italian architects (then and now) Scarpa was forced to find alternatives to building, yet these necessary excursions into other branches of design and his parallel teaching career only deepened his mastery of the mother art.

The architect's design work from 1926 to 1947 was most distinguished by his efforts in Murano art glass, the leading industrial production of the Venetian lagoon. He worked out many of his major ideas in that "minor" medium well before he was able to address them in building. Among the vases, bowls, and other vessels that indicate their designer's innate feel for the inherent qualities of the material at hand (another gift that he shared with his hero Wright) are several pieces that display his virtuosic ability to take historical forms—whether Roman, Chinese, Islamic, or Renaissance—simplify them greatly, inflect them wholly and credibly in a contemporary direction, and thereby make them fully his own. Taken in its entirety, Scarpa's command of a wide range of glass-fabrication techniques, refined sense of color, and belief in research as the fount of creativity confirm him as the supreme Italian glass designer of the twentieth century.

Complicating the reuse of history for Scarpa throughout his career—which began in the early years of Mussolini and ended in the worst year of the Red Brigades—was the way in which the Classical tradition was sullied in Italy under the Fascists. Mussolini encouraged a watered-down but pumped-up simulacrum of the Classical vocabulary to evoke Roman Imperial antecedents in the cynical service of his brutal regime, thereby discrediting historical form in his country long after his downfall. As a result, Scarpa and his postwar contemporaries sought a figure who embodied "the architecture of democracy" and they found Wright, who detested all overt revivalism and was basking in the critical acclaim that greeted his late-life creative resurgence. In 1951 Wright went to Venice (where he met Scarpa) for an exhibition of his work, and a year later was asked to design a small palazzo on the Grand Canal for an architectural library dedicated to the memory of Angelo Masieri, Scarpa's collaborator on the Veritti Tomb and one of his closest friends, who had recently died in a car crash soon after visiting the master at Taliesin. This project fell through because of the growing sentiment that contemporary architecture—even a scheme as suitable as this crypto-Gothic palazzo—would compromise the touristic charm of the historic city.

Wright's use of integral ornament—worked directly into building materials such as molded concrete block or handcrafted into details that reiterated themes stated elsewhere in the structure—ran counter to the International Style's ban on applied decoration. He thereby inspired Scarpa to use embellishments that are *of* a building rather than *on* it, just as he maintained that a house should be of a hill rather than on it. Such characteristic Scarpan motifs as horizontal rows of lines stepped inward or outward to imply a Classical molding can be traced directly to Wright, who seemed to offer a viable third way between politically tainted Classicism and globally generic Modernism. Yet the American's architecture, with its profoundly rooted sense of place, could not be transplanted as readily as the aptly named International Style, which could be erected on virtually any site anywhere. Scarpa found in his native region's indigenous crafts, traditional materials, and characteristic colors—Carpaccio pink, Titian red, Bellini ocher, and Byzantine gold—a territorial grounding that no foreign influence could alter.

If one spends time among Italian architects, the word *interventi* (interventions) is bound to come up in the first few minutes of almost any conversation, and it is essential to understanding Scarpa. Confrontations with and alterations of existing buildings have long formed the basis of architectural practice in Italy, whose ancient history and omnipresent artistic heritage have always encouraged the recycling of old buildings. The American-style obliteration of the still-usable past seems in the Italian setting not merely economically profligate but also culturally suicidal. That intelligent repurposing was sequentially applied over several centuries to the Palazzo Abatellis in Palermo, which was badly damaged during World War II. Scarpa was nearing fifty when in 1953 he received his first major museum commission: to remodel the palazzo to house the medieval and modern art collections of the Sicilian state. He was brought into the project once the physically compromised structure was stabilized by other architects and, working against a tight deadline and on a small budget, was charged with the creation of gallery spaces and new installation components.

He rejected the notion that a building's past lives should, or even could, be effaced or concealed, and thus openly treated the historic survivor as a palimpsest. The accidental contributions of time and fate were welcomed by Scarpa, who did not seek superficial perfection. Reopening a disused quarry to find the exact match for old stonework—a practice not unheard of among historic preservationists—would never have occurred to him. In his work, awkward joints between earlier portions of a building and his *interventi* were exalted rather than eradicated.

Writing in the 1999 CCA catalog, the architect Jorge Silvetti sums up the master's noninvasive and yet revelatory strategy:

The slab of travertine that he adds next to a medieval stone wall acts as an emblem of his architecture. Such a sliver of space joins them...yet at the same time it literally separates them, puts air in between, and...makes unequivocal what is new and what is old; that slice of space is also the space of his signature.

Scarpa would study closely the color and texture of the buildings he was entrusted to improve, but was improvisational enough to know that handsome results could be achieved in a variety of ways and often worked directly with craftsmen on-site to do so. Some of the walls at the Palazzo Abatellis were plastered in a natural off-white tone or tinted a velvety light olive-green, while others were left in their original exposed masonry, but all were deemed worthy as backdrops for painting and sculpture. The architect's unpretentious but exquisitely wrought display devices, which received their first major exposure here, helped change the way in which art objects are presented to the public. Plinths of rough concrete, sculpture bases combining raw welded steel with smoothly polished ebony, and clamp-like metal brackets jutting out from walls and even suspending objects in midair knocked traditional art off its cliché pedestal and gave a modern immediacy to works centuries old, a technique now followed in museums around the world, though rarely with Scarpa's inventive attention to detail. Sensitive to how certain artworks were originally meant to be viewed, he tried to approximate such settings wherever practicable. At the Palazzo Abatellis, for example, he positioned an anonymous fifteenth-century fresco of *The Triumph of Death* in the apse of the Gothic chapel of the former monastery, the better to convey the painting's emotional impact at the end of a long enfilade as part of a sequence of religious images dealing with the life cycle.

Scarpa's most impressive installation, daring in its simplicity, is his addition to the Canova Plaster Cast Gallery of 1955–1957 in Possagno, in the Veneto, which preserves the working prototypes of the preeminent Neoclassical sculptor. In a period when white walls had become a museological article of faith, Scarpa was not afraid to use color, often deeply saturated pigment, when he thought it best for specific galleries. Yet rather than contrasting Canova's pale monochromatic sculptures against darker backgrounds, he made a riskier decision and kept the walls of his galleries light to maximize reflectivity, and used tall, narrow cuts at right angles into the upper corners of the cubic galleries to flood the casts with natural illumination. Though Canova was termed "the erotic Frigidaire" by the critic Thomas B. Hess, his figures have never seemed more fleshly, animated, or sensuous than they do in Scarpa's warming bath of daylight.

His third great (and most complex) gallery scheme was for the Castelvecchio Museum of 1956–1973 in Verona, a fourteenth-century fortress that became a barracks under the Napoleonic occupation and a museum in the 1920s, when the bastion was gussied up with pseudo-Gothic detailing and fake Renaissance decor. As Ranalli has written of this scheme:

Rather than viewing restoration as the opposite of renovation, Scarpa embarked on an intriguing strategy of demolition, change, and modification. He layered history, allowing each historical moment to come alive and take its place next to the others. Eventually functioning as a curator in deciding how to treat each fragment of the existing structure, he removed some elements, restored others, and interspersed new ones. He was able to achieve this while setting up a dialogue between old and new, provoking the older elements into conversation with wholly invented new forms, surfaces, textures, and motifs.

The jewel of Castelvecchio is Scarpa's *sacello*, or treasure chest, a small reliquary-like structure built to house a few remarkable Longobardic antiquities. The exterior of this severely cubic masonry container is faced with a syncopated, mosaic-like checkerboard pattern of small rose- and cream-colored stone squares, alternatingly rough-hewn and matt-finished, which impart an almost Byzantine sparkle and sumptuousness. Inside, dark olive-green plaster walls and a concealed skylight add to its air of mystery and concentrate attention on the precious objects within. Epitomizing Scarpa's genius for revitalization is his placement of the Castelvecchio Museum's most famous artifact, a white marble equestrian statue of the fourteenth-century condottiere Cangrande della Scala. Scarpa perched it atop a second-story bridge in a loggia that he created to separate the Napoleonic addition from the medieval fortress. He angled the effigy of horse and rider to emphasize its autonomy from the architecture and to increase its visibility from several directions, and put it where visitors must pass several times during their route through the galleries and thus encounter it each time from a different and newly telling perspective.

Scarpa's masterpiece is the Brion Family Tomb and Chapel of 1969–1978 in San Vito d'Altivole in the Veneto (see Illustration 10). If modern religious architecture fell on hard times because of a concomitant crisis of belief and the growing secularization of Western culture, then twentieth-century funerary art fell into the abyss. There are but a handful of other great modern structures that deal effectively with death, most notably Gunnar Asplund's Crematorium of 1935–1940 at Stockholm South Cemetery and Aldo Rossi's San Cataldo Cemetery of 1971–1984 in Modena. Giuseppe Brion was the founder, with his wife, Onorina Tomasin, of Brionvega, the Milan-based electronics manufacturer renowned during the 1950s and 1960s for its elegantly designed radios, televisions, and sound equipment. A year after her husband's death in 1968 at the age of fifty-nine, the widow Brion thought in the same terms of aesthetic excellence and commissioned Scarpa to create an equally superb final resting place in her husband's native village.

The architect saw the project as a chance to give full expression to ideas that he had been nurturing for some time. "All great architecture is rational," he declared, "but great art is created only when spiritual and imaginative elements appear in it—the irrational, which constitutes its inspired, creative function." Above all, he wished to address in built form what he called "the great open questions in which modern rational thinking has no place." Scarpa conceived the large, inverted-L-shaped Brion plot in an outer corner of the town burial ground in terms of a spiritual journey through a metaphorical landscape—*del cammin di nostra vita*" (the pathway of our life), in Dante's deathless phrase.

An inward-tilting, concrete peripheral rampart sets the site apart from its varied surroundings—farm fields on one side (where crops grow to the full height of the wall and completely obscure it from view in that direction), houses on another, with the cemetery's conventional grave monuments ranked in grid patterns within the arms of the L. With its several reflecting pools, water channels, and clusters of columnar cypresses, the Brion precinct appears to float like an island, recalling the cemetery of San Michele in the Venetian lagoon, which Scarpa knew from earliest childhood and where he built several tombs in the 1940s, or the much-reproduced painting *Die Toteninsel* (The Isle of the Dead), produced in several versions during the 1880s by the Swiss Symbolist Arnold Böcklin.

The visitor's progress through the grounds of the Brion Tomb is as carefully controlled as that through a classical Japanese stroll garden, with sightlines restricted and perspectives directed to foster an impression of limitless space in a relatively small area. The disposition of three major elements in three corners of the site further maximizes one's experience of the whole. The cubic chapel (rotated ninety degrees within the grid of the cemetery) and the rectangular water pavilion each occupy a different far end of the L, with the circular burial vault of the Brions equidistant at the right angle between them. Scarpa's illusion of infinite extension begins with the propylaeum, a tightly enclosed concrete entry corridor that recalls Wright's restricted transitional spaces, which make the areas beyond them seem larger in contrast.

At the entry to that covered walkway, one wall is punctuated by an aperture of two large overlapping circles, outlined in blue and gold mosaic, an ancient motif known in Latin as the *vesica piscis* (fish bladder), also used as a proportioning device in Gothic architecture and as a ritualistic symbol by Freemasons. (Scarpa repeated that motif in small marble inlays behind the chapel altar.) This modern reiteration of an archaic symbol of marital fidelity and eternity—two intertwined rings, but also a diagram in silhouette of a solar eclipse—frames a poignant first glimpse through the opening of the actual gravesite, with its pair of marble sarcophagi set just below grade beneath a low, bridge-like canopy, angled to be visible from the far ends of the L. Hugely affecting, this vista through the double-ringed opening brings to mind the words from Oscar Wilde's *Salome*: "And the mystery of love is greater than the mystery of death."

The propylaeum leads both to the water pavilion, a contemplative space with an atmosphere of absolutely Eastern tranquillity, and in the opposite direction, around a corner toward the chapel. That Catholic sanctuary, though strikingly devoid of Christian symbolism, is a deeply moving place, one of those rare works of modern religious architecture (Le Corbusier's Ronchamp chapel being another prime example) that communicates not intellectually but viscerally. The precast concrete exterior is almost Classical, with its symmetrically placed entry door and rhythmically repeated motifs—tall, narrow windows framed by pilaster-like panels beneath a step-banded cornice.

The chapel's interior, a dark, angular volume of concrete walls beneath a ziggurat-stepped ceiling, is unremitting in its solemnity. A grave-size slab of marble set flush into the mosaic floor at the foot of the lectern-like altar—a minimalist abstraction of the catafalque—leaves no doubt about this space's funerary function, a place that awaits the inevitable hour. The narrow, ceiling-high windows, the skylight at the apex of the coffered ceiling, and a series of four small, square, hinged alabaster panels on either side of the altar all admit slanting rays of light that mitigate the gloom and allude to the cosmos. The scale is at once intimate and monumental, focusing on the individual and inescapable nature of death while elevating the personal into the realm of the transcendent.

This, in the end, is what the sublimely enigmatic architecture of Scarpa at its best accomplishes. His work has sometimes been dismissed as too personal and hermetic to be widely emulated, but such a criticism misses the entire point of what he achieved. Scarpa wanted architecture to be more alive to its own time but also more alive to all that had gone before it; to be one with its surroundings but also to make a place more vivid than it had been before. "The problems involved are the same as ever," he said of modern architecture. "Only the answer changes." The Brion Tomb had just been finished when its architect traveled to his beloved Japan, whose design ethos so profoundly influenced his own. While in the northern city of Sendai, he fell down a flight of concrete steps, was critically injured, and died ten days later. His body was returned to the Veneto, where it was wrapped in a linen winding sheet and immured in a peripheral wall of his newly completed necropolis, standing up in the manner of a medieval knight, befitting a heroic condottiere of the building art.

11

JAMES STIRLING

FEW YOUNG AFICIONADOS of the building art now realize how large James Stirling loomed on the international architecture scene during the two decades before he died, in 1992, at the age of sixty-eight. Apart from the eager embrace of his avant-garde colleagues, who saw in him the harbinger of thrilling new design directions, Stirling in his white-hot heyday was as celebrated by youthful fans as Rem Koolhaas is today—a veritable rock star of the profession who lectured to capacity audiences, was lionized by critics, became a fixture on short lists for prestigious cultural commissions, and attracted applicants from all over the world to study with him at Yale, where he was an influential and much-loved visiting professor for nearly a quarter of a century. (One characteristically idiosyncratic representational method that he popularized among several generations of Yale architecture students was his novel "worm's-eye-view" perspective drawing, which depicts a building as if seen from below ground.)

Now Stirling is best remembered for his dramatic mid-career stylistic shift from mechanistic forms and industrial-looking materials associated with the early Heroic Period of the Modern Movement —the post–World War I concatenation exemplified by the revolutionary schemes of Le Corbusier, Ludwig Mies van der Rohe, the Russian

Constructivists, and Holland's De Stijl group—and his move to Post-modernism. That eclectic architectural style, popular from around 1975 to 1990, borrowed motifs from earlier periods in implicit sympathy with the alleged communicative power of the building art's age-old signs and symbols. Stirling's Postmodern designs derived in part from the English Baroque (particularly Nicholas Hawksmoor and John Vanbrugh, both with strong Mannerist tendencies) and German Neoclassicism (including Friedrich Weinbrenner and Karl Friedrich Schinkel). But he mixed ideas explored by those architects with early Modernist engineering concepts and vernacular industrial construction techniques, which gave his work a hybrid character that made him difficult to categorize among his peers. His nearest contemporary analogue was the Milanese architect Aldo Rossi, who likewise mined the Classical tradition to impressive effect on occasion.

Stirling—whom I got to know somewhat when my wife, the architectural historian Rosemarie Haag Bletter, and I worked on an eponymous 1986 documentary film about him commissioned by the BBC in conjunction with German and Swedish television and directed by Michael Blackwood—objected vehemently to my having written that his body of work divides quite evenly into two distinct phases marked by his volte-face of the mid-1970s, when he started to combine Modern and Classical styles. Instead, he insisted that all his designs shared an inner consistency despite superficial disparities. But even a cursory examination of his life story reveals equally sharp divergences that in retrospect seem of a piece with the often jarring contradictions that define his architecture, and his character as well.

James Frazer Stirling was born in Glasgow in 1924 and grew up in Liverpool, though he was fond of telling American lecture audiences that he had been conceived aboard a ship anchored in New York harbor, which may or may not have been true. He also habitually claimed to have been two years younger than he really was, just as

Frank Lloyd Wright had done, no doubt to make himself seem more impressively precocious, a discrepancy revealed only after Stirling's death by his designated biographer, the architectural historian Mark Girouard, in the invaluable *Big Jim: The Life and Work of James Stirling* (1998). The architect's father, a naval engineer often absent on sea voyages, was a harsh character, the one person whom his only son, rather a bully himself, said he had ever been afraid of. Stirling's dour upbringing seems to have left him emotionally stunted; as one of his lovers, the African-American novelist Barbara Chase-Riboud, told Girouard: "He built a psychological wall around his inner self, which was difficult for others to penetrate."

As a boy Stirling found an emotional outlet in his love of bird-watching, and became so proficient an amateur ornithologist that while still a teenager he earned an acknowledgment in Eric Hardy's classic *The Birds of the Liverpool Area* (1941). Conscripted into the British army in 1942, he found military life an ordeal, but after the war quickly got his footing during the ascendancy of the postwar Labourite welfare state. That he harbored far grander aspirations than his background promised is clear from his so-called "Black Notebook," in which he recorded exceptionally acute perceptions about architecture, and both added to and referred back to throughout his career. Like many working-class strivers in postwar Britain, Stirling tried to camouflage his desire to rise socially and professionally by setting himself apart from the all-pervasive class system in ways both big and small.

He married above himself when, in 1966, he wed the furniture designer Mary Shand, a daughter of Philip Morton Shand, the socially connected wine connoisseur and early champion of Modernist architecture in Britain who wrote several popular books on those subjects. (Another of Shand's daughters, Elspeth, married Geoffrey Howe, successively Britain's chancellor of the exchequer, foreign secretary, leader of the House of Commons, and finally deputy prime minister under Margaret Thatcher, a grand link that pleased the upwardly mobile Stirling immensely; in 2001 Elspeth was created a baroness in her own right. One of Shand's granddaughters is Prince Charles's second wife, née Camilla Shand.) Mary Shand followed an age-old propensity by taking a husband exactly like her cantankerous and self-destructive father. As she recalled to Girouard, "My mother... thought [Shand] was a genius, you see, and geniuses had to be looked after," so even though Stirling was "a handful, and I realised that,... I thought that with my background I could cope." Girouard's commendable determination to tell the whole truth and nothing but the truth—including a detailed account of the late-life affair that came close to ending his subject's marriage—led Stirling's widow to withdraw her support for what had started out as the architect's authorized biography.

Stirling's early works in England—especially his university commissions of the 1950s and 1960s at Oxford, Cambridge, and Leicester universities, his so-called Red Trilogy (so named for the coloration of their redbrick cladding, the building material that became synonymous with the expansion and democratization of British higher education in the postwar years)—would alone justify a long-overdue reassessment. The first of the two uncontested peaks of Stirling's career was his and James Gowan's Engineering Building of 1959–1963 at the University of Leicester (see Illustration 11a), which reiterated readily identifiable early Modernist details in a way that had been unthinkable in a profession that had only lately abjured the direct copying of Greek, Roman, Romanesque, Gothic, Renaissance, and other historical prototypes. But now it is easy to see Stirling's borrowings from early Modernist antecedents in the 1960s as a forerunner of his Classical appropriations during the 1980s, a kind of Postmodernism *avant l'heure*.

For Leicester, Stirling and Gowan (who ended their association soon after that job was finished) designed two wedge-shaped lecture theaters that thrust outward from the base of the slender office tower like giant diving platforms. These were modeled after Konstantin Melnikov's Rusakov Workers' Club of 1927–1929 in Moscow, one of the canonical masterworks of Russian Constructivism. A cylindrical glass-enclosed spiral staircase repeats a similar configuration in Walter Gropius and Adolf Meyer's model factory at the Deutscher Werkbund Exhibition of 1914 in Cologne, while Leicester's wraparound strip windows bring to mind Wright's S. C. Johnson Research Tower of 1944–1951 in Racine, Wisconsin. The Red Trilogy also owes a huge debt to Alvar Aalto's University of Jyväskylä in Finland, begun in 1951, although Stirling's sense of site planning at that point in his development was nowhere near as sophisticated as that of the older and more experienced Finnish architect.

Some critics have maintained that the Leicester Engineering Building (subsequent work by Gowan supports his partner's primary authorship here) in effect puts quotation marks around some of the best-known motifs of early twentieth-century architecture and thus treats the Modern Movement as a swipe file rather than a set of philosophical principles. But as Stirling would later do in very different ways in his and Michael Wilford's Neue Staatsgalerie of 1977–1983 in Stuttgart (see Illustration 11b), he united these potentially discordant elements with consummate assurance and complete coherence and, early or late, could never be defined or dismissed as a mere pasticheur.

Once Stirling's practice finally started to prosper in the late 1960s with corporate commissions from Olivetti and Siemens, he assembled an important collection—which he installed in his Arts and Crafts–style house in London's Belsize Park—of vigorously scaled, museum-quality Regency furniture by such then-undervalued figures as George Bullock and Thomas Hope. These pieces he mixed among biomorphic 1930s bent-plywood chairs and tables by Aalto, Le Corbusier and Charlotte Perriand's boxy leather-and-chrome Grand Confort chair, contemporary plastic-cased stereo equipment by the Italian firm Brionvega, and potted avocado trees. It was one of the emblematic interiors of Swinging Sixties London, and the high/low look was widely imitated by Stirling's American confreres.

The ways that win, the arts that please play a crucial role in successful architectural practice, as proven par excellence by Philip Johnson and I. M. Pei, two born charmers and diplomats whose relative lack of native talent was far outweighed by their ability to court, land, and keep clients. Nikolaus Pevsner, the godlike doyen of British architectural historians, let his judgment stray from the professional to the personal when he bitterly remarked that "Stirling is a rude man, and the buildings he designs are rude as well." Such personal animus aside, one cannot but conclude that Stirling's abundant architectural gifts were subverted by his deep-seated personality flaws. Problems were evident early on. The property developer who commissioned Stirling and Gowan's Ham Common Flats of 1955–1958—a skillful tripartite grouping of thirty low-rise apartment units inserted behind a landmark Georgian mansion in the London suburb of Richmond, a scheme heavily influenced by Le Corbusier's Maisons Jaoul of 1951–1956 in the Paris suburb of Neuilly—found the young Stirling (as the developer's son later told Girouard) to be

> a terrible prima donna.... He has a very feminine side to him. He's rather like a dressmaker producing a dress, and there are terrible scenes if I want the windows to be two inches lower or higher, because I don't think that the people buying them would like them.

Stirling's biographer struggled manfully to show a kinder, gentler side of his rumbustious subject, but there is no denying that the architect was self-defeatingly off-putting to would-be supporters and potential clients alike. For example, his most strenuous advocate was the critic Charles Jencks, who saw in the Stuttgart Neue Staatsgalerie perfect justification for his belief in Postmodernism as the wave of the architectural future. However, Jencks had one cavil about the new museum: he disliked an off-the-rack industrial storm drain that Stirling placed at the center of the rotunda pavement, and suggested instead a representational sculpture to glorify the building's symbolic omphalos. Stirling repaid his thankless exponent by referring to him in public lectures thereafter as "Charlie Junk."

Certainly the frustrations of keeping an avant-garde architectural practice solvent in postwar Britain were enormous, and no doubt took their psychic toll on Stirling, whose office on more than one occasion was without any work whatever. During the 1970s, a recessionary decade when the worldwide dearth of construction prompted architects to produce hypothetical schemes or publish dossiers of their earlier designs, he magnified his status with the instant cult classic *James Stirling: Buildings & Projects, 1950–1974*, a precursor of Koolhaas's best-selling and considerably thicker *S,M,L,XL* (1995). Stirling's strikingly laid-out automonograph was a self-promotional picture book, and its close resemblance to Le Corbusier's *Œuvre complète* was hardly coincidental.

The architectural historian Anthony Vidler has plausibly interpreted Stirling's mid-career recourse to Classical motifs as a natural by-product of his architectural training at the University of Liverpool during that postwar interregnum in English design education when the Beaux Arts Classical tradition still lingered on but Modernism had not yet fully taken root. Even if one accepts Stirling at his word that he made his big stylistic shift not for opportunistic reasons, when Postmodernism became the latest architectural fashion, but to find greater expressive range than the restrictive Modernist vocabulary allowed, there has been little evidence since his death to change one's view of a markedly bifurcated oeuvre. Stirling's posthumous reputation has languished largely because of diminished critical regard for Postmodernism. He was arguably its most successful practitioner, as demonstrated by his and Wilford's indisputable masterpiece, the Neue Staatsgalerie, the first (and, some would say, only) evidence that the Classical vocabulary could still yield the expressive force Stirling ascribed to it.

The Stirling and Wilford office was at a near standstill when the firm received this major commission, part of the extraordinary spree of German museum construction in the years just before reunification. Nominally an addition to a mid-nineteenth-century Neoclassical art gallery, this ingenious synthesis of monumental architecture and humane city planning not only ameliorated some of the more egregious blunders of Stuttgart's postwar urban renewal but created, in the museum's majestic roofless rotunda, one of the finest civic spaces in modern Europe. Although its conventional picture galleries are adequate and nothing more, the entire ensemble has aged handsomely, unlike the dated appearance and shabby condition of so many public works from that period.

The Neue Staatsgalerie is loaded with visual jests, mainly insider jokes best appreciated by architectural cognoscenti, including a Weinbrenneresque columned portal that seems to sink into the rotunda's pavement through a "trapdoor," and sandstone walls that lack connective mortar and flaunt (to specialists who notice such things) their nonstructural nature by revealing how the steel framework behind actually does the heavy lifting. Yet this extensive composition, which covers several city blocks, is at once boldly assertive and deferentially adaptive. It meshes so smoothly with its surroundings that one can only agree with Jencks, who called it "more an articulation of urban tissue than a conventional building."

Stirling's most effective use of color was at the Neue Staatsgalerie, with a palette initially controversial but in due course widely emulated. To take the curse of bourgeois stodginess off the sober sandstone cladding, he specified that his exaggeratedly fat metal handrails be painted shocking pink and electric blue, with the metal framing of the undulating glass window-walls of the reception hall painted an even more jolting poison green, the same shade as the Pirelli raised-disk rubber-tile flooring the visitor encounters on entering the building. Although Stirling fancied himself an adept colorist, sometimes he clearly did not know when to stop. Many of the widely admired monochromatic drawings that emerged from the Stirling and Wilford office during the 1970s were in fact rendered by Léon Krier (the Luxembourg-born architect who went on to design the neotraditional Dorset new town of Poundbury for Prince Charles). The bilious greens and dingy blues that Stirling subsequently superimposed on Krier's delicate black-and-white originals—several of which include Hitchcock-cameo depictions of Stirling and his favorite pieces of Regency furniture—led Girouard to report that

> Krier was quite rightly infuriated to find that Jim had coloured many of his drawings for the Black Book and elsewhere. Among others the wonderful worm's-eye axonometric of the Florey Building [at Oxford], and the famous drawing of Jim and his Hope furniture were, in effect, ruined in this way. There may have been an element of jealousy or mischief in what Jim did.

The causes of Stirling's creative decline during his final decade are impossible to ascertain, but he was to some extent a casualty of the jet-age architectural treadmill that he mordantly termed "the circus" —a punishing nonstop international round of pitches for competitive commissions, speaking engagements to generate publicity, participation in conferences to validate his peer-group credentials, and visiting professorships to guarantee a steady cash flow. As with many experimental architects whose uncertain workload requires outside sources of income to help keep an office and staff afloat, Stirling's peripatetic existence was further necessitated because he was suspect in Britain for questionable technical abilities that subverted his job prospects there. That bum rap stemmed from functional problems that plagued his poorly maintained Cambridge University History Faculty Building of 1964–1967, the reading room of which is covered by a gigantic tentlike glass roof that leaked incessantly. (An unexpected supporter of the design was Isaiah Berlin, who liked it because it was not a pastiche of antique forms.) Not until the following decade, when Stirling was taken up by a series of sympathetic German patrons (and aided by German engineers, contractors, and craftsmen far superior to their often lackadaisical British counterparts), did he shed the stigma of lax execution.

His personal presentation worked against him as well. The Pavarotti of architecture, Stirling weighed more than three hundred pounds—how much is unknown, for his physician's scale went no higher—and if not an outright alcoholic he was certainly a very heavy drinker. (I recall taking this Falstaffian figure to dinner at the trendy North London restaurant Carrier's in the early 1980s, when he guzzled bottle after bottle of some costly Rothschild wine as if it were water on a hot summer's day. He brought along his uninvited teenage son, Ben, whom he importuned, to the young man's evident embarrassment, "Drink up, boy, you won't get claret like this every day!") In 1984, the impending decision about who would win the coveted commission for the Getty Center in Los Angeles, which came down to two finalists—Stirling and Richard Meier—prompted a member of the selection committee, the great British architectural historian and Stirling admirer Reyner Banham, to tell me pessimistically that the decision would hang on whomever Getty officials preferred to dine with over the next several years. Quite possibly the prospect of endless boozy, gluttonous evenings with Stirling pushed them into the arms of Meier, though as the loser sourly but accurately predicted, "They'll get another washing machine." However, by the time this thirteen-year project was completed, the unlucky Stirling had been dead for half a decade. He succumbed to complications from abdominal surgery twelve days after the queen knighted him.

Nothing Stirling and Wilford did after Stuttgart ever rose to that level of excellence. As often happens in an underappreciated architect's homeland once he is acclaimed for work built abroad, Stirling was rediscovered by the British after his German *coup d'estime*, and his office again began to receive important commissions in England after nearly a decade of stony indifference. Among those jobs was Number One Poultry of 1985–1998, a mid-rise mixed-use commercial building for a prestigious triangular site in the City of London facing Mansion House, the lord mayor's official residence. This Postmodern project was backed by the property developer Peter Palumbo, whose two-decade struggle to erect Mies's International Style bronze-and-glass Mansion House Tower of 1967—a nineteen-story mini–Seagram Building—ran aground thanks to the outspoken opposition of Prince Charles. No doubt Palumbo calculated that in the afterglow of his Stuttgart museum, Stirling was the man of the hour who could propel the long-stalled effort to completion. Palumbo thought his intuition was confirmed when Charles told him, "You can rest assured that this is one scheme I shan't be saying anything about." However, the fickle prince later denounced it on television as a "1930s wireless set." In fact, Number One Poultry—clad in alternatingly toned horizontal sandstone stripes, much like Stuttgart—more closely resembles a decapitated Sphinx, its subliminally Egyptoid aura reinforced by a bloated scale that overwhelms its decorous surroundings far more than Mies's elegant Minimalist tower would have done.

In 1986, Stirling and Wilford were also passed over in favor of the Americans Robert Venturi and Denise Scott Brown for the Sainsbury Wing, an extension to London's National Gallery. The following year the British partners completed their Clore Gallery, a substantial wing at the city's Tate Gallery for the work of J. M. W. Turner. The Clore was conceived by Stirling as a metaphorical garden pavilion, which he clad in a superscale gridwork pattern that gives the inverted L-shaped pairing of two shoe-box-like volumes a repetitive, rectilinear, mock-Elizabethan air. But any Tudor revivalism was countered by the incorporation of a massive limestone entry surround with Mycenaean overtones. It says a great deal that the Clore looks best late at night, dimly lit. The upper-story interiors, however, were meant to be viewed in the full natural light of day, and some of the colors Stirling selected for those display spaces were hideous, especially a cloying raspberry-mousse hue that has fortunately been replaced with neutral tones more hospitable to the Turners hung there.

Emboldened by his way with color at Stuttgart, Stirling went to even greater extremes in his and Wilford's pink-and-blue-banded Wissenschaftszentrum Berlin für Sozialforschung of 1979–1987 in the German capital, their expansion of a social-sciences think tank adjacent to the city's Kulturforum, a jumble of dissonant high-style Modern architecture that includes Mies's Neue Nationalgalerie of 1959–1965 and Hans Scharoun's Philharmonie of 1959–1963. This was perhaps the most idiosyncratic work Stirling ever brought to fruition. A gleeful contrarian, he always professed to detest picturesque design—buildings in which a preconceived arrangement of exterior forms takes precedence over internal organization and mimics painterly or theatrical effects to create an eye-catching image. But the Wissenschaftszentrum's multifarious agglomeration of Tuscan-inspired components is by any definition picturesque. Stirling asserted that this grouping of four office structures, cranked around at various angles, stemmed from his rejection of a typical Modernist superblock solution. The complex includes a barracks-like street-front block three stories high; an octagonal flat-topped tower of eight stories; and a semicircular wing (dubbed the amphitheater) and a cruciform volume with one apsidal end, termed the basilica, of five stories each.

The Wissenschaftszentrum's overall affect of carnivalesque excess and manic gaiety—the result of its loud exterior treatment in alternating layers of baby blue and Pepto-Bismol pink—prompted one Berlin wag to spray-paint a curving wall of the complex with the word *Geburtstagstorte* (birthday cake). Stirling, with characteristic perversity, wanted to leave that epithet in place, but his staid academic client demurred. The architect's apparent need to upstage the adjacent competition of Mies and Scharoun was not unlike a typically infantile propensity remarked upon by Girouard, who relates that if his subject felt he was not the cynosure of attention at social gatherings he would sometimes resort to making funny faces and antic gestures to gain attention.

An artist of sporadic genius, a thoroughly inspiring educator, and a critic of uncommon insight, Stirling remains a figure of continuing interest at the very least because his highly uneven output so strongly illuminates a significant transitional moment in architecture. Even though he produced only two buildings that can be deemed true classics—in Leicester and Stuttgart—those are enough to assure his place in the modern canon, if not in the top tier of all-time master builders. Faute de mieux, perhaps, but Stirling was the preeminent British architect of the third quarter of the twentieth century (and even a bit beyond). One can only honor his deeply abiding passion for architecture and his desire to impart that enthusiasm through his own buildings. In one of the most telling passages of "The Black Notebook," Stirling records his reaction to Anthony Mann's biopic *The Glenn Miller Story* (1954), which he terms "a poor film enlivened by 5 minutes of Louis Armstrong":

> [Armstrong's] whole personality and more directly his music expresses "the joy of living." Obviously he is no longer innovating, he is not producing with the same deliberate intention or innovation of the early days—yet his now non-progressive music is still greater than any other living jazzman. He can't help it—so easy—like Corb who has said "I shit architecture." Again the combination of man and instrument and music producing something which has the grace of inevitability.

That fundamentally joyous and inevitable quality suffuses his architecture at its best—one might even say that Postmodernism was a poor style enlivened by five minutes of Jim Stirling. The narrative of modern architecture would be far less lively without this formidable, unruly, and paradoxical figure, whom the journalist Colin Amery once described, a bit maliciously but nonetheless quite aptly, as "a great rogue elephant."

12

RENZO PIANO

RENZO PIANO, WHO turned seventy-five in 2012, may be best known as the preeminent museum designer of his time, but he has also amply demonstrated organizational and technical skills that have won him prestigious, horizon-altering jobs of the sort once deemed the summit of architectural attainment—the skyscraper. Piano's increasingly taller office towers trace his progress from the twenty-one-story Debis Haus of 1993–1997 in Berlin, to the forty-one-story Aurora Place of 1996–2000 in Sydney, and then to the fifty-two-story *New York Times* headquarters of 2000–2007 in Manhattan. His most spectacular and in several respects best skyscraper is not only his tallest but was also the loftiest habitable structure in Western Europe at the time of its completion: the 1,016-foot-high Shard of 2000–2013 in London (see Illustration 12a), a ninety-five-story mixed-use development that combines offices, apartments, a hotel, restaurants, and an observatory. The flight path to Heathrow Airport along the undulating pewter ribbon of the Thames is now spiked—in Southwark on the river's South Bank, near Tower Bridge—by Piano's crystalline form of angular, sloping glass-sheathed planes, which taper upward like a colossal stalagmite and stand out all the more because of the Shard's medium-rise surroundings and glazed exterior, both of which contrast dramatically with the skyscraper's masonry-clad neighbors, which average about fifteen stories.

A generation after the widespread public debate set in motion during the 1980s by the architecturally retardataire Prince Charles as to whether or not London should permit further high-rise development near the city center, a 2000 Urban White Paper issued by the Labour government of Prime Minister Tony Blair, "Our Towns and Cities— the Future," laid out incentives to promote the construction of skyscrapers in the British capital to spur economic development. Even though the 2001 terrorist attack on New York's World Trade Center raised urgent questions about the safety of extremely tall buildings, that catastrophe barely delayed a new wave of ambitious high-rise construction around the globe, including several claimants to record-breaking height in their city, country, continent, or the world at large.

The skyscraper first emerged in the late nineteenth century as a means of maximizing land use in the downtown financial centers of Chicago and New York, but that format turned out to be a potentially lucrative venture even where property values were not excessively high, because repeatable stories are a relatively cheap method of repetitive design and standardized construction. The profit motive has been at the root of the resurgence of the very tall building despite increasing doubts about the form's sustainability and security. Yet for all those reservations, in purely architectural terms Piano's dazzling London tower is difficult not to admire.

Although at first glance the Shard's general shape might bring to mind William Pereira's Transamerica Pyramid of 1969–1972 in San Francisco, that 850-foot-high office building looks much more static than the London skyscraper because its four canted sides meet neatly at right angles and rise continuously to a single pinnacle. In contrast, Piano's more animated and ambiguous composition (a fragmentary eight-sided arrangement in which the outer wall planes diverge obliquely from right angles and overlap at the edges rather than meeting directly) culminates in individual points that converge but do not quite come together at the very top. Thanks to the architect's specification of an unusually clear iron-free glass, the Shard exhibits an extraordinary transparency both when viewed from the exterior and particularly when experienced from within. That impression is especially pronounced as one stands close to the floor-to-ceiling window walls on one of the office levels, which occupy floors 2 to 28 (with restaurants on 31 to 33, the Shangri-La Hotel on 34 to 52, private residences on 53 to 65, the observatory on 68 to 72, and the spire from 73 to 95, with the stories in between those divisions taken up by mechanical equipment floors). Thanks to the slightly irregular, angled periphery of each story, the tower's gentle upward tapering, and the unobtrusive external framing, the predominant sensation the Shard imparts is one of a gossamer weightlessness, wholly unexpected in a structure of such magnitude.

The most unfortunate aspect of the Shard is a rectangular nineteen-story wing appended perfunctorily to the structure in fulfillment of the developer's demand for 900,000 square feet of rentable space. A newly imposed zoning regulation capped the maximum height of the tower at 1,355 feet, a 25 percent reduction from the architect's original configuration that necessitated an addition to make up the difference. Nicknamed the Backpack, this blocky and banal annex, which could just as well be found in a suburban American office park, disfigures the sculptural integrity of the beautifully proportioned tower and reminds us that although Piano was hired because of his highly marketable name, the Shard was driven not by artistic aspiration (as was Ludwig Mies van der Rohe and Philip Johnson's Seagram Building in New York, commissioned by the Bronfman family) but as a money-making speculation.

Yet for all the skyscraper commissions that will come to Piano because of the Shard, during the three decades that preceded it he consolidated his place as the most sought-after specialist in the defining architectural category of his time—the museum. As of 2012 he had completed nineteen museum buildings in Europe, the United States, and Asia, and was planning another six in the thriving offices he maintains in Paris and his native Genoa. Taken as a whole, these twenty-five commissions make up a self-contained body of work within his larger oeuvre and comprise virtually all of the museum's myriad present-day incarnations. Among them Piano has designed eight museums for major modern art collections, four single-artist museums, three expansions for Old Master collections, two national or regional cultural centers, two large additions to encyclopedic institutions, two science and technology museums, as well as a *Kunsthalle*, an ethnographic museum, a natural history museum, a university museum, and a motion picture museum—a roster unequaled by any of his peers.

Foremost among Piano's museums is the quartet of exquisite private galleries on which his unrivaled reputation in that field justifiably rests: the Menil Collection of 1982–1987 and the Cy Twombly Gallery of 1992–1995 in Houston; the Beyeler Foundation Museum of 1991–1997 near Basel; and the Nasher Sculpture Center of 1999–2003 in Dallas. These jewel-like showcases elevate the viewing and contemplation of art to an exalted level unsurpassed in modern architecture save for the Kimbell Art Museum of 1966–1972 in Fort Worth, by Louis Kahn, in whose office the young Piano briefly worked at the time of that commission. (In 2013 Piano completed a new building for the Kimbell adjacent to the revered original.) The triumph of Kahn's universally admired Kimbell led to his commission from the Houston collectors John and Dominique de Menil for a small private museum, but that scheme was not fully developed when the architect died suddenly in 1974, and the job in due course passed to Piano. His

Menil Collection building has probably won Piano more work than any of his other buildings, but it has not had the immense impact of his and Richard Rogers's controversial Georges Pompidou Center of 1971–1977 in Paris, which more than any other museum altered the conception of the modern art institution—for good or ill, depending on one's opinion of the widespread changes it set in motion.

Given the proliferation of Piano's museum practice, his later clients have sometimes found themselves in the unanticipated position of struggling for press attention despite having hired an architectural superstar. But there was no lack of publicity for his Broad Contemporary Art Museum (BCAM) of 2003–2008 at the Los Angeles County Museum of Art (LACMA), which opened to considerable (if discordant) fanfare. It was presented by the parent institution as most emphatically *not* a new wing but as a museum-within-a-museum. The building's redundant nomenclature was adopted at the behest of the $56 million endeavor's mastermind and principal patron, Eli Broad, who prospered by building Southern California tract houses and providing investment services to retirees, and was estimated at one point to have a net worth of $7 billion.

An exceptionally munificent benefactor of several institutions, he gave $100 million each to MIT and Harvard, but attracted even more réclame as a collector and gallery builder, having also endowed the Eli and Edythe Broad Art Museum of 2007–2012 at his alma mater, Michigan State University in East Lansing, a small but nonetheless flamboyant gallery designed by Zaha Hadid. Perhaps most notably, he established himself as an aggressive but price-conscious player in the ferocious postmillennial global market for high-priced contemporary art, which became a kind of supranational currency among the world's burgeoning mega-plutocracy. With more than 1,800 artworks —about four hundred owned by him personally and upward of 1,400 held by his Broad Foundation (with assets of some $2.5 billion)—the tycoon's collection was considered so desirable that some felt LACMA should do whatever it took to secure this coveted prize. Accordingly, Broad, a LACMA trustee since 1995, was allowed to choose the architect for the BCAM building and to have his foundation's curator participate in its installation. Furthermore, in 2006 Broad was instrumental in luring Michael Govan away from his job as director of the Dia Art Foundation in New York to replace Andrea Rich as LACMA's director after she quit, reportedly because of her repeated run-ins with Broad, who is often portrayed in press accounts as a tough, demanding, and intrusive executive.

An essay in the official book that accompanied the Piano building's debut, *BCAM/LACMA/2008: The Broad Contemporary Art Museum at the Los Angeles County Museum of Art,* was noteworthy for a frankness almost unheard of in such celebratory publications. Written by the then LACMA curator Lynn Zelevansky (who in 2009 became director of the Carnegie Museum of Art in Pittsburgh), "Ars Longa, Vita Brevis: Contemporary Art at LACMA, 1913–2007" retraces the museum's sad history as a champion and repository of new art. Perhaps LACMA officials imagined that such a critical account would make the Broad enterprise seem like a Hollywood happy ending, though in fact it unintentionally came off as an ironic commentary not unlike Robert Altman's mordant movie-industry satire *The Player* (1992). Zelevansky's litany of self-interested meddling by earlier donors unconcerned about the destructive effects of their behavior was all the more topical and troubling because it drew obvious parallels between erstwhile LACMA trustees and the museum's latter-day big kahuna. As Adrian Ellis wrote in *The Art Newspaper* in 2008, the museum's acquiescence to Broad poses

a very real danger that the appropriate conservatism of the museum sector will be challenged aggressively by a new generation of proprietorial museum board members who feel that, as in their own professional lives, "rules are for other people" and that, whatever the formal legal status, these institutions are an extension of their own private property and can be run as such.

A month before BCAM was inaugurated, the donor gave an interview to the *New York Times* reporter Edward Wyatt, in which he revealed that rather than giving his art to LACMA as many had anticipated, his holdings will remain the property of his foundation, which will make decisions normally reserved by a museum for works in its possession. Observers viewed this stunning news as an ominous portent for American arts philanthropy. Govan tried to put the best possible spin on Broad's ill-timed announcement, but there was no disguising the worst public relations disaster to befall an art institution since the reopening in 2006 of the Getty Villa in Malibu was eclipsed by the international antiquities scandal that implicated that museum. Although Govan gamely told Wyatt that "I don't think most people care when they walk in the door whether the museum owns the works or not," the consensus in the art world echoed the *Time* magazine critic Richard Lacayo's blunt blog posting: "LACMA got screwed."

The prior architectural history of this institution offers a classic, perhaps unsurpassable, example of how an inferior design can bedevil sponsors years after a project was finished. In light of later depredations, Pereira's LACMA of 1963–1965 doesn't look so terribly bad. Apart from the scheme's bastardized Modern-Classical styling and the off-putting moat that originally surrounded the three-building complex, this ensemble of freestanding pavilions took advantage of the region's benign climate and avoided the claustrophobia endemic to so many conventional museums. In 1984, the superbly intelligent architect Charles Moore surprised his fellow Postmodernists when he called LACMA "on the inside, one of the finest museums in Southern California." Although LACMA tried to improve its physical plant bit by bit, things got worse and worse. Its expansion of 1982–1986, by Hardy Holzman Pfeiffer Associates, burdened the site with a ponderous PoMo-Deco addition reminiscent of a 1930s Hollywood soundstage. The museum's quest for architectural cohesion was further doomed by Bruce Goff and Bart Prince's bizarre Pavilion of Japanese Art of 1978–1988, a zoomorphic folly that evoked a fossilized mammoth, the resemblance underscored by sub-Disney dinosaur replicas placed around the adjacent La Brea Tar Pits. (In 2013 the museum announced that it would demolish Pereira's pavilions and the Hardy Holzman Pfeiffer addition and replace them with a $650 million building by Peter Zumthor, the Swiss Minimalist and Pritzker Prize winner.)

LACMA's one great chance for architectural redemption came and went with the master plan of 2002–2003 by Rem Koolhaas and the Office for Metropolitan Architecture. With one breathtaking gesture—Koolhaas wanted to lop off the upper levels of the entire complex and encase the remains under a rectangular, translucent plastic dome—he would have given it a new architectural identity of stupendous power. But the museum's officials balked because the radical plan required closing the institution to the public for three years, whereupon Broad approached Piano, who in 2003 agreed to design the collector's dream monument to himself, but only if LACMA would also implement the architect's master plan. On paper, at least, Piano's rethinking of the museum seemed so logical as to be irrefutable, and sensible enough for the most conservative trustee. Instead of Koolhaas's scorched-earth approach, his successor called for the demolition only of the ugly multilevel parking garage next to the Pereira complex. In place of that eyesore, he positioned BCAM as the fulcrum of the expanded campus, which is now entered via a new plaza on Wilshire between BCAM and the original LACMA ensemble. The first phase of Piano's three-part master plan exacerbated some of the site's defects. It comprised BCAM, the BP Grand Entrance (an 8,100-square-foot piazza shaded by a graceful, unenclosed, and flat-roofed minimalist canopy, named for British Petroleum, which donated $25 million to the museum), and the covered walkways that now link the Piano and the Pereira buildings. Phase two added Piano's Resnick Pavilion of 2006–2010 for changing exhibitions, with phase three a planned overhaul of the oldest structures. BCAM's boxy form and forbidding Wilshire elevation reiterated the monolithic muteness of the Hardy Holzman Pfeiffer addition. To enliven the twin-square façade of his building's street elevation, Piano suggested that they be hung with superscale, scrim-like banners commissioned from local artists. Without such embellishment, however, BCAM would be virtually indistinguishable from a public utility substation. The symmetrical gallery wings are clad in beige travertine, and to emphasize the H-shaped ground plan Piano gave the slightly recessed midsection, which contains elevators and stairways, a transparent glass skin. The absence of an entrance on Wilshire clearly acknowledges that almost all visitors to LACMA come by car and enter through the parking garage rather than from the street.

The BP Grand Entrance pavilion employs the same red-painted steel Piano used for BCAM's side-wall fire escape and the beams that protrude horizontally above it, as well as the escalator-cum-stair tower and the concourse that connects BCAM with the original complex. The interior wall colors Piano specified for his New York Times Building (including several infelicitous shades of red) exposed his deficiencies as a colorist. The screaming fire-engine red he picked for BCAM's exterior metalwork looks awful against the pale masonry.

Mixing bold, even loud colors with neutral stonework is not an impossible task, as was proven by James Stirling and Michael Wilford's majestic Neue Staatsgalerie in Stuttgart, where the architects used acid-green mullions and hot-pink railings to jazz up the museum's stolid limestone-and-sandstone veneer. Here Piano's unconvincing chromatic contrast comes across as no more than a mixed metaphor.

BCAM is meant to be entered on its third and uppermost story, via the open escalator or the stairway housed within the scaffold-like red-painted steel structure Piano has dubbed "the spider," but which more closely resembles an outsize jungle gym. Not since the gigantic Plexiglas tube he and Rogers snaked up one flank of their Pompidou Center has Piano designed such a flamboyant people mover. Indeed, this overelaborate appendage seems a nostalgic bid to recapture the brashness of his breakthrough commission. Whatever the architect had in mind here, the mildly embarrassing entry sequence is soon forgotten as one approaches the main event: the galleries for which Piano is so celebrated. At the building's 2008 press preview, Govan extolled the "crystal clear" light of Piano's loftlike, columnless exhibition spaces. But after one entered the building and passed through the top-floor lobby (dominated by a vast, glass-fronted elevator shaft containing a three-story-high, black-white-and-red montage commissioned from Barbara Kruger), the first gallery on the north side (devoted to Jasper Johns) came as a shock. Despite perfect weather— as bright a day as can be expected of Southern California in winter— the light was gray and gloomy. A nearby room devoted to enormous unstretched canvases by Leon Golub fared somewhat better, but it too seemed inadequately illuminated. The only truly impressive gallery was a spacious room hung with tier after tier of large color photographs by Cindy Sherman, where the lower artificial light level was likely dictated by conservation requirements for works on paper.

Another telling portion of the museum's surprising inaugural publication—the transcript of a discussion among Broad, Govan, and Piano—hints at a possible source of the trouble:

> EB: …I was very concerned with the cost of the roof. Renzo and I had quite a few discussions about how to get it down to $200 a square foot.
> RP: The good thing about the roof is that we needed the roof. I lost on the basement, and I won on the roof.
> EB: The roof's great, except it cost more than the rest of the building.
> RP: Eli, do you remember one day, we were around the table and you said, "How much do we save if we take the roof away?" Well, you save a lot, especially on the architectural fees!

By way of comparison, BCAM cost about 66 percent less per square foot than the Nasher. (LACMA never itemized the final cost-per-square-foot of the BCAM roof.) By any reckoning, Broad cannot be called a cheapskate. Nevertheless, his dickering over the architectural element Piano is most famous for—his ingenious overhead light filters—might have led to the architect's use of rows of relatively rudimentary mesh ceiling panels below the rooftop's factory-style sawtooth skylights, which evidently do not perform at the high level achieved by the intricate, custom-designed ceiling systems he created, without regard to expense, for the Menil and the Nasher.

Southern California is often said to be America's proving ground for trends that later go nationwide. Although the private museum was pioneered on the East Coast (and also at the Huntington Library near Los Angeles) in the early twentieth century, its postwar resurgence was largely a Los Angeles phenomenon, with the J. Paul Getty Museum in Malibu and Brentwood, the Norton Simon Museum in Pasadena, and the Armand Hammer Museum in Westwood. It is impossible not to wonder what the cultural life of Los Angeles would now be like if those three men had given the billions they lavished on art and architecture to LACMA instead. However, those buccaneers were not the only hometown models Broad could have emulated. For decades, one of LACMA's biggest and most reliable supporters was the fabulously rich, publicity-shy Anna Bing Arnold, who died at the age of one hundred in 2003. Her first husband was the New York real estate magnate Leo S. Bing, who with his brother Alexander M. Bing funded such seminal housing reform schemes as Clarence Stein and Henry Wright's Sunnyside Gardens of 1924–1928 in Queens, New York, and the new town of Radburn, New Jersey, of 1928–1932. The $24 million she bequeathed to the museum for its education program was just a fraction of her lifetime gifts to LACMA, where she was esteemed for her unconditional readiness to pay for acquisitions curators deemed imperative—the Blanchette Rockefeller of the West, and the antithesis of Broad's all-strings-attached modus operandi. In 1978, Arnold addressed a Los Angeles conference on the arts in education, and in phrases that harked back to the nineteenth-century notion of the museum as vehicle for spiritual uplift and social cohesion, she emphasized what a unifying force art can be:

> Art is a universal language which binds people to one another and to humane and ideal aims.... Art can still be the leaven to help us fulfill our emotional needs, to accept the restrictions in our daily lives, and to become all that we are.

To have the crucial role of museum professionals usurped by self-serving tycoons in the name of economic imperative threatens not only the integrity of individual institutions but the very principle of art held in public trust. Not all California crazes have caught on elsewhere in America, which raises hopes that the cautionary example of LACMA, seduced and abandoned, might deter other museums from entering into such dangerous liaisons. It is a commonplace that museum architecture must be subservient to the needs of the works displayed within it, but what a museum chooses to exhibit is sometimes less important than the building itself. Such is the case with Piano's Astrup Fearnley Museum of Modern Art of 2009–2012 in Oslo (see Illustration 12b), a privately owned contemporary art gallery built to house works—predominantly paintings and sculptures but also including photography, video, and installation pieces—assembled by the Norwegian shipping firm Astrup Fearnley starting in the 1960s and formalized by the creation of the eponymous museum in 1993, for which Piano created its first purpose-built home almost two decades later.

Piano's great foursome of the Menil, Twombly, Beyeler, and Nasher museums not only are alike in being his finest essays in exhibition design but are equally distinguished by their exceptional holdings. The contents of the Astrup Fearnley collection, on the other hand, were not generally well known beyond art-world insiders until the opening of the Piano building, though word had spread within the New York trade about the Norwegian institution's vigorous acquisition of high-priced pieces from leading contemporary dealers. The extent of the Fearnley foundation's purchases in the run-up to its museum's completion astounded viewers when they were finally put on view in 2012, for the results amounted to a veritable checklist of the trendiest (and most expensive) artists of the period, including Maurizio Cattelan, Damien Hirst, Jeff Koons, Takashi Murakami, and Richard Prince, in what certainly must have represented an outlay of many tens if not several hundreds of millions of dollars. Although other figures of considerably greater merit are also represented —Robert Gober, Bruce Nauman, and Cindy Sherman among them—

along with a number of young Norwegians little-known outside their homeland, the overall impression of the collection was one of immense but sadly misallocated resources. If there was ever a modern museological equivalent of the term "fashion victim," this was it.

Whatever one makes of the Astrup Fearnley Museum's contents, the building itself is a great success in urbanistic terms. In hopes of this becoming the cultural anchor of the city's newly gentrified district of Tjuvholmen (the name means "thieves' home," alluding to a former penal colony), property developers offered the institution a spectacular waterfront site on the Oslo Fjord to the southwest of the city center. Piano, who grew up in the Ligurian port of Genoa and has always been attuned to the sea, responded to the site with a nautically inspired structure quite unlike any of his many other museums. Here the dominant architectural feature is a vast, billowing glass-and-steel roof canopy that swoops over the three distinct components of the complex beneath it like a gigantic ship's sail and unites the trio of buildings: the harborfront gallery for changing exhibitions, and across a narrow channel a parallel structure for the permanent collection and administrative offices, next to which is a six-story office building leased to a major Oslo law firm.

In piquant contrast to Piano's high-tech roof element—which touches down on one point like a barely tethered tent in the grassy sculpture park that fronts the fjord—the three buildings are clad in unfinished vertical wood siding that suggests maritime piers. It has been claimed that any building looks twice as good if it is sited next to a major body of water, and that could also be said of Snøhetta's Oslo Opera House, which likewise abuts the city's coastline but in a much more industrial segment of its inner port. Echoing Le Corbusier, Piano said at the Astrup Fearnley Museum's dedication, "Light is the most important material for architecture," and went on to add, "The next is water—water is magic because it is never the same."

Looking back on the quite mixed results of Piano's unprecedented volume of museum design, there seems little doubt that the success of his individual projects owes less to the felicities of site than to the exigencies of patronage. His quartet of galleries in Texas and Switzerland are perhaps most remarkable for the way in which they transcend largely unpromising environmental conditions to create sympathetic spaces for viewing art. But they no doubt owe their transcendent quality to their enlightened benefactors—the connoisseurs Dominique de Menil, Ernst Beyeler, and Raymond Nasher. They stand in telling contrast to Eli Broad, who received one of Piano's least satisfactory efforts, even though it is widely assumed that a single strong client is more likely to obtain a good result than a consensus-seeking committee. As Renzo Piano's finest museums indicate, at his best he can be an architectural alchemist, but at the other end of his creative spectrum it is clear that he is not a magician.

13

REM KOOLHAAS

WITH HIS PRODIGIOUS gift for invention, shrewd understanding of communication techniques, and contagiously optimistic conviction that modern architecture and urban design still possess enormous untapped potential for the transformation of modern life, no master builder since Le Corbusier has offered a more impressive vision for a brighter future than the Dutch architect Rem Koolhaas, who has somehow managed to preserve his long-standing reputation as the bad boy of his profession even while executing the most impressive body of built work by a member of his generation. To be sure, there are other present-day architects who do certain things better than he does. Robert Venturi is a finer draftsman and a more elegant writer; Denise Scott Brown has a more empathetic feel for the social interactions that inform good planning; and Frank Gehry displays a sharper eye for sculptural assemblage and a keener instinct for popular taste. But when it comes to sheer conceptual audacity and original thinking about the latent possibilities of the building art, Koolhaas today stands unrivaled.

Through his Rotterdam-based practice, the Office for Metropolitan Architecture and its research-and-development division, AMO, Koolhaas has conceived some of the most daring schemes of the past

four decades, ranging in scale from mammoth undertakings like Euralille of 1987–1994 (the reconfiguration of the northern French city
of Lille with a new high-speed railway hub, commercial center, and
convention hall) and De Rotterdam of 1997–2013 (three interconnected mixed-use towers that together comprise the biggest building
in Holland) to exquisite smaller structures including the Casa da
Música of 2001–2005 in Porto, Portugal (an ark-like concert hall),
and the Netherlands Embassy of 1997–2003 in Berlin (the finest
work to rise in the German capital since reunification). But there is a
dark side to Koolhaas as well, signified by the laissez-faire stance he
takes toward social issues and the morally neutral attitude he brings
to his architecture and urbanism, especially his cynical acceptance of
the world as it is in all of its post-capitalist corruption and squalor, a
stance diametrically opposed to the high-minded reformist ideals of
the Modern Movement.

I witnessed a startling outburst that exemplified Koolhaas's deep
disdain for the social welfare planning at which his homeland excels
during a visit to his Rotterdam office in 1994. We walked past a recently built old-age home in an inoffensively mild Postmodern style
that brought to mind the redbrick Begijnhof in Amsterdam, a late-
medieval courtyard of almshouses notable for its humane scale and
quiet dignity. Eyeing the new facility, Koolhaas suddenly exclaimed,
"That's *exactly* what I hate about Holland, that horrible sentimentality!" The widespread perception of Koolhaas as a Manichean opportunist whose undeniable brilliance is diminished by an essential
coldheartedness was summed up in a cruel but telling passage in
Chip Kidd and Dave Taylor's architectural-themed graphic novel
Batman: Death by Design (2012), in which this polarizing figure is
transparently disguised as a Dutch architect named Kem Roomhaus.
As Batman observes, "Roomhaus may be an insufferable, affected,
narcissistic creep, but he's also a genius." Yet the same could be said

of Le Corbusier, and like that similarly chilly and determined careerist, Koolhaas knows that the power of presentation, verbal as well as visual, is a crucial (and perhaps the decisive) element in the realization of the building art.

Following the great Swiss-French master's profitable example, Koolhaas has produced several hugely popular books, including *Delirious New York: A Retroactive Manifesto for Manhattan* (1978) and *S,M,L,XL* (1995). Koolhaas's *Project Japan: Metabolism Talks*... (2011), written with Hans Ulrich Obrist, pays tribute to the Metabolists, the mid-twentieth-century Japanese architects at the forefront of that country's near-miraculous rebuilding after the devastation of World War II, led by the elder statesman of non-Western modernism, Kenzo Tange. This heavily illustrated and engagingly discursive oral history was undertaken in 2005 (the year of Tange's death at the age of ninety-one) to record the testimony of the surviving Metabolists.

In common with all of Koolhaas's publications, one can readily detect that *Project Japan* actually concerns the author and his own interests as much as its ostensible subject. The Metabolists' obsessive fixation on futuristic megastructures—stupendous agglomerations of superscaled buildings with integrated urban transport and other infrastructure meant to extend over many square miles, sometimes atop shallow bodies of water like Tokyo Bay, none of which were fully executed—has long been shared by the Dutch architect, who like his older Japanese counterparts in the Metabolist group has sought ingenious ways to overcome the severe geographic constraints of his tiny, sea-bound, populous homeland.

Another means of mass communication is perhaps even more important to Koolhaas than the printed word: film, which he studied as a young man. Few makers of architectural films exploit the full potential of the medium to create a convincing sense of what it is like to move through a sequence of interiors, which was made much easier with the introduction of the Steadicam in 1976. A rare exception was Ila Bêka and Louise Lemoine's documentary *Koolhaas Houselife* (2008), with which the architect was not directly involved and which presents a warts-and-all portrait of his House in Bordeaux of 1994–1998, a country residence outside the village of Floriac and overlooking the river Gironde. This rectangular three-level flat-roofed structure—already under the protection of France's Caisse Nationale des Monuments Historiques—was commissioned by Jean-François Lemoine, a newspaper editor who was paralyzed in an automobile accident and died only three years after his home was completed. Characteristically, Koolhaas flouted received wisdom about architecture for the handicapped with his House in Bordeaux, which American building inspectors would deem a potential death trap. Yet Lemoine did not want to live in a private Hôtel des Invalides but rather in a dwelling that did not advertise his disability, a fact that *Koolhaas Houselife* suggests only obliquely—an odd decision given that one of the film's two directors is Lemoine's daughter.

She and her collaborator came up with an inspired organizational conceit. The scenario comprises twenty-four brief segments, separated by short blackouts accompanied by the twang of a stringed instrument, like a *Seinfeld* episode. The production's unlikely star is the Lemoines' middle-aged Spanish housekeeper, Guadalupe Acedo, who seems to have wandered in from an Almodóvar comedy about a dysfunctional upper-middle-class Madrid family. Her nonstop, throwaway commentary is by turns gossipy, sagacious, pragmatic, and critical, like a canny servant girl in a Mozart opera, but she remains self-effacing and sympathetic to her unseen employers (Lemoine's widow still uses the house) and their bizarre but essentially wonderful domain. Acedo makes her initial appearance in the movie's opening scene as she ascends with her cleaning equipment on the hydraulic platform elevator that Koolhaas placed at the heart of the house to give his wheelchair-bound client easy access to all levels of the three-story structure. Koolhaas surmounted the breathtakingly open ground-level public living areas with a bedroom-and-bathroom story ponderously sheathed in Cor-Ten steel and punctuated with portholes like an outsize slab of rust-colored Swiss cheese. Several scenes expose the deplorable physical condition of the building, which is falling apart after little more than a decade. Leaks are far from the only problems, not least of which is the rapid degradation of the internal concrete core that holds up the house and frees large portions of the exterior from load-bearing encumbrances.

Artists of genius generally wish to appear as though they emerged fully formed, and Koolhaas is no exception. A scion of the Dutch avant-garde cultural elite, Remment Lucas Koolhaas was born in Rotterdam in 1944, at the onset of the *Hongerwinter* (hunger winter), the final ordeal of the five-year Nazi occupation of Holland. His polymathic father, Anton Koolhaas, was an esteemed journalist, author of beloved fables about anthropomorphic animals in the manner of Kenneth Grahame and George Orwell, and the scenarist for two Academy Award–nominated documentaries. The elder Koolhaas was also an ardent advocate of independence for the Dutch East Indies. In 1949 the Netherlands granted autonomy to Indonesia, and three years later Sukarno, the new country's first president, invited him to run a cultural program there, whereupon the writer moved his family to Jakarta. That four-year immersion in a third-world society—"I really lived as an Asian," the architect has reminisced—was a central factor in fostering his uncommonly broad worldview, which gave him a distinct advantage when the globalization of architectural practice began to accelerate as he hit his professional stride decades later.

Following his father's example, the young Koolhaas initially turned to journalism and screenwriting. In 1963, when he was eighteen, he began working for *De Haagse Post*, a right-liberal weekly published in The Hague, where he designed layouts and wrote on a wide range of political, social, and cultural topics. He later collaborated on an ultimately unproduced movie script, *Hollywood Tower*, for the soft-porn director Russ Meyer, auteur of such camp classics as *Faster, Pussycat! Kill! Kill!* (1965). There were other family influences as well. Koolhaas's maternal grandfather was Dirk Roosenburg, a vanguard architect in whose studio the boy made some of his earliest architectural drawings. Roosenburg's best-known work was the Philips electronics company's Lichttoren (light tower) of 1920–1928 in Eindhoven, a concrete-and-glass Art Deco office, laboratory, and factory building internally illuminated throughout the night like some twentieth-century Pharos—just the sort of romantic Modernism that Koolhaas evokes in his most imaginative speculations.

After studying at the experimentally oriented Architectural Association in London and later at Cornell (where he sought out the influential theorist O.M. Ungers), Koolhaas became the prime mover behind the Office for Metropolitan Architecture (OMA), which he founded in 1975 with the Greek architect Elia Zenghelis (under whom he had studied in London) and their respective spouses, the artists Madelon Vriesendorp and Zoe Zenghelis. Koolhaas has enjoyed a domestic life not unlike that in Anthony Kimmins's film comedy *The Captain's Paradise* (1953), in which Alec Guinness plays a ferryboat skipper who shuttles between a wife and a mistress in separate ports. Vriesendorp makes her home in London, but since the mid-1980s her husband has lived in Holland with the Dutch designer Petra Blaisse, who has collaborated on several OMA projects, including the interiors of the Seattle Central Library. (The Koolhaases' daughter, Charlie, is a photographer who did the principal illustrations for *Project Japan*, and their son, Tomas, is a cinematographer who is making a documentary on the architect titled *Rem*.)

Vriesendorp created the most celebrated image in *Delirious New York*, which first brought her husband to international attention. The painter's architectural fantasy *Apres l'amour* depicts an apparently postcoital Empire State Building and Chrysler Building lying side by side on a rumpled bed. In between them is what looks like a discarded condom but turns out to be a deflated Goodyear blimp—a sly reminder that the Empire State's spire was originally intended as a dirigible mooring mast (an idea abandoned as too dangerous). Beyond such provocative erotic metaphors—the antithesis of the coolly technocratic renderings that typified postwar corporate Modernism—what makes *Delirious New York* so unforgettable is its author's insights into the psychohistory of urbanism: the ways in which the often unacknowledged or unexpressed ethos of a city is embodied in its architecture. Koolhaas's almost cinematic exploration of Manhattan's subconscious architectural mystique had an especially tonic effect on the collective civic consciousness when it first appeared, just three years after the fiscal crisis of 1975 brought the city to the brink of bankruptcy. Even at Gotham's lowest ebb, Koolhaas never lost sight of the imaginative heights this greatest of metropolises could yet again attain.

An entire book could (and in due course undoubtedly will) be written about Koolhaas's spectacular trio of failed American museum proposals immediately before and after the millennium: an expansion of the Museum of Modern Art (1997) and an addition to the Whitney Museum of American Art (2001–2003), both in New York City, and a reconfiguration of the Los Angeles County Museum of Art (2003). (In 2001, he completed the Guggenheim Hermitage Museum at the Venetian casino-hotel in Las Vegas, but that small branch gallery, a consortium between the eponymous art institutions in New York and St. Petersburg, closed in 2008 after it lost too much money.) Koolhaas's inability to win any of these three high-profile assignments in

the most conspicuous architectural category of the past several decades says much about the frequently confrontational nature of his
vision. In the limited competition for the MoMA job, ten invited
participants (among whom Koolhaas was by far the best-known)
were asked to present broadly conceptual ideas. His irreverent scheme
included two elements that irreparably offended the search committee's amour propre: he proposed transforming Philip Johnson and
James Fanning's sacrosanct Abby Aldrich Rockefeller Sculpture Garden of 1953 into a sunken plaza not unlike the Rockefeller Center
ice-skating rink. Even more insolently, he would have surmounted a
seven-story addition atop Johnson's 1964 wing with a billboard emblazoned "MoMA, Inc."

Had the nonagenarian Johnson, a big fan of Koolhaas's, not been
in his dotage and thus out of the selection process, he might have
defended such bad-boy tactics as precisely the reinvigorating shock
MoMA needed to jolt it back to its revolutionary roots. But absent the
crafty old power broker, the merits of Koolhaas's scheme were overlooked and the job—which many seasoned observers had assumed to
be his for the asking—passed instead to Yoshio Taniguchi. That decorous but chilly design, which combines the dismal immensity of an
airport terminal with the disorienting placelessness of a convention
center, fulfilled the Dutchman's sardonic prophecy about the once-
pathbreaking museum's increasingly corporate character. Though
Koolhaas's impudence could be interpreted as professional suicide,
one still cannot help but marvel at his critical bravery.

Four years after the MoMA debacle, the Whitney turned to Koolhaas in another attempt to add to Marcel Breuer's stubbornly unex-
pandable Brutalist monolith of 1963–1966. During the 1980s, Michael
Graves had produced three increasingly unsatisfactory versions of a
pompous Postmodern enlargement that would have engulfed the original building in a welter of fussy classicizing polychromy, which was

dropped after strenuous community opposition. Koolhaas's far more radical plan called for a curved superstructure to be inserted behind the landmarked brownstones adjacent to the museum, which would have risen up and hovered over the Breuer building like a monstrous cobra. The Whitney abandoned that nonstarter after two years of even more vocal neighborhood protest. Koolhaas took the loss of the Whitney commission particularly badly. Not long after the New York museum cut him off, I saw him at the press preview for his McCormick Tribune Campus Center of 1997–2003 at the Illinois Institute of Technology in Chicago, the International Style campus designed by Ludwig Mies van der Rohe between 1943 and 1951.

As I looked around Koolhaas's excitingly inventive structure (which incorporates an adjacent elevated railroad by enclosing part of it in an enormous extruded tube, an idea proposed by Edgar Chambless for Roadtown, his visionary linear-city scheme of 1910) the architect pulled me into an empty conference room, shut the door, and urged me to write an exposé on the Whitney's longtime board chairman and principal benefactor, the cosmetics tycoon Leonard Lauder. He promised to provide me with enough damning information on his erstwhile patron to "ruin" him, but when I declined to be his mouthpiece, he disgustedly exited the room.

The best of Koolhaas's three lost museum schemes was for the Los Angeles County Museum of Art, which asked him to bring coherence to its jumble of dated 1960s pavilions. He immediately envisioned a drastic but brilliant solution: he called for the architectural equivalent of cutting the entire complex off at the ankles, leaving the footprints of the existing galleries and circulation routes intact, and then covering everything inside the oblong periphery of the multi-acre site with a gigantic bubble roof that suggested an inflatable tennis court shelter. In one bold stroke, LACMA would have gained the unified and monumental civic presence it has always lacked. Instead, like the

Whitney, the Los Angeles museum turned to Renzo Piano, the master of predictably safe and supposedly timeless institutional modernism. Alas, Piano's incremental boxes (the compromised Broad Contemporary Art Museum of 2003–2008 and the warehouse-like Resnick Pavilion of 2006–2010) have only exacerbated LACMA's organizational mess. Rather than returning to him for further installments of his proposed master plan, the museum in 2013 hired the Swiss architect Peter Zumthor to design a $650 million structure that will replace its buildings from the 1960s and 1980s while retaining Piano's postmillenial additions.

Apart from his short-lived Vegas display space, Koolhaas's only executed art gallery remains his Kunsthal of 1987–1992 in Rotterdam, a temporary exhibition facility with flexible galleries arranged around a squared-off helix of interior ramps that lead visitors almost effortlessly from level to level, without the now-ubiquitous escalators that give so many contemporary museums (especially Taniguchi's MoMA and Herzog and de Meuron's Tate Modern) the air of a shopping mall. Koolhaas used this same low-tech internal circulation for his largest work in the US, the Seattle Central Library of 1999–2004 (see Illustration 13a), which was enthusiastically received upon its completion. His solution demonstrates his fundamental disdain for a major preoccupation of bien-pensant architects since the 1960s—"contextualism," or designing a building to fit in with earlier structures near it. Given the dreary array of banal 1960s and 1970s high-rises that surround the entire city block dedicated to the new library, one can second his belief that it would have been futile to make any accommodating gestures toward such a negligible setting.

Wisely, he devised a blockbusting composition: an angular pile-up of prism-like glass layers wrapped in white-painted, diamond-patterned steel latticework that forcefully establishes itself by ignoring everything around it. In continuation of a Modernist tradition that began with the Crystal Palace, the open, soaring, light-flooded interior of the Seattle Central Library provides a majestic public space that suggests that the activities taking place within it are of singular importance to the community—something that architectural neoconservatives have wrongly insisted lies beyond the emotional capacity of the modern design vocabulary and solely within the writ of the Classical tradition.

Koolhaas is inexorably drawn to the architecture of state power and is fascinated by earlier architects attuned to power regardless of its source. None of the great twentieth-century masters was more assiduous in his willingness to work for clients of any political stripe, from Communists to Nazis and all stops in between, than Koolhaas's idol Mies van der Rohe. But whereas Mies's design genius might excuse much guilt by association, it is hard to fathom Koolhaas's perverse fondness for Wallace K. Harrison, a modestly accomplished establishment Modernist known mainly as the Rockefeller family's de facto court architect. Harrison's in-law relationship to the Rockefellers gave him initial entrée, and he went on to oversee several gargantuan commissions under their sponsorship, including the collaboratively designed United Nations Headquarters of 1949–1952 and Lincoln Center for the Performing Arts of 1959–1969, both in Manhattan, and the Empire State Plaza of 1959–1976 in Albany, which he designed (at the behest of Governor Nelson A. Rockefeller) with his longtime partner, Max Abramovitz. Koolhaas—who mounted a quixotic exhibition honoring the aged and démodé Harrison at New York's avant-garde Institute for Architecture and Urban Studies in 1979—has been particularly intrigued by the architect's hypothetical X-City of 1946, proposed by the real estate developer William Zeckendorf for the Manhattan site later donated by John D. Rockefeller Jr. to the UN, a configuration resurrected by Koolhaas in Euralille's dated enfilade of slab-sided high-rises.

As for his own relations with power, Koolhaas harbors no discernible qualms about abetting a state-controlled propaganda agency of the current Chinese dictatorship. Following the example of architects from time immemorial, he has gone where the work is, and during the first postmillennial decade that meant China, where his major projects include the Shenzen Stock Exchange of 2006–2011, a monolithic, Miesian tower surrounded by a projecting "base" hoisted six stories above ground level by massive diagonal struts. Likely to remain Koolhaas's most controversial commission is the 5.1-million-square-foot China Central Television Headquarters of 2004–2012 in Beijing (see Illustration 13b), with an estimated cost of more than $800 million. (A disastrous 2009 fire, which destroyed the OMA-designed Television Cultural Center, a multiuse hotel, theater, restaurant, and retail complex next to the giant main structure, was largely responsible for a three-year delay in the project's completion.)

The CCTV building brings to mind a twice-as-large, deconstructed version of Johann Otto von Spreckelsen's Grande Arche de la Défense of 1982–1989 in Paris, one of the most visible, if least distinguished, of the *grands projets* initiated by President François Mitterrand. (Significantly, OMA lost the 1991 competition for an extension to La Défense, the office-building district created just outside the city limits to spare central Paris from high-rise development.) Despite their striking disparity in size—the CCTV structure is 768 feet high, the equivalent of a seventy-story tower, while the Grande Arche is the equivalent of only thirty-five stories—both are approximate cubes that inscribe a vast void within their clearly defined outlines. But whereas Spreckelsen's slab-sided squared-off arch is dully static, the vertiginously off-kilter CCTV headquarters is a tour de force of high-tech engineering, orchestrated by Cecil Balmond of the London-based structural consultancy Arup.

Not the least controversial aspect of the CCTV project has been one of the most deplorable and widely decried preservation disasters in recent memory: the systematic devastation of the city's historic *hutong*, or alleyway quarters. Among the most shocking victims of this replay of the barbaric sacking of artistic treasures during Mao's Cultural Revolution was the *siheyuan*, or courtyard house, of the revered early-twentieth-century architects, historians, and preservationists Liang Sicheng and his wife, Lin Huiyin, an aunt of the American architect Maya Lin. In order to escape notice, the authorities suddenly razed it in January 2012 during Lunar New Year festivities; the demolition set off an international uproar. Nonetheless, there are some who believe that historic preservation has gotten out of hand and thwarts innovative architecture and city planning. Those contrarians include Koolhaas, who advanced that idea in his exhibition "Cronacaos," which was first seen at the Venice Architecture Biennale in 2010.

In this visually deficient show, Koolhaas asserted that some 12 percent of the earth's surface is now barred from new construction because of various restrictive regulations—historic preservation, land conservation, and the like—and thus the full creative potential of the building art is stiflingly inhibited internationally by what he sees as an excessive, sentimental attachment to older architecture. That proposition sounded rather ironic coming from the author of the stupendous CCTV headquarters, which caused such unconscionable destruction in its veritable shadow. In a 2007 article in *The Guardian*, the architecture critic Jonathan Glancey called the CCTV building, which occupies a forty-five-acre site that was cleared for its construction, "the most dramatic of these *hutong*-gobblers," but noted how Koolhaas showed him snapshots of the endangered landmarks and wistfully commented that "people, I think, miss their old life down below in the courtyards." Glancey cited this contradiction as "exactly the kind of paradox [Koolhaas] revels in. In public, he is the master of sock-it-to-me design; in private, he looks with affection at ... an old way of oriental life likely to vanish."

The glass-and-metal-skinned Beijing behemoth is basically a pair of slightly inward-leaning L-shaped towers on two opposing corners of a vast square, joined at the top by a breathtaking right-angled cantilevered overhang that imbues the composition with gravity-defying bravado. The horizontal and vertical elements interconnect in a continuous series of eight segments, a snakelike circulation system quite unlike that of any other office-and-broadcasting facility. Experimental architecture by its very nature is more prone to the depredations of time and natural elements than buildings made from conventional materials through traditional methods. Avant-garde architects often simply do not know how the products of their imagination will perform when implemented, especially if untested components are involved. Yet the titanium-zinc-alloy cladding of the CCTV building began to show the dire effects of Beijing's poisonous air pollution only four years after the material was installed and even before the megastructure was fully occupied.

With a plethora of bizarre new architecture engulfing them—some three hundred new high-rises in the city's specially zoned central business district alone—baffled Beijingers devised a new architectural lexicon recalling the wry coinages long perfected by witty Berliners, who, for example, dubbed the glass dome of Norman Foster's Reichstag renovation of 1992–1999 *die Käseglocke* (the cheese cover). Thus the two-legged CCTV colossus became colloquially known as *da kucha* (big pants crotch). In trying to preempt a sarcastic nickname of this sort, officials wanted to get locals to refer to the CCTV building as *zhi chuan* (knowledge window) a pretentious choice that backfired because of its close homophonic echo of *zhi chuang*—hemorrhoid. But whatever moniker people adopt, one can predict that they will be beguiled by the highly unusual and equally controlled tourist route that is being built through the CCTV nerve center, large portions of which are vacant spaces that fill out vast internal volumes but serve no functional purpose, a wasteful allocation solely in service of the structure's gigantic and admittedly breathtaking form. Visitors will be able to navigate the premises in one nonstop loop while never disturbing day-to-day activities, a surefire public relations coup that will confer a bogus semblance of transparency on what is anything but an open operation.

CCTV arises amid the urban free-for-all of Beijing's central business district, a chaotic cityscape that makes 1980s Houston seem like Haussmann's Paris. To counter that urban miasma, Koolhaas (and his design partner for this project, the German architect Ole Scheeren) applied a strategy explicated in Koolhaas's 1994 manifesto, "Bigness, or the Problem of Large." It enumerates five "theorems," some of them evident in the Beijing scheme:

1. Beyond a certain critical mass, a building becomes a Big Building. Such a mass can no longer be controlled by a single architectural gesture, or even by any combination of architectural gestures....

2. ...Issues of composition, scale, proportion, detail are now moot.

The "art" of architecture is useless in Bigness.

3. In Bigness, the distance between core and envelope increases to the point where the façade can no longer reveal what happens inside. The humanist expectation of "honesty" is doomed....

Where architecture reveals, Bigness perplexes; Bigness transforms the city from a summation of certainties into an accumulation of mysteries. What you see is no longer what you get.

4. Through size alone, such buildings enter an amoral domain, beyond good or bad.

Their impact is independent of their quality.

5. Together, all these breaks—with scale, with architectural composition, with tradition, with transparency, with ethics—imply the final, most radical break: Bigness is no longer part of any urban tissue.

It exists; at most, it coexists.

Its subtext is *fuck* context.

Such morally indifferent attitudes infuriate Koolhaas's detractors, who see him as pandering to the basest market-driven impulses in a world that has largely abandoned the social vision of the early Modernists as either pragmatically impossible or impossibly utopian. As if to endow his free-floating *Realarchitektur* with legitimate parentage, he championed a reappreciation of the work of Robert Venturi and Denise Scott Brown, who during the full flood of socially responsive design in the 1960s and early 1970s were similarly denounced for what some saw as their all-too-willing embrace of commercialism, epitomized by their incendiary study *Learning from Las Vegas* (1972) and its codification of the American roadside vernacular. Venturi and Scott Brown's position, however, was no unprincipled acquiescence to capitalist imperatives but a resigned acceptance that these are conditions that all present-day practitioners—even high-style architects—must deal with, like it or not. A similar uproar greeted the 2001 publication of *The Harvard Design School Guide to Shopping*, a comprehensive analysis of retail design that emerged from a course that Koolhaas taught at the university and focused on today's all-pervasive global consumer economy.

Two other books have emerged from similar studies led by Koolhaas as part of his Project on the City at Harvard's Graduate School of Design, where he has been a visiting professor since 1995. Investigating what he has described as "a new type of metropolis that we have called a 'city of exacerbated difference,'" Koolhaas and his students have focused on such immense ad hoc conurbations as five rapidly expanding cities in China's Pearl River Delta (Guangzhou, Hong Kong, Macau, Shenzen, and Zhuhai), subject of *Great Leap Forward* (2002), and Nigeria's biggest city, analyzed in *Lagos: How It Works*. These seminars were based on Scott Brown and Venturi's now-famous 1968 Yale course that led to *Learning from Las Vegas*. But whereas they and their class gathered data by driving along and photographing the Strip, Koolhaas has admitted that he and his team were too scared by Lagos's chaos to exit their vehicle, and instead rented the president of Nigeria's helicopter to survey the city by air. "What seemed, on ground level, an accumulation of dysfunctional movements, seemed from above an impressive performance, evidence of how well Lagos might perform if it were the third largest city in the world," he later wrote. Traffic jams became occasions for people to make sales.

Some critics consider both his subject matter and methodology de haut en bas slumming. As George Packer wrote in *The New Yorker* in 2006:

> That impulse to look at an "apparently burning garbage heap" and see an "urban phenomenon," and then make it the raw material of an elaborate aesthetic construct, is not so different from the more common impulse not to look at all.

In much the same way that artists like Jeff Koons, Damien Hirst, and Takashi Murakami have appropriated ideas put forward by Andy Warhol and taken them to extremes their originator could scarcely have imagined, so Koolhaas has proceeded from Venturi and Scott Brown's premises and transmogrified them in ways that can seem like grotesque parodies rather than sincere homages. There can be no doubt whatever about Koolhaas's once-in-a-generation talent. What remains very much still in question is whether his seeming indifference to progressive values will make future observers wonder why this cultural potentate was so reluctant to confront Chinese oligarchs with the same fearlessness he once marshaled against captains of capitalism on American museum boards.

14

BERNARD TSCHUMI

AN UNSEEN YET palpable presence seemed to hover over the Greek capital of Athens in June 2009 during the inaugural festivities for the New Acropolis Museum (see Illustration 14b), which was designed by the Swiss-born, New York–based architect Bernard Tschumi. This pervasive emanation was not the aura of Athena Parthenos (Athena the Virgin), dedicatee of her namesake city's principal temple atop the Acropolis—the Parthenon of 447–432 BC, long esteemed as the apex of Classical architecture. Neither was it the shade of Ictinus, the building's architect; nor that of Phidias, who sculpted the gold-and-ivory effigy of the goddess that nearly touched the inner sanctum's forty-foot ceiling. Nor was it Agoracritus, putative head of the sizable Parthenon workshop that carved tons of white Pentelic marble into numerous fully dimensional figures for the two triangular pediments; ninety-two high-relief panels, called metopes, for the frieze above the oblong structure's peripheral colonnade; and the bas-relief that wrapped like a ribbon around the exterior of Athena's inner sanctum and depicted the Great Panathenaic procession (the citizenry's celebration of their divine protector's birthday).

Instead, the regnant spirit of the New Acropolis Museum's consecration turned out to be a departed diva of the silver screen, Melina

Mercouri, the actress-turned-politician whose name was repeatedly invoked at the ceremonies, and over whose grave in Athens's First Cemetery prayers were said as part of the elaborate observances. Those middle-aged or older film fans who recall Mercouri (if at all) only as a midcentury sex symbol outshone by her more renowned contemporaries Marilyn Monroe and Brigitte Bardot might be bemused by the exalted place she now occupies in the modern Greek pantheon, rather as if in this country Angie Dickinson had become head of the National Endowment for the Arts and ultimately a patriotic demi-deity akin to Betsy Ross. But more than anyone else, Mercouri vivified the continuing campaign to bring Greece's long-lost archaeological treasures back to their homeland.

Three decades ago, she began agitating for the unconditional return of marble carvings that were sawed off the Parthenon between 1801 and 1812 under the direction of Thomas Bruce, 7th Earl of Elgin, an amateur antiquarian and British ambassador to the Sublime Porte (as the seat of the Ottoman Empire in Constantinople was called in diplomatic parlance). Elgin's representative in Athens exploited loopholes in a vaguely worded permit from Greece's Ottoman overlords and stripped both the Parthenon and an adjoining shrine, the Erechtheum, of their choicest surviving sculptures (many had already been destroyed in the infamous bombardment by the Venetians in 1687). Elgin's removal of the marbles provoked immediate outrage, not least from Lord Byron, who castigated him in *Childe Harold's Pilgrimage* of 1812 as "the last, the worst, dull spoiler" who "rive[d] what Goth, and Turk, and Time hath spar'd."

Four years later, the British government bought the booty from the cash-strapped earl for £35,000 (about $4 million today), and the Elgin Marbles, as they became known, remain in the British Museum. Sporadic demands for their return to Greece have flared up and died down over the years. But by the time the sculptures were reinstalled, to breathtaking effect, in John Russell Pope's purpose-built Duveen Gallery of 1936–1938 (after they received an ill-advised acid scrub), the Elgin Marbles had attained the transcendent status shared by those very few artworks universally agreed to be the common spiritual inheritance of all mankind—and thus just as legitimately held in London as in Athens or anywhere else, so long as they remain accessible to the public and are safeguarded for future generations.

This Olympian view of global custodianship was vehemently rejected by Mercouri, who in 1981 became her country's minister of culture (a post she held, save a four-year interregnum, until her death in 1994). Self-described as the Parthenon's La Pasionaria, she reignited a smoldering controversy and turned the sculptures' restitution into an international crusade that her countrymen have continued. Those efforts reached an emotional crescendo with the unveiling of Tschumi's $200 million showplace, which seemed less an architectural event or a museological accomplishment than the costliest and craftiest weapon in a *Kulturkampf* of Homeric intensity and duration. That perception was underscored by the foreign press brigade flown in at considerable expense by the Greek government for the sumptuously produced, strenuously orchestrated opening, a rare promotional extravaganza at a time of retrenchment for cultural institutions worldwide and a harbinger of the financial crisis that would plunge the country into deep turmoil just a few years later.

Any prior pretense to the lack of a political agenda was dropped at the dedication of the New Acropolis Museum when the Greek minister of culture, Antonis Samaras, spoke of the building's true function in the bluntest of terms:

We cannot dedicate this magnificent new museum with full hearts. We cannot illuminate fully the artistic achievement created in fifth-century Athens, because almost half of the sculptures from the Parthenon were taken from here 207 years ago to reside in enforced exile 4,000 kilometers away.

The abduction of these sculptures is not only an injustice to us Greeks but to everyone in the world, the English included, because they were made to be seen in sequence and in total, something that cannot happen as long as half of them are held hostage in the British Museum.

Samaras went on to quote a reluctantly compliant American museum head who surely had forced his honeyed words through gritted teeth:

After three decades of trying to avoid the inevitable[, i]n explaining the decision to return the [Euphronios] vase [to Italy], the Met's director, Philippe de Montebello, said: *"The world is changing and you have to play by the rules."*

Then, in the evening's coup de théâtre, the minister put on a pair of white conservator's gloves, lifted a fragmentary marble relief of a boy's head toward the massed photographers, inserted the shard into a shattered metope, and beamed like a clever child who had completed his first jigsaw puzzle. Several foreign-owned (and insignificant) bits of the Parthenon sculptures were donated to the new museum in time for the opening, but the one Samaras brandished was on loan from the Vatican Museum for only a year. Days before the opening, he indignantly rebuffed the British Museum's offer to lend the Elgin Marbles to Athens for three months in return for Greek recognition of British ownership. According to Samaras's communiqué, "Accepting it would legalise the snatching of the Marbles and the monument's carving-up." But he nonetheless seized upon the Holy See's paltry benefice as though it were a papal endorsement and milked it to maximum effect as the Platonic ideal of a photo-op prop.

Mercouri's strategy has emboldened other countries to press for possession of artworks they likewise judge essential to their national identity, and in many cases those efforts have succeeded. However, the proliferation of such suits clearly endangers the free and open diffusion of culture in the higher service of international understanding. Masterpieces of art possess immense potential to advance a worldview that could help assuage the societal terrors posed by globalization, the most thoroughgoing socioeconomic upheaval since the Industrial Revolution, which has set off a pandemic of retrogressive nationalism, regional separatism, and religious extremism. In the cultural sphere, this unfortunate development was anticipated by Mercouri's discovery of the hot-button issue that would secure her second career. Daughter of a high-ranking Athens politician, she shared the leftist sympathies of her American-born husband, the director Jules Dassin, who was blacklisted during the McCarthy period and moved to Europe. Most memorable of their eight films together was Dassin's *Never on Sunday* (1960), in which she portrayed a definitive golden-hearted whore.

But Mercouri's finest hour came as a fearless opponent of the right-wing dictatorship that seized power in Greece in 1967. When the military despots revoked her citizenship, she spat out: "I was born a Greek and I will die a Greek. Mr. Pattakos [a leader of the junta] was born a fascist and will die a fascist." After democracy was restored in 1974, she was elected to parliament and made the Elgin Marbles into a cause that not only played irresistibly to the Greek national psyche but reunited her country after decades of partisan strife. In the role of a lifetime, she morphed from earthy sexpot to Euripidean avenger and vividly personified what until then had been but a vague legal abstraction. For her final, posthumous metamorphosis, Mercouri's compatriots erected a white marble herm—with a bust of her that is classically correct save for its anachronistic hairdo and facsimile movie-star autograph—across from Athens's Arch of Hadrian and Temple of Olympian Zeus, the perfect place to immortalize the woman they called "the last Greek goddess."

Bernard Tschumi was born in Lausanne in 1944, son of Jean Tschumi, an estimable yet little-remembered Swiss-French architect who was trained in the Classical tradition at the École des Beaux-Arts but became a committed Modernist. The elder Tschumi's somewhat conservative aesthetic and high standard of execution (much like his contemporary Marcel Breuer) won him large corporate and institutional commissions in Europe, including two major Swiss projects: the Nestlé headquarters of 1959–1960 in Vevey and the World Health Organization headquarters of 1962–1966 in Geneva. Tschumi *fils* lived with his family in Paris until he was ten, when they moved back to Switzerland. Following his father's career path he studied architecture at the Federal Institute of Technology in Zurich, but was repeatedly drawn back to Paris, which remains his spiritual home. He was there during *les événements de mai* 1968, a year before he graduated, and though the precise nature of his involvement in the protests remains hazy, ever since then he has advertised his *soixante-huitard* sympathies with a ubiquitous revolutionary-red scarf, a trademark akin to Frank Lloyd Wright's porkpie hat and Le Corbusier's round spectacles. At the Acropolis museum press preview, Tschumi's *écharpe rouge* was a summery chiffon, but as one fashion-conscious journalist at the Athens opening noted, "In winter it's red cashmere."

After Tschumi received his diploma, he taught for several years in London at the Architectural Association, and in 1976 resettled in New York. He taught at Cooper Union as well as Princeton, and gravitated toward the theoretically minded architects and scholars associated with the now-defunct Institute for Architecture and Urban Studies, the avant-garde think tank and academy that exerted an enormous influence on advanced architectural thought between 1967 and 1984. His big career breakthrough came when he won the design competition for one of François Mitterrand's lesser-known *grands projets*: the Parc de la Villette of 1983–1986 in Paris (see Illustration 14a), a redevelopment of 135 acres in the city's northeast section formerly occupied by cattle yards, abattoirs, and meatpacking plants. In this intriguing if rather overworked attempt to reconceive the urban park, he dispersed twenty-six red-painted metal-clad follies (most of them two or three stories high) in a grid pattern that blanketed the site. These fantasias recombined snippets of familiar early Modernist motifs—especially the dynamic forms of Russian Constructivism—and although charming, they soon seemed of little consequence.

Tschumi's stalled building career prompted him to become the dean of Columbia's architecture school, and thanks to the exposure and contacts the position provided, he began to get more work. But his executed oeuvre is hardly extensive, and includes (in addition to his Athens and Paris commissions) only about half a dozen completed buildings, among them the Florida International University School of Architecture in Miami (2003), the Vacheron Constantin watch company headquarters in Geneva (2004), the Limoges Concert Hall in France (2007), and the Alésia Museum Visitor's Center at a Roman archaeological site in Burgundy (2012).

In 2003, after fifteen years at Columbia, Tschumi left to concentrate on the Athens project, by any measure one of the most prestigious commissions of the past quarter-century, on a par with I. M. Pei's Grand Louvre of 1983–1993 in Paris, Robert Venturi and Denise Scott Brown's Sainsbury Wing of 1985–1991 at the National Gallery in London, and Norman Foster's Reichstag of 1992–1999 in Berlin. The hiring of foreign architects for all those highly coveted assignments in national capitals reflected the increasing globalization of the profession, reconfirmed when Tschumi was called to the Acropolis.

These selections may well have indicated the sponsors' desire to attract worldwide attention or to avoid the appearance of cultural chauvinism, or both. But by choosing the cosmopolitan Tschumi, exemplar of today's *architectes sans frontières*, his Greek clients found both an adept practitioner and a perfect camouflage for their underlying nationalistic motivations.

As a work of architecture, the New Acropolis Museum brings to mind Mark Twain's deadpan observation that "Wagner's music is better than it sounds," for in certain respects Tschumi's design is better than it looks, especially after one recovers from the terrible first visual impression it makes. This triple-decker sandwich of latticework concrete at the bottom, angled panels of corrugated metal in the middle, and dark-gray glass at the top appears more like a provincial convention center than a national treasure house. Athenians have complained that the hulking structure—as high as a seven-story building—is out of scale with its low-rise residential surroundings. But the museum's site is ideally positioned in relation to the Acropolis, which rises three hundred yards to the northwest, and a public institution of such extraordinary importance could hardly have been confined to a domestic scale.

The museum's ground floor and piano nobile are trapezoidal in plan and parallel the surrounding streets. However, the rectangular top story is shifted on a diagonal to align with the Parthenon. This contrary inflection recalls Tschumi's premillennial Deconstructivist phase (he was one of seven architects, along with Peter Eisenman, Frank Gehry, Zaha Hadid, Rem Koolhaas, Daniel Libeskind, and the Viennese firm Coop Himmelb(l)au, included in Philip Johnson and Mark Wigley's 1988 Museum of Modern Art exhibition "Deconstructivist Architecture"). Happily, the Athens museum is much more low-key than the most extreme example of that trend in Tschumi's work, his Alfred Lerner Hall of 1996–1999 at Columbia University, a dizzying and pointless mash-up of frenetic angular tricks.

Perhaps he intended the infinitely calmer Athens museum's tripartite elevations to evoke the base/shaft/capital format prescribed by the Five Orders of Classical architecture. Particularly unfortunate is the structure's ground level, with deeply recessed concrete panels that were quickly colonized by pigeons as a readymade dovecote. The main entrance is dramatized by a long, upswept concrete canopy that extends toward the broad pedestrian promenade where tourists begin the ascent to the Acropolis. This flamboyant porte cochere, which unfortunately brings to mind a Miami Beach or Las Vegas hotel rather than any loftier association, is raised on four fat concrete cylinders typical of the building's ungainly and overabundant concrete supports (forty-three in all). According to the architect, the massive columns dictated by building codes for the earthquake-prone Attica region also allowed him to make fewer incursions into Roman-era ruins that were unearthed as the foundation was dug. Remnants of a fourth-to-seventh-century-AD commercial neighborhood are visible through a large aperture in the entry plaza pavement beneath the canopy, but are unlikely to excite anyone but archaeologists.

Where, one thought, is Renzo Piano now that we really need him? In fact, he was at work on the other side of town, where his Stavros Niarchos Foundation Cultural Center (which comprises a new national library, opera house, and park, the latter by the American landscape designer Deborah Nevins) is scheduled to open in 2015. Much sought after for his dependable Modernist variations on the Classical colonnaded pavilion, Piano would have seemed the self-evident choice for the Acropolis project, but he eschews design competitions and accepts only direct commissions. (Best known among the dozen contenders for this job, which Tschumi won in 2001, were

Arata Isozaki and Daniel Libeskind.) Not only would Piano's hallmark style have been most appropriate at its veritable source, but his aptitude for more lightweight engineering would likely have assured a much more elegant structural outcome.

Visitors to the New Acropolis Museum pass under the entry marquee, move into a disappointingly generic low-ceilinged reception lobby, and then are directed toward the Gallery of the Slopes, named for its ramped floor (segments of which are glass to offer more glimpses of the lackluster subterranean ruins). This vast central hall expands the recent tendency for museum concourses to mimic airport terminals (exemplified by Yoshio Taniguchi's Museum of Modern Art expansion of 1997–2003 in New York and Piano's Modern Wing of 1999–2009 at the Art Institute of Chicago) but more specifically suggests an airplane hangar. The gallery's lateral walls are paneled with dot-patterned concrete rectangles that resemble superscale dominoes, while beneath them are vitrines chockablock with ancient objects discovered on the site (similar to displays in the Athens airport). At the far end of the space, a wall-to-wall flight of steps rises to the second-floor exhibition areas for works from the surrounding Attica region, Athens, and the Acropolis, though not the Parthenon itself.

One is greeted on that next level by a fragmentary reconstruction of the pediment from an earlier Acropolis temple of Athena destroyed by fire. To the right of this assemblage one passes into the wedge-shaped Archaic Gallery, and all at once another unimaginably sublime world materializes. The exterior glass walls of this sculpture hall are coated with tiny white ceramic dots (called frits) that screen distracting city views and suffuse a supernal glow heightened by filtered daylight that streams down from deeply inset skylights—an effect equal to the widely esteemed lighting of Piano at his best—made possible when Tschumi rotated the story above this middle level of the museum. The sculptures are thus shown to much better advantage than comparable works at Athens's drab National Archaeological Museum, where several top-rank masterpieces are undermined by poor one-source illumination.

Under the lambent daylight of the Archaic Gallery, marbles disclose translucence that eludes even the finest high-resolution photography and reveal rare traces of original pigment—a shock to those unaware that the ancient Greeks painted their statuary in bold (and to modern tastes garish) polychrome. The pedestals here were individually calibrated to the center of gravity of each object as a seismic precaution. Only breakable artifacts are kept behind glass, and one's ability to view pieces from all angles lends further credence to the free-form display concept. This lively convocation of gods, goddesses, demigods, kouroi, korai, horses, mythical beasts, and grave stelae is electrifying, all the more so because the ensemble includes such Ancient Art 101 mainstays as the *Kritios Kouros* and the torso of the *Rampin Rider* (fitted with a casting of the horseman's head, now in the Louvre).

Some critics have deplored the Archaic Gallery's lack of clearly differentiated display and traffic zones. But to me this seems a well-nigh-perfect installation, perhaps a result of the museum's staff having devised the arrangement not solely through the usual scale models and cutout replicas of artworks but rather by experimenting with the actual sculptures in the space itself. That almost unheard-of method was afforded by the twenty-month lead time between the initial transfer of the collection from the old Acropolis Museum of 1874 (a small, undistinguished structure next to the Parthenon) and this building's debut. The Archaic Gallery demonstrates, better than any other museum space in recent memory, that when great works are superlatively presented, architectural deficiencies can seem practically irrelevant.

With the exception of the Archaic Gallery, all the rest of the New Acropolis Museum, until one arrives at the top-floor Parthenon Gallery, is a disappointment. That is especially true of the museum's worst organizational blunder. Increasing levels of air pollution in Athens have prompted removal of the Acropolis's remaining sculptures to prevent further erosion from acid rain. (They are being replaced with facsimiles made from the same Pentelic marble as the originals.) Among those pieces are five caryatids (columns in the form of draped standing women) that formerly supported the so-called Porch of the Maidens on the Erechtheum, a small temple just to the north of the Parthenon. (One maiden was abducted by Elgin, who in addition to decorative sculptures took away architectural elements as study models for Britain's burgeoning building-products industry.) In the New Acropolis Museum, this quintet of the four Greek-owned caryatids and one replica have been reinstalled in their original configuration, but what ought to have been a showstopper is a fiasco. These celebrated chiton-clad figures were placed on a mezzanine balcony under which visitors pass into the Gallery of the Slopes on the first floor, and the sculptures are easy to miss if one does not turn around and look up. Furthermore, even though much of that soaring hall receives natural light, the caryatids are diminished by inept artificial illumination.

At last visitors come to the museum's make-or-break moment at the very top of the building, the Parthenon Gallery, which might be called Exhibit A in Greece's case before the court of world opinion. Here we are immediately confronted by a thrilling panorama framed by the floor-to-ceiling wraparound window wall: we see the invincibly glorious sanctuary of Athena Parthenos from a vantage point superbly calibrated in orientation (the temple seems illuminated in even northern light, like a model in an artist's studio), proximity (from this three-hundred-yard remove, the full length of the monument can be encompassed in a single glance), and perspective (the gentle thirty-one-degree sightline from the gallery up to the Acropolis does not unduly foreshorten the Parthenon).

Less felicitously, this majestic vista is distractingly broken up by two overlapping, discordant metal grids: one holds the oblong panes of the top story's curtain wall, the other supports an inner screen of glass panels with steel cables and square gaskets. The two-and-a-half-foot interstice between the two layers maximizes the circulation of cooled air mandatory for a glass-skinned building in the desertlike Attic climate. But this plethora of superimposed, misaligned rectangles recalls David Hockney's mosaic-like composites of pieced-together photographs. One yearns for glazing details as seamless as the hyper-Minimalist transparency achieved by the Japanese firm SANAA for their nearly invisible Glass Pavilion of 2001–2006 at the Toledo Museum of Art in Ohio.

Architects often purport to have reached design decisions that were so logical as to be inevitable and irrefutable, whereas almost all such choices are in fact arbitrary to some extent. Tschumi maintains that the Parthenon Gallery had to echo its subject as closely as possible. It was easiest for him to approximate the outline of the Parthenon's ground plan within the confines of the museum's loftlike, 128-by-276-foot top story. That story's outer dimensions allowed a broad ambulatory for viewing the sculptures on all four sides of the floor-to-ceiling rectangular structure that the architect positioned at the center of the space. However, he could not also replicate the prototype's 40-foot height in a building that already towers over its surroundings as it is. Thus, in the 23.5-foot-high Parthenon Gallery, the metopes are seen from a vantage point lower than they originally were on the temple. The architect's dutiful adherence to Modernism's ban on outright imitation is reflected in a display that is schematic enough to avoid "Disneyfication," an unforgivable sin in the Eurocentric intellectual circles Tschumi frequents. Therefore, although the Parthenon Gallery has the exact number of columns placed around the central display rectangle in the same arrangement visible in the near distance, these supports are chilly stainless-steel tubes rather than warm fluted-marble drums.

In one crucial respect, this commendable installation creates an impression quite the opposite of the client's desired result. Mixed among the pristine plaster metopes and Great Panathenaic procession frieze—molded during the nineteenth century from the British Museum's holdings—are the degraded and discolored pieces lately saved from the Parthenon. Granted that even the Elgin Marbles themselves are no longer as white as these immaculate reproductions, anyone who has seen the London originals will agree that they are in far better shape than the Athens remnants, some of which appear to have been marinated in tobacco juice.

Other pieces here seem like half-dissolved sugar cubes, and it takes a good visual imagination and knowledge of Classical iconography to figure out what some panels represent. (Helpfully, small reproductions of the precise drawings made by the French artist Jacques Carrey thirteen years before the 1687 bombardment have been placed next to the sculptures they document.) Present-day Greeks dismiss any suggestion that Elgin may have actually performed a great service by ensuring the protection of many masterworks that otherwise would likely be in the same state of deterioration. But this side-by-side, before-and-after evidence speaks for itself.

Given the highly charged political imperative of this project, one had half expected a polemical presentation on the order of the artist Hans Haacke's scathing installation pieces, in which he takes deadly aim at the sinister symbiosis between cultural institutions and corporate interests. But instead of rhetorical stunts—pedestals standing empty under spotlights, vacant walls emblazoned with accusatory texts—Tschumi's neutrally detailed, gray-painted matrix makes Greece's portion of the Parthenon legacy seem unexpectedly abundant, and the facsimile inserts are not so jarring as anticipated. No matter what the eventual outcome of the Elgin Marbles saga, this long-suffering treasure will never be complete because of the many irretrievable losses it has suffered, even if all the surviving pieces were reassembled in one place.

Bernard Tschumi's Parthenon Gallery conveys a remarkably full impression of the original ensemble. Given the riches on display one story below this, and the even more stupendous holdings in Athens's National Archaeological Museum, the modern Greeks' relentless determination to own every last one of the Parthenon marbles seems more than a bit selfish. These are not trading cards with a wrapper urging "Collect them all!" Greece is to be congratulated for finally improving upon the dumpy old Acropolis Museum. But monopolizing a common inheritance of all mankind is anything but desirable, and it would be a far greater boon to the entire world if both the British Museum and the New Acropolis Museum continue to share this glory that was Greece.

15

TOD WILLIAMS AND BILLIE TSIEN

NOTHING LESS THAN a latter-day miracle—a wholly unexpected and an unbelievably lucky one at that—occurred in Philadelphia in 2012, when the most acrimonious and protracted power struggle in the recent history of museums finally came to a glorious and uplifting conclusion with the opening of the long-anticipated new gallery of the Barnes Foundation Collection (see Illustration 15a), the finest concentration of French Impressionist and Postimpressionist painting in the Western Hemisphere. Despite jeremiads by the scheme's many implacable and vociferous opponents, and the nagging doubts of even some of the project's bien-pensant supporters, this decades-long drama turned out to be a triumph for all concerned. The combined talents of the New York–based husband-and-wife architectural team of Tod Williams and Billie Tsien (see frontispiece), their senior associate Philip Ryan, and the landscape architect Laurie Olin resulted in a wholly sympathetic and virtually perfect setting for a superabundance of treasures by such modern masters as Cézanne, van Gogh, Seurat, Matisse, and Picasso, miscellaneous Old Masters, and many unnamed African tribal artists.

How such a fortuitous outcome could have emerged from a tortuous tangle of circumstances unequaled in the annals of modern art and architecture is a question that will surely fascinate analysts of the museum industry for years to come. But there is no doubt about who the big winner is: the general public, which now can enjoy unprecedented access to a peerless cultural patrimony long fettered by restrictions imposed by the high-minded, visionary, yet maniacally controlling Albert Coombs Barnes. This pioneering early-twentieth-century collector's fierce determination to manipulate his enviable legacy from beyond the grave nearly caused his beloved possessions to be sold off by his designated legatee, Lincoln University, a traditionally black college in southeastern Pennsylvania, which he empowered, many believed, as a rebuke to the Philadelphia elite that had long snubbed him. As one cultivated doyen of Philadelphia high society dryly remarked years later of this self-made pharmaceutical tycoon and perpetually embittered outsider, "Perhaps we ought to have invited Barnes to our parties."

Thanks to a coalition of concerned institutions and individuals that banded together early in the new millennium—including the Pew Charitable Trust, the Annenberg and Lenfest foundations, along with the Getty, Luce, and Mellon foundations, among others, as well as numerous private benefactors—the impending dissolution of this stupendous hoard was staved off and a huge cultural calamity thereby averted. A malign and melodramatic documentary film opposed to the new Barnes, Don Argott's *The Art of the Steal* (2009), attempted to portray the institution's relocation to Philadelphia's Museum Mile from its original home in the Main Line suburb of Lower Merion as an act of naked thievery. But this civic rescue mission was actually comparable to a desperate family's intervention aimed at saving a shared inheritance from being irrevocably squandered by an incompetent, out-of-control relative.

The saga's tumultuous backstory, reported by John Anderson in his thoroughly researched and extensively reported book *Art Held*

Hostage: The Battle over the Barnes Collection (2003), makes it obvious who the real villains and heroes were, and for once the good guys won. To summarize briefly, Barnes's overly conservative investment directives (which foolishly demanded that his endowment be placed in low-yield tax-free public bonds even though the trust already enjoyed tax-free status) reduced his foundation's solvency by the inflationary 1970s. As the value of his art soared exponentially—in inverse proportion to the shrinking endowment—the Barnes's resources were further diminished by a costly lawsuit over a proposed parking lot on its property that was opposed by upper-class local residents, and sapped through extravagant spending by some of its officials.

Although substantial funds were realized during the 1990s through a major book deal and a lucrative international tour of the collection while the Lower Merion gallery building was being restored, the Barnes was effectively bankrupt by the turn of the millennium. In 2002 the foundation's beleaguered board members petitioned a court to let them break Albert Barnes's trust indenture and move his art to the center of Philadelphia in order to make it more convenient to the general public—admission had been by appointment only and was severely limited—and thereby alleviate the institution's fiscal crisis, a remedy enabled by the financial backing of foundations and individuals who supported the departure from Lower Merion and made their funding contingent on it. Barnes had insisted that none of his eight hundred paintings or thousands of other objects could ever be sold, loaned, or removed from the elaborate installations he contrived for them. Thus, the court agreed to the relocation after Barnes officials guaranteed that the collector's displays would be strictly maintained in the institution's new home.

Barnes, whose father labored in a Philadelphia slaughterhouse, put himself through the University of Pennsylvania and earned a medical degree, but he saw greater financial potential in manufacturing medicines. He teamed up with a more technically adept colleague who devised the formula for an antiseptic eyewash that prevented congenital gonorrheal infections in newborns. A skillful marketer, Barnes bought out his partner for a relative pittance and went on to make a fortune from the soon-ubiquitous optical solution, which he named Argyrol. The elder Barnes was a friend of Peter Widener, a fellow abattoir worker who later became a trolley magnate and an important art patron. Widener's example likely inspired the younger Barnes to assemble his own, far more significant collection once the big money began to roll in.

In 1912 Barnes asked an old Philadelphia high school classmate, the artist William Glackens, to buy paintings for him in Europe, and his friend's selection of choice works by Cézanne, Renoir, van Gogh, and Picasso set the tone for the collection. Starting with Glackens's choices, Barnes, relying on his own formidable artistic judgment, went on to build a collection of 46 Picassos, 59 Matisses, 69 Cézannes, and 181 Renoirs, as well as Old Master pictures by Hans Baldung Grien, Tintoretto, Veronese, El Greco, Frans Hals, Salomon van Ruisdael, Claude Lorrain, and Goya, along with Modernist works by Courbet, Daumier, Degas, Manet, Monet, Gauguin, Toulouse-Lautrec, the Douanier Rousseau, Redon, Braque, Modigliani, Utrillo, de Chirico, Soutine, Klee, Miró, and the Americans Maurice Prendergast, Charles Demuth, Glackens, Marsden Hartley, and Horace Pippin. (Barnes's Renoirs—the one instance when his superlative eye failed him—are his collection's weakest link. His taste tended toward the artist's excruciating late female nudes, grotesque creatures with puny craniums and colossal bottoms—wobbly orange-tinted images of flesh so bloated that they seem eerily prophetic of our country's current pandemic of morbid obesity.)

To house them, in 1922 Barnes engaged the French-born Beaux Arts architect Paul Philippe Cret (now best remembered as Louis

Kahn's teacher at the University of Pennsylvania) to build an imposing limestone-clad mansion in Lower Merion, a township bordering Philadelphia to the northwest. There he intermingled his pictures in galleries further crowded with Pennsylvania German painted furniture, Native and Early American pottery, Navajo jewelry, Greek antiquities, classical Chinese sculpture, and any other rare and beautiful objects that caught his all-encompassing eye. Certainly the oddest component of these eclectic ensembles was the array of metal hardware and utensils he hung all around his paintings like nimbuses emanating from saints—curlicues of antique wrought iron that often echo sinuous linear elements in canvases or decorative objects near them. Detached from their functional setting, these finely crafted door knockers, escutcheons, hinges, keys, ladles, latches, padlocks, and other implements serve as calligraphic glosses on the pictures they surround.

An even more effective display element is the ocher-colored burlap Barnes specified for the gallery walls, a color so harmonious with most of his pictures that one wonders why it is not widely copied elsewhere. Another controversial aspect of the installation was his practice of "skying" pictures in tiers two or three rows high, a vertical arrangement traditionally employed by the Académie des Beaux-Arts in Paris and the Royal Academy in London for their annual exhibitions. Yet the Barnes galleries are so well proportioned and the pictures so intelligently disposed that there is almost never any difficulty in seeing even things positioned high on the walls. Certain pictures, the Cézannes in particular, are strong enough to be read without difficulty across a large room even when hung eight feet up, as his *Large Bathers* is. The only serious exception is Seurat's *Poseuses*, a tableau of artist's models that possesses the transcendent equilibrium of a Botticelli. In an instance of complete aesthetic overkill, Barnes placed that shimmering Pointillist apparition, which begs to be seen at close range as well as from a further remove, over Cézanne's somewhat smaller but monumental *The Card Players.*

On occasion, Barnes's juxtapositions, all of which are maintained in the new museum, can be breathtaking. For example, in Room 22, on the second floor, the face-off between two ferocious Picasso oil studies of African-masklike heads (1907), contemporary with his revolutionary *Demoiselles d'Avignon*, sets up a reciprocal magnetism further intensified by three late-medieval figures of the crucified Christ hung between these small but terrifying pictures. Barnes may have been a crank, but he was also touched with some kind of genius. That appears especially clear now that visitors can see these fabled works better than at any time since Barnes bought them. The Lower Merion galleries were immersed in a depressingly subfusc gloom because the curtains were always drawn to keep out harmful ultraviolet rays.

Thus the most welcome aspect of the new Barnes is the veritable visual resurrection occasioned by the lighting designer Paul Marantz's exquisite calibration and mixture of natural and artificial illumination—only two of the twenty-three display rooms do not have some daylight—which made even those well acquainted with the collection wonder if the works were cleaned as part of the reinstallation, though they were not. Perhaps the luckiest beneficiary of this transformation is Matisse's tripartite mural *The Dance* (1932–1933), which Barnes commissioned for the lunettes just below the ceiling of the triple-height Main Room. This jazzy composition has always fairly vibrated with kinetic energy, but now its plummy colors strut their stuff, too.

Although several informative new books were issued in conjunction with the opening of the Philadelphia gallery in 2012, the finest publication on the collection remains *Great French Paintings from the Barnes Foundation: Impressionist, Post-Impressionist, and Early Modern* (1993). It was the first book to reproduce these works in color, which Barnes had prohibited because he believed that his pictures' true tonalities would inevitably be misrepresented. This classic volume is especially commendable for the art historian Joseph J. Rishel's entries on Cézanne, which include some of the finest writing on that artist by any scholar, including the brilliant Meyer Schapiro, whom Barnes spitefully barred from Lower Merion while he let Cub Scout packs and the odd working Joe roam his overwhelming galleries.

The design for the new Barnes emerged through an invitational competition organized in 2007 by Martha Thorne, executive director of the Pritzker Architecture Prize, who was assisted by several well-informed advisers, including the veteran architectural editor Suzanne Stephens. Portfolios were solicited from some thirty firms, and the selection committee, which included Barnes trustees and representatives of institutions backing the move, evaluated a well-chosen short list of six finalists: Tadao Ando, Thom Mayne of Morphosis, and Rafael Moneo (all Pritzker Prize winners), as well as Diller Scofidio + Renfro, Kengo Kuma, and Williams and Tsien. The latter's powerful little drawing, titled "Gallery in a Garden, Garden in a Gallery," depicts an oblong ensemble of the same approximate outlines as Cret's Barnes. Williams and Tsien's proposal was likewise centered amid a landscape reminiscent of the original building's graceful arboretum, with the addition of a small garden within a three-story-high glass-enclosed cloister inserted into the heart of the gallery wing in place of a light well in the Cret original. (That building is being retained by the foundation for horticultural programs.)

The exterior of the new Barnes is as well considered as the site planning, and both are perfectly enhanced by the elegant and appropriately Gallic landscape design by Laurie Olin, which features ranks of low hedges, allées of specimen trees, serene reflecting pools, and pathways of *terre pisée*—rammed earth. The long elevation of the building is set parallel to the north side of the Benjamin Franklin Parkway of 1917, the broad tree-lined boulevard that the French urban planner and architect Jacques Gréber sliced at a diagonal into William Penn's symmetrical grid plan of 1683 in a fanciful bid to give the staid Quaker City some Parisian élan. This Beaux Arts–inspired outburst of Francomania was also responsible for Cret and Gréber's jewel-like Rodin Museum of 1926–1929, directly northwest of the Barnes, devoted to the foremost modern French sculptor.

Williams and Tsien's $150 million structure is surfaced in pale beige Negev limestone, which harmonizes beautifully with the limestone-clad Rodin next door. The architects' handling of the masonry is ravishing. They deployed large rectangles of the tawny material in rhythmic patterns reminiscent of the geometric kente-cloth motifs woven by the Ashanti and Ewe peoples of West Africa, and interspersed the stone with thin, straight-edged, hammered-bronze "fins" that protrude slightly beyond the wall plane. This subtle detailing creates intriguing shadow patterns and alludes obliquely to the artisanal metalwork hung in the galleries within. This likeness to tribal textiles is most fitting, given Albert Barnes's determination to accord African tribal objects the same exalted status as European art, and his deep interest in African-American culture. Beyond that specific reference, the exterior stonework is a compositional masterstroke, for the architects' division of the cladding into three huge horizontal bands at once brings the structure down to human proportions while at the same time giving it a civic monumentality.

One's first view of the Barnes is reminiscent of the approach to Cret's Folger Shakespeare Library of 1929–1932 in Washington, D.C., which is sited similarly, shares the same approximate dimensions, and is likewise masonry-clad but lacks the columns, balustrades, rounded pediments, and other traditional detailing of the slightly earlier Lower Merion gallery. The close resemblance of

Barnes I and Barnes II is of course not surprising given that the new building was designed to follow the layout of the original installation exactly. That determination—which fortunately did not extend to replicating the original building's Neoclassical exterior as part of the bargain—meant that Williams and Tsien decided to retain the arrangement of windows and doors dictated by the rooms within. This has been all to the good, because the faultless proportions characteristic of the Classical tradition were scrupulously observed by Cret, whose oeuvre evolved from the conventional Beaux Arts proprieties of Barnes I to the more modern Stripped Classicism of the Folger.

Apart from their superscale handling of the exterior stonework, Williams and Tsien's boldest conceptual gambit was to surmount the 93,000-square-foot Barnes with a gigantic horizontal superstructure they call the Light Box: an immense translucent white-glass bar that dramatically cantilevers forty feet beyond the building's north end and sixty feet beyond the south end. I will admit to having been highly skeptical of this particular aspect of the scheme at first, but upon completion instantly understood its correctness. When illuminated from within at night, the Light Box serves as a wordless marquee that announces this singular new presence and imparts a boldly contemporary quality that makes it apparent, even from afar, that the new Barnes is not some gorgeously preserved cultural corpse laid out for solemn visitation. The full impact of the capacious Light Court beneath the Light Box—an internal plaza that measures 170 feet long, 45 feet wide, and 52 feet high at its apex—is felt with particular force as one exits the gallery wing. After the at times claustrophobic impact of Barnes's jam-packed installations, you experience an astonishing whoosh of open space that comes as a liberating relief.

To the rear of the site the architects placed a reverse-L-shaped office-and-temporary-exhibition wing, parallel to and touching the gallery structure, between which the Light Court serves as a central gathering space. Entry to the Barnes is by advance ticket sale only and timed to a maximum of 125 visitors per hour, with a total of 250 allowed in the galleries at any one time. Educational services, including a lending library, auditorium, and classrooms to accommodate the art-appreciation lessons Barnes so passionately believed in—he was a follower and friend of the philosopher John Dewey, whose pragmatism informed his ideas about culture in a democracy—are housed in a subterranean story.

The offer by the Barnes Foundation to reproduce the old galleries made many observers fear that this concession would limit the designers to an exercise in cultural taxidermy, with little scope left for architectural originality. Remarkably, Williams and Tsien found unexpected expressive range within the confines they were bound to observe. In that respect the outcome of this project is dazzling—the new Barnes is infinitely superior to the vast number of museums designed with a completely free hand, and in hindsight, Judge Stanley R. Ott's 2004 ruling in favor of the move to Philadelphia seems Solomonic in its wisdom.

Williams and Tsien are among several first-rank husband-and-wife architectural teams to emerge in the generation that followed such pioneering coprofessional couples as Alison and Peter Smithson in Britain and Robert Venturi and Denise Scott Brown in the US. Tod Culpan Williams was born in 1943 to a well-to-do WASP family in Michigan—his father, an automotive engineer, invented the electrically controlled seat-adjustment device—and graduated from the private Cranbrook School (part of Eliel Saarinen's celebrated campus of 1926–1943 in the Detroit suburb of Bloomfield Hills) four years before Mitt Romney. He went on to study architecture at Princeton, and after an apprenticeship with the neo-Corbusian Richard Meier, set up his own Manhattan office in 1974. Billie Tsien was born in 1949 in Ithaca, New York, to Chinese-American parents; her father was an electrical engineer, her mother a biochemist. She received degrees in fine arts at Yale and architecture at UCLA, and joined Williams's firm in 1977. They married six years later, officially became professional partners in 1986, and have one son, Kai Tsien Williams, an industrial designer. Apart from their extraordinary individual talents and complementary balance of design skills—he concentrates on structural aspects, she attends to materials and finishes, though neither confines themselves exclusively to these tasks—Williams and Tsien stand out among their contemporaries for a determination to keep their staff small enough to maintain the hands-on control they deem essential to an art-based practice. Their firm generally takes on only two new assignments each year, has never had more than forty employees, and currently numbers around twenty.

As a result, their output has been relatively small: twenty-seven institutional buildings completed thus far, and seven houses. Unlike several Pritzker Prize winners, they have never designed one of those increasingly common retail showplaces or high-end condominiums exploited as signature "branding" by international luxury-goods conglomerates. They prefer to work solely for educational and cultural institutions, following the example of Louis Kahn, who likewise sidestepped involvement with corporations. Among the couple's best designs is the Williams Natatorium of 1998–1999 at his high school alma mater, Cranbrook, to which his parents bequeathed $2 million toward the $10 million cost of the project. Because Eliel Saarinen's vision for the campus was so comprehensive, it has been very hard for other architects to add to his minutely coordinated ensemble. Far and away the most successful post-Saarinen structure there is this majestic indoor swimming-pool hall, which numbers among the handsomest sports facilities of recent decades.

Williams and Tsien evoke the spiritual essence of Saarinen's Nordic Arts and Crafts aesthetic through a combination of strong but

simple massing, substantial but never ostentatious materials, sub-
dued colors, contrasting textures, hand-wrought details, and an
overall sense of self-contained dignity. Indeed, they surpass Saarinen
by imbuing a workaday athletics building with a mysterious aura
akin to that attained by his greatest fellow Finnish architect, Alvar
Aalto, peerless humanist of the Modern Movement. The ceiling over
the Cranbrook swimming pool is painted midnight blue and features
two retractable ovoid skylights that open to the sky, evoking the
"clearing in a forest" motif found time and again in Aalto's interiors.

Another of their outstanding efforts offered an unfortunate demonstration of the vulnerability that even high-style architecture is
subject to in an age of cultural gigantism. The American Folk Art
Museum of 1997–2001 (see Illustration 15b) was erected on two narrow adjacent townhouse plots on Manhattan's West 53rd Street, just
west of the Museum of Modern Art. That property once belonged to
the longtime MoMA benefactor Blanchette Rockefeller, who gave
the land to the folk art museum much to the later chagrin of MoMA
when it embarked on Yoshio Taniguchi's massive aggrandizement of
1997–2003. The American Folk Art Museum opened in the economically shaky aftermath of the 2001 terrorist attacks and its financial
footing was further undermined by the Great Recession later in the
decade. By 2011 its trustees felt compelled to sell the Williams and
Tsien building to MoMA, which two years later announced that it
would demolish this architectural gem to make way for yet another
expansion, thereby setting off heated public protests.

Sadly, Williams and Tsien's brilliant maximizing of an absurdly
constrained mid-block site—which they overcame with illusionistic
sleights of hand much like those John Soane used to turn his London
house-museum of 1808–1824 into a marvel of soaring top-lit spaces—
never won an enthusiastic audience beyond design professionals. By
ingeniously engineering a veritable exoskeleton of concrete, Williams

freed almost the entire volume of the building envelope from the interior steel supports of conventional high-rise construction. All the same, a good deal of the space he gained had to be devoted to vertical circulation—stairways and elevators—and the museum's display areas sometimes felt hemmed in. Still, architectural aficionados marveled at the ingenuity and care Williams and Tsien invested in this difficult task and were outraged by what more than one critic termed MoMA's act of architectural vandalism.

Completed several months after the Barnes, the Reva and David Logan Center for Creative and Performing Arts of 2007–2012 at the University of Chicago (see Illustration 15c) is situated at the southwest corner of the school's Midway campus. Logan Center was envisioned not only to consolidate related cultural activities—music, theater, film, dance, studio art, and art history—that had been scattered throughout the sprawling complex but also to act as a gateway between the university and the South Side community, whose residents (well over 90 percent of whom are African-American) have long felt alienated from an institution they view as elitist and indifferent to them. The striking 170-foot-high tower that makes Logan visible from afar—a syncopated flat-topped high-rise pylon that subliminally channels the Art Deco flair of Chicago's 1933 Century of Progress exposition—signifies the welcome being offered there to neighborhood performing arts groups.

The $114 million Logan Center cost about 20 percent less than the Barnes but at 184,000 square feet is twice as large. The rich materials of the Barnes are contrasted here with far more modest components—steel instead of bronze, tile instead of mosaic, cork instead of parquet flooring, industrial felt wall coverings instead of custom silk weavings. The exterior is clad in supersized "bricks" of midwestern limestone four feet long, four inches high, and four inches deep, which the architects wanted to relate to the limestone employed throughout the campus but also to allude to the elongated Roman brick that Frank Lloyd Wright used for his nearby Robie house of 1906–1910. Yet the architects' commitment to quality and attention to detail are identical in both the Logan and the Barnes schemes, as is the intricate organizational planning that fits a bewildering array of functional requirements—at Logan, rehearsal rooms, recital halls ranging from black-box experimental spaces to a full-dress auditorium, screening room, classrooms, offices, and common areas—into a coherent and thoroughly satisfying whole.

The Barnes, however, will be very hard for Tod Williams and Billie Tsien to surpass no matter how long their project list grows over time. It must now be included among the tiny handful of intimately scaled museums in which great art and equally great architecture and landscape design coalesce into that rare experience wherein these three complementary mediums enhance the best qualities of one another to maximum benefit. Such institutions include, for example, Jørgen Bo and Vilhelm Wohlert's Louisiana Museum of Modern Art of 1958–1966 outside Copenhagen, Louis Kahn's Kimbell Art Museum of 1966–1972 in Fort Worth, and Renzo Piano's Nasher Sculpture Center of 1999–2003 in Dallas. The incorrigibly contentious and gleefully litigious Albert Barnes—who loved a good lawsuit as much as a good Cézanne, it would seem, and who got no end of pleasure from rebuffing the great and the good of the art establishment—would probably have railed against the ultimate disposition of his life's work. Yet what cannot be disputed is that with the final withering of his posthumous grip, a generous vision of art's life-enhancing potential at long last came into full focus.

16

KAZUYO SEJIMA AND RYUE NISHIZAWA

FOR MORE THAN three decades an often dolorous springtime ritual for lovers of the building art has been the announcement of the latest winner of the Pritzker Prize for Architecture. Skepticism about the Pritzker seemed hardly misplaced from its inception, when in 1979 Philip Johnson, the dark prince of Modernism, was named its first recipient, a choice that hinted at a certain cynicism and want of imagination. The $100,000 award had been instituted a year earlier by the Chicago-based Pritzker family, owners of the Hyatt hotel chain, whose claim that this would become the Nobel of architecture struck some observers as quite presumptuous, to say nothing of rather ironic, given that the donors have erected so many banal structures in cities around the world. Particularly vexing was their central role in promoting John Portman, the Atlanta-based architect and developer whose glitzy but hermetic atrium hotels made the Pritzkers billions but had a deeply destructive effect on American urbanism. Though more admirable figures immediately followed Johnson (Luis Barragán in 1980 and James Stirling in 1981), thereafter the prize too often went either to stars with overinflated reputations—Kevin Roche (1982), Hans Hollein (1985), Gordon Bunshaft (1988), and Jørn Utzon (2003)—or lesser-known architects whose critical standing remained essentially unchanged by the accolade, including Gottfried Böhm (1986) and Christian de Portzamparc (1994).

Thus the revelation in 2010 of what were widely perceived as surprise winners, Kazuyo Sejima and Ryue Nishizawa—the principals of the Tokyo-based firm SANAA (Sejima and Nishizawa and Associates)—was cause for rejoicing among those who treasure the honorees' delicately calibrated and deeply humane sensibility. They are further unusual in architecture as a female-male pair who are not married to each other and, rarer still, one in which the senior partner is a woman. The selection of Sejima and Nishizawa marked a significant and encouraging departure from past Pritzker practices—including at least one that adversely affected the prize's credibility. In 1991 the award went to Robert Venturi but not to his collaborator and wife, Denise Scott Brown, with the specious explanation that it is bestowed on individual practitioners, not firms. Persistent rumblings about that gratuitous snub—made worse because there were thirteen male winners before Venturi but no women whatsoever—evidently prompted the Pritzker to play catch-up by selecting the first team to jointly win, Jacques Herzog and Pierre de Meuron (2001), and the first female recipient, Zaha Hadid (2004).

Kazuyo Sejima was born in 1956 in Ibaraki prefecture, northeast of Tokyo. She studied at Japan Women's University, and upon graduation became an assistant in the Tokyo office of Toyo Ito, winner of the 2013 Pritzker Prize and one of the leading architects of the preceding generation, which also includes Tadao Ando. Ito's designs are noteworthy for a particular lightness of touch, a quality very much in evidence in the work of Sejima, his most celebrated protégé. Her exceptional talent was recognized early on. During a visit to Japan in 1984 to see Ito's buildings, I heard reports from other young architects of a prodigiously gifted Miss Sejima in his studio who mesmerized her male colleagues with both her fluent design skills and considerable personal charms. In 1987 she struck out on her own and set up Kazuyo Sejima and Associates, the name of which she changed in 1995 to SANAA to reflect her new partnership with Ryue Nishizawa. Ten years her junior, he was born near Yokohama in 1966 and earned a degree at Yokohama National University. The two architects' pairing had its difficulties from the outset—she is known to be as equable as he is volatile—and in 1997 the younger partner set up an independent practice, Office of Ryue Nishizawa, to pursue projects apart from Sejima, an unusual accommodation that has allowed their sometimes contentious but nonetheless highly fruitful creative collaboration to continue.

Personal presentation plays an important role in architects' advancement. Philip Johnson's access to corporate boardrooms unquestionably benefited from his impeccable bespoke navy pinstriped suits and commanding black Corbusier spectacles. Hadid's outsized éclat derives in large measure from her famously tempestuous demeanor and dramatic dress sense, which make her seem the prima donna in her own private Aïda. Thus a photograph of Sejima and Nishizawa released at the time they won the Pritzker was refreshingly antithetical to the norms of architectural power portraiture. In it, Nishizawa resembles an amiable novice yoga instructor in his rumpled white shirt, while the adorably dorky Sejima, wearing a doll-like frock (quite likely by her favorite fashion designer, Rei Kawakubo of Comme des Garçons) and droopy eyeglasses, brings to mind a Roz Chast cartoon character in the flesh, bemused and a bit bewildered. Yet whether they look stylish or not, Sejima and Nishizawa's architectural merit is so self-evident that it negates any suspicion of remedial tokenism or backpedaling for the Pritzker's prior lapses.

The partners are best known in the United States for two exceptional museum commissions: the Glass Pavilion of 2002–2006 at the Toledo Museum of Art in Ohio and the New Museum of

Contemporary Art of 2003–2007 on New York City's Bowery. Along with their 21st Century Museum of Contemporary Art of 1999–2004 in Japan, this nearly contemporaneous trio of public galleries offers an impressive demonstration of the designers' virtuosity within one functional category, and shows the remarkable breadth of expression they are able to wrest from the restricted Minimalist palette. Minimalist architecture is thought to require an extraordinary degree of perfection in materials, finish, and detailing in order to compensate for the lack of range inherent in this severely reductive aesthetic. Yet SANAA's repeated (though never repetitive) use of pure geometric forms, unadorned white surfaces, and large expanses of clear glass (seemingly held in place by little more than the designers' willpower) is not in the least dependent on the top-of-the-line specifications characteristic of Ludwig Mies van der Rohe's early and late Minimalist masterpieces: his jewel-like German Pavilion at the Barcelona International Exposition (1928–1929), with its rare golden-onyx interior wall, and the vastly larger though no less exquisite Seagram Building (1954–1958) in New York City, clad in costly bronze. Unlike many other Minimalist architects, Sejima and Nishizawa pay little obvious attention to the finer points of rich materials, precise joints, and immaculate surfaces, but instead focus our attention through masterful handling of light and space.

That particular ability was first evident in their 21st Century Museum of Contemporary Art in the small provincial city of Kanazawa (see Illustration 16a). This one-story circular structure, set in a centrally located park, functions not only as a municipal art gallery but more importantly as the focal structure for the city, a rarity in traditional Japanese urban planning, which puts little store in public buildings and civic spaces. To encourage this new institution's acceptance among people unfamiliar with viewing art, the architects demystified the museumgoing experience by sheathing the undifferentiated, nonhierarchical exterior in transparent glass all around, giving a clear view of the activities that take place inside it and making none of the intimidating gestures common to this kind of building, whether traditional or modern in style. The result might have been boring to the point of nothingness were it not for the exhilarating lightness and unexpected warmth Sejima and Nishizawa bring to Minimalism, which in the wrong hands can be harsh and pleasureless.

Toledo's Glass Pavilion is the architects' haunting and highly original reiteration of the see-through box, a recurrent High Modernist theme from the Crystal Palace to Philip Johnson's Glass House of 1949–1950 and many other examples thereafter. With its diaphanous exterior and transparent inner partitions, the single-story structure retains all the enigmatic subtlety of SANAA's earlier work in Japan, even though the partners' delicate aesthetic can expose the sort of minor mistakes that other architects camouflage with a host of diversionary tricks. This freestanding exhibition wing, which houses the museum's noteworthy glass collection, makes highly effective use of transparency and reflectivity, but more than being just an extra-large vitrine, this gently contoured, intriguingly layered, and teasingly ambiguous display space offers a complex essay on varying degrees of visual penetration in modern architecture. The 74,000-square-foot steel-framed and -roofed structure is clad with 360 glass panels, many of them curved, which measure eight by thirteen-and-a-half feet and weigh between 1,300 and 1,500 pounds each. That this superb work cost a mere $30 million seems almost as miraculous as its designers' feat of lightweight engineering.

Far more expensive was SANAA's $198 million Le Louvre-Lens of 2005–2012, a satellite exhibition space for France's national art museum, named not (as Anglophones might suspect) for the optical refracting device but rather the down-at-the-heels industrial town in the Pas-de-Calais region where the branch was located in an attempt to lift the depressed local economy through cultural tourism. Covering 301,000 square feet of a disused sixty-acre brownfield site that until 1960 was used for coal mining, Le Louvre-Lens is four times larger than the Toledo pavilion but cost six-and-a-half times more. It comprises a series of five separate but contiguous pavilions (four rectangular and one square, several with slightly curving elevations) arranged in a somewhat skewed enfilade not unlike the elongated linear layout of the historic Palais du Louvre in Paris, with its accretion of wings added end-on-end over several centuries. (The architects likened the grouping to a flotilla of boats coming in to dock and bumping lightly against one another.) Though the Lens gallery is neither as transparent as the Kanazawa museum nor as layered as the Toledo pavilion, its translucent glass walls, held in place by vertical polished-aluminum frames, impart a feeling of openness and accessibility much like those earlier SANAA designs. Furthermore, its highly flexible display spaces are well suited to a changing array of works from the Louvre's revered core collection (not its forgotten deep-storage holdings, as some have incorrectly assumed).

SANAA's Rolex Learning Center of 2004–2010 at the École Polytechnique Fédérale de Lausanne, a library and campus hub underwritten by the eponymous watchmaking company, is a 37,000-square-foot rectangular low-rise structure that undulates gracefully, with the building's wavelike floor and ceiling planes always in parallel, curvilinear alignment. Fourteen biomorphically shaped atria of various sizes punctuate the ground plan, and from the air the 398,000-square-foot facility brings to mind a gigantic slice of melting Swiss cheese (or one of Claes Oldenburg's incongruous *Projects for Monuments* series of the 1960s). Regrettably, the architects' well-intentioned attempt to give this large facility an enlivening degree of spatial variation is counteracted by a noteworthy amount of virtually unusable space where billowing horizontal planes approach and meet the ground, and also by surprisingly crude, un-Swiss craftsmanship (likely a reflection of the comparatively low $118 million budget).

Sejima and Nishizawa's ability to overcome physical and financial limitations is most apparent in their New Museum of Contemporary Art in Manhattan (see Illustration 16b), a slender, off-kilter high-rise shoehorned into an improbably tiny mid-block site that the architects exploit with all the cunning of urban planners inured to the impossibly tight building lots of Tokyo. The New Museum is one of those rare, clarifying works of architecture that makes most recent buildings of the same sort look suddenly ridiculous. This mesmerizing 174-foot-high tower demonstrates the power of understatement more convincingly than any Manhattan structure since Mies's Seagram Building was completed five decades earlier.

Some museum boards think that choosing an architect can be reduced to a science, but in the final analysis it comes down to a matter of taste, though also of courage in those instances when a patron is willing to hire a relatively untested designer. A short list of prospective designers speaks volumes about the likely outcome. If the candidates' styles are too divergent, the search committee doesn't know what it wants. If one contestant seems the odd man out, the fix might be in. Thus many observers were both surprised and impressed with the New Museum's unconventional but highly informed short list, comprising five experimentally minded firms esteemed by architecture aficionados but otherwise unknown, and they were even more impressed by the ultimate selection of Sejima and Nishizawa, who were poised on the threshold of greatness but still needed a brave client to give them their big international break. When SANAA won this commission in 2002, the firm had not yet built beyond Japan. In Manhattan the architects displayed the same engaging qualities they

evidenced in Kanazawa, although this high-rise scheme for a cosmopolitan audience could hardly be more different from that Japanese
museum in form and social setting.

What constitutes "contemporary" art is an interesting question in
itself. The big international auction houses now define contemporary
art as works made during the past thirty-five years, with earlier
pieces designated as "modern." The New Museum, an exhibition
space freed from the burdens of building a permanent collection, can
concentrate on the present in a way no longer possible for mainstream institutions, including what wags have called the Metropolitan Museum of Modern Art. Provocative contemporary art of the
kind championed by the New Museum since its founding by Marcia
Tucker in 1977 looks best in settings that aren't overly refined—one
reason why recycled warehouses and factories have made such effective galleries.

On Manhattan's still gritty if increasingly fashionable Lower East
Side, SANAA captured a utilitarian spirit without resorting to the
pseudo-industrial effects of Renzo Piano and Richard Rogers's Pompidou Center in Paris. Here Sejima and Nishizawa managed to wrest
a series of flexible, loftlike exhibition spaces from a site so tiny that
the designers' sleight of hand approaches architectural alchemy. The
New Museum seems even more of an accomplishment than SANAA's
venture in Ohio because the New York client couldn't afford costly
finishes on a no-frills, $50 million budget. Despite their commitment
to Minimalism, Sejima and Nishizawa generally make perfection a
nonissue save in instances such as their Lausanne building, where
minimal standards dip too low. They escape the tyranny of costly
detailing and sidestep the Modernist obsession with finely wrought
specifics in favor of boldly conceived generalities, and thereby get
more bang for the buck (or euro, or yuan). SANAA is also renowned
within the profession for a relentless work ethic that helps explain

how this firm extracts so much from so little and for so relatively little money, a skill that doubtless will be the subject of study in architecture schools.

Many perplexed observers find present-day museum design a choice between outlandishly sculptural structures that ignore the proper display of art on the one hand, and on the other hand neutral containers so submissive to art that all architectural presence is lost. But the New Museum persuasively demonstrates that honoring art and architecture need not be an either-or proposition. For Sejima and Nishizawa, whose expansive imaginations refuse to be cramped by the postage-stamp-size building plots typical of Tokyo, the challenge of working with the New Museum's L-shaped mid-block plot—a mere 71 feet wide and 112 feet deep—was evidently no big deal. Their previous experience with such restricted conditions encouraged the New Museum's prescient director, Lisa Phillips, to push for SANAA among the contenders, and to her must go a great deal of the credit for this miracle on the Bowery.

The shimmering two-ply exterior of the building—metal layered with an outer skin of perforated metal, which can look variously silver, gray, or off-white, depending on the time of day and the weather—imparts a mirage-like aura when the sunlight cooperates, an effect intensified by the irregularity of the nonaligned boxes comprising the off-kilter tower. However, this slight syncopation, which makes the almost windowless tower seem much larger at a distance, is far from the chaotic angular cascade proposed by Daniel Libeskind in his unexecuted Spiral addition of 1996 for London's Victoria & Albert Museum, which evoked a collapsing stack of cartons. The varied height-and-width proportions of each rectangular component at the New Museum are no mere aesthetic whim but rather a practical strategy to create setbacks that provide most of the museum's galleries with skylights, allowing the natural lighting that many artists hope for and seldom get. (Those rooms that lack natural toplighting have been reserved for video installations and works requiring low illumination.)

Natural lighting has become something of a fetish in contemporary museum design. Although technological advances have made artificial illumination every bit as effective as (and far more manageable than) the real thing, museum officials and donors cling to the sentimental notion that natural light is inevitably preferable. It's easy to think that is so at John Soane's Dulwich Picture Gallery of 1811–1817 in London, or Louis Kahn's Kimbell Art Museum of 1966–1972 in Fort Worth, the two most frequently invoked examples of natural toplighting among latter-day patrons. But what is suitable for the display of the Old Master pictures in those marvelously illuminated interiors is not universally desirable for other kinds of art elsewhere. The skylights in the New Museum galleries have a negligible effect in improving one's experience of the works on view there, and fluorescent ceiling fixtures largely cancel out the meager amount of daylight that filters through the thin strips of overhead glazing in several rooms. Any benefit from the skylights is primarily architectural, giving the galleries added breathing space, as it were, and allowing the several sprawling sculptural installations to be properly assessed from multiple vantage points without feeling backed into a dark corner.

One serendipitous gain from the New Museum's tight site is the structure's necessary vertical emphasis, which gives unusual volumetric integrity to its one-per-story display areas on the second, third, and fourth floors, ranging in height from eighteen to twenty-four feet and in area from three to five thousand square feet. There's none of the lost-in-space disorientation many visitors have complained about at Yoshio Taniguchi's MoMA expansion. Nowhere is that contrast more evident than in the New Museum's humanely scaled lobby—enlivened by an undulating metal mesh partition reminiscent of Alvar Aalto's designs and screening the gift shop—which makes MoMA's megascale entry concourse feel even more like the airport terminal of nightmares.

Contemporary art museums now face the dilemma of trying to anticipate what kind of spaces will be needed for unimaginable creations likely to emerge over the coming decades. The one-size-fits-all approach of hangar-like enclosures with movable partitions is no solution, as demonstrated time and again since the *grandpère* of them all, the Pompidou Center. It will take quite some time to fully determine how well the New Museum responds to the demands of an organization founded to disregard, indeed flout, art-establishment convention. What is not in question is the instant urban impact the New Museum's new home had on its immediate surroundings and the city in general.

Among the most delightful aspects of the SANAA scheme is the seventh-floor Sky Room, a glass-walled, wrap-terraced lounge with exhilarating views of the downtown skyline. It is easy to imagine this space as a reincarnation of the old members' dining room and lounge atop the original Museum of Modern Art building, fondly remembered by many as a space that encouraged socializing in a way that no other place in the city offered at the time, almost domestic in its intimacy and informality. The current emphasis on the museum experience as a form of elevated consumerism is as pernicious as it is pervasive, and the Sky Room, where ideas about the art on display might be exchanged in a stimulating, noncommercial atmosphere, could be a useful bulwark against the museum as entertainment complex.

Beyond doubt the New Museum was a high point of New York's postmillennial construction boom. For example, the grand publishing skyscrapers of Midtown West—Piano's New York Times Building of 2000–2007 and Norman Foster's Hearst Tower of 2001–2005—are,

MAKERS OF MODERN ARCHITECTURE, VOLUME II

respectively, dull and overbearing. With the exception of Michael Arad's triumphant National September 11 Memorial, the adjacent rebuilding of Ground Zero will remain a glaring example of ineptitude and architectural mediocrity in urban planning. It is no longer to be taken for granted that a new museum building will embody a society's highest aspirations—in fact, recent evidence indicates quite the contrary. Thus, the audacious New Museum augurs well because it speaks of a discernment about contemporary architecture that may promise equal astuteness about contemporary art. An implicit rebuke to MoMA's bombast, this dimensionally modest but subliminally monumental landmark transcends its stated function, sometimes in unanticipated ways. As you stand on the Bowery just north of the New Museum and look downtown toward the clustered spires of lower Manhattan, it's hard not to think of SANAA's hypnotic addition to the city's skyline as a poetic meditation on America's quintessential architectural contribution, and loss.

17

ELIZABETH DILLER, RICARDO SCOFIDIO, AND CHARLES RENFRO

ALTHOUGH THERE ARE countless tangents that a career in the building art can take, it is nonetheless most unusual for a major architectural practice to emerge once a firm's principals are well into what is loosely called middle age. Thus one of the most extraordinary emergences in the building art during recent decades has been the husband-and-wife team of Ricardo Scofidio and Elizabeth Diller, who first attracted attention beyond avant-garde architectural circles in 1999, when they were awarded a MacArthur Foundation "genius" grant at the respective ages of sixty-four and forty-five. Along with Charles Renfro, who is ten years younger than Diller, they comprise the New York firm Diller Scofidio + Renfro. Scofidio and Diller (who founded their office in 1979 and made Renfro a full partner in 2004) had long appeared determined to be among the theoreticians and educators who infuse architectural thought with vivid imagination but construct little if anything at all. In that regard they followed the lead of their Cooper Union colleague John Hejduk, the school's longtime dean, a poète maudit who fantasized in drawings and philosophized in print but built almost nothing.

The prevailing impression of this maverick couple as consummate architectural luftmenschen was heightened by the Whitney Museum of American Art's enigmatic 2003 exhibition "The Aberrant Architectures of Diller + Scofidio." Devoid of almost anything the lay public could comprehend as architecture or urbanism, the show presented a series of the subjects' more-or-less whimsical installation pieces. These displays included *Mural* (2003), a robotic power drill that moved along 330 feet of wall-mounted track and randomly bored holes in a partition between two galleries. It was all great fun, but the designers' hermetic cleverness left many visitors baffled.

The first structure that Diller and Scofidio executed—their Blur Building of 2000–2001 in Switzerland—was commissioned by the Swiss national exhibition Expo.02. This aqueous caprice was created atop an ovoid open-air platform in Lake Neuchâtel at Yverdon-les-Bains. Connected to the shore by a pair of long gangways, the Blur Building was created by a sophisticated system of 31,500 high-precision high-pressure water jets. This mysteriously cloudlike water-vapor "pavilion," which measured more than three hundred feet wide, nearly two hundred feet deep, and sixty-six feet high, could contain as many as four hundred visitors, who were given waterproof ponchos to wear within the wraparound canopy of fine mist expelled from the lightweight metal framework.

In its shifting contours and indeterminate outlines, the phantom structure obliquely commented on what the architect Greg Lynn in 1996 termed "blob architecture"—free-form constructs enabled by new computer-aided technologies. Diller and Scofidio's beguiling jeu d'esprit became the hit of the Swiss fair. The idea of fashioning an inhabitable space from water—a tantalizing contradiction in architectural terms—has fascinated visionaries for centuries, especially writers in Islamic Spain who during the Middle Ages fantasized about fountains with liquid domes that one could enter. That evanescent dream was finally brought to dazzling life in this triumph of the architectural imagination.

Ricardo Scofidio was born in New York City in 1935 and grew up in a small town in western Pennsylvania. He has said that his family never discussed its ethnicity, and apparently only in adulthood did he learn that some of his ancestors were black. He studied at New York's Cooper Union, and after taking an architectural degree from Columbia returned to teach at his undergraduate alma mater, where he is now a professor emeritus. Elizabeth Diller was born in 1954 in Łódź, Poland, to Holocaust survivors who emigrated to America when she was six. After receiving her undergraduate diploma from Cooper Union she enrolled in the school's architecture program in 1976, where one of her teachers was Scofidio. Their relationship moved from the professional to the personal, and Scofidio, who was married with four children, left his family and moved in with Diller. They set up their architectural practice in 1979 and were later married. Charles Renfro was born on the Texas Gulf Coast in 1964, studied architecture at Rice and Columbia, and joined Diller and Scofidio's office in 1997. In an act of exceptional collegial generosity, the couple made him an equal partner and added his surname to their firm's title seven years later.

In the decade following the frisson of the Blur Building, Diller, Scofidio, and Renfro executed several exemplary public spaces that provided pragmatic, cost-efficient solutions to underutilized or ineffective urban settings. The most justly celebrated of these commissions is New York City's High Line (see Illustration 17b), begun in 2004, for which the firm's partners were a major part of the collaborative design team. A pressing question that arises as cities mature is what to do with outmoded infrastructure. Many architectural preservationists were slow to concede the historical merit of utilitarian landmarks until the 1960s and 1970s. The case for the imaginative greening of brownfields—derelict industrial sites, in planners' jargon—has been tremendously advanced by the High Line, a linear park superimposed on the eponymous long-defunct cargo railroad trestle that wends through nearly a mile and a half of Manhattan's West Side from Midtown to Greenwich Village. The High Line was erected some thirty feet above street level, between 1929 and 1934, by the New York Central Railroad, to speed delivery of materials and foodstuffs directly to factories and processing plants. Unlike the elevated trains that still clattered above the vehicular traffic of Manhattan's Second, Third, Sixth, Ninth, and Lexington Avenues, the High Line followed a mid-block, back-door path in the Chelsea district between and through buildings, which made the tracks virtually invisible except at crosstown intersections. It began a veritable disappearing act in 1980 when the tracks carried their last shipment and by the end of the century, this disused vestige of the city's once-vital manufacturing economy had more or less faded from memory.

The collaborative retrofitting of the High Line was headed by James Corner Field Operations (a firm specializing in converting urban infrastructure) with Diller, Scofidio, and Renfro as architectural partners, and the Dutch landscape architect Piet Oudolf in charge of the horticultural aspects. The High Line team remained firmly committed to the project's two fundamental principles: to retain as much of the infrastructure's gritty character as practicable, and to ensure that all new interventions reinforced the site's original qualities. The Corner office largely focused on shoring up the decaying freight rail trestle to make it safe for heavy pedestrian traffic, whereas Diller, Scofidio, and Renfro addressed broader questions of how this new kind of park might best be used and enjoyed.

Well versed in such theoretical concerns as "the gaze"—the ways in which visual perception translates into social (and sexual) interaction—the architects devised a host of basic but effective ways to encourage visitors to the High Line to view the city and its inhabitants from a variety of new perspectives. Rather than relying on traditional park benches or movable chairs in the manner of London and Paris parks, they designed several built-in seating areas, ranging from banquettes to recliners to stadium-style bleachers. These socially attuned partners' encouragement of people-watching emanates from their canny understanding that seeing and being seen—voyeurism and exhibitionism, if you will—are central to the civic transaction. They abetted this universal pleasure with devices as uncomplicated but potent as a dramatic cascade of bleacher seating called the Tenth Avenue Square, a glass-walled amphitheater perched above the thoroughfare at West 17th Street.

The decade-long struggle to save the High Line from demolition and turn it into a civic amenity began in 1999, when Joshua David (then a magazine writer and editor) and Robert Hammond (at the time a consultant for commercial and nonprofit organizations) met at a local community board meeting, discovered their mutual enthusiasm for the moldering railroad spur, and eventually devoted themselves full time to its salvation. These oft-thwarted civic crusaders remained cheerily undaunted as they confronted and overcame opposition from every quarter. Not the least of their many impediments was an obstructionist neighborhood group, Chelsea Property Owners, which for a decade and a half had been trying to have the High Line torn down as a nuisance and an eyesore. City officials proved no less hostile. Joseph Rose, head of New York's City Planning Commission during the Giuliani administration, called the decaying High Line "the Vietnam of old railroad structures" and declared, "It must come down." And as Hammond later wrote, "The property owners who opposed the High Line had hired Rudy Mastro, one of [Mayor Rudolph] Giuliani's former deputy mayors, who paid him a lot of money to lobby Giuliani, and that's why Giuliani was opposed, in my view."

A turning point came in 2000–2001, when the photographer Joel Sternfeld took a breathtaking series of images of the picturesquely decrepit train bed—a veritable urban prairie lush with nodding wildflowers and shimmering grasses. Sternfeld's stunning color photos were exhibited and published in a book that became a fund-raising kit beyond the dreams of the canniest public relations consultant. Yet the High Line is hardly the first of its kind. The most frequently cited prototype is Jacques Vergely and Philippe Mathieux's Promenade Plantée of 1988–1993 in Paris, also known as Le Viaduc des Arts or La Coulée Verte (the green stream), a three-mile-long masonry viaduct that extends between the Place de la Bastille and the Bois de Vincennes, with a landscaped pathway atop the structure and shops inserted into the archways below.

The High Line begins near the intersection of Gansevoort and Washington Streets in the northwest extremity of Greenwich Village known as the Meatpacking District (most of whose wholesale butchers have been supplanted by upscale boutiques, galleries, and restaurants). The sleek, silvery stairway ascending to the High Line at its southernmost terminus leads up to the promenade platform, where the centered walkway is paved with oblong concrete blocks laid end-to-end like wood-plank flooring and studded with dark gray stones to mimic fine terrazzo. Flanking the path (which varies in width along the meandering route) are planting beds meant to evoke the lush, self-sown greenery that thrived on the High Line during its three decades of desuetude. To recapture some semblance of that volunteer vegetation, Oudolf—the best-known exponent of the wild-garden movement dubbed "New Wave Planting"—applied his distinctive formula of expansive, irregular drifts of softly toned, small-blossomed perennials interspersed with rippling waves of tall grasses, with strong emphasis on native species. This windswept, painterly approach looks spontaneous to all but experienced gardeners, who are aware of the labor-intensive artifice needed to achieve a convincing illusion of utter naturalness. One only wishes that the collaborators had made it possible for visitors to sit directly among the flowers, bushes, and trees, and not just view them like pictorial dioramas.

Though at first glance the High Line seems surprisingly modest, it marks a radical departure from the Classical model of the public park as *rus in urbe*—"country in the city"—epitomized by Frederick Law Olmsted and Calvert Vaux's Central Park of 1857–1873 in Manhattan, that sweeping synthesis of farsighted urbanism, scenic wizardry, and social engineering, which allows one to imagine having been transported to an idyllic countryside. In contrast, what makes walking the High Line such an intriguing experience is the way in which it celebrates rather than obviates the collision of natural and man-made environments. The incongruous delight of strolling through a leafy glade three stories above the roaring traffic's boom is made more piquant by the omnipresence of buildings crowded close to both sides of the walkway, especially at those points where it passes a towering new structure and shoots straight through a cavernous old one, recalling the fanciful multilayered Manhattan imagined by illustrators for the turn-of-the-twentieth-century journal *King's Views of New York*.

Seldom in modern city planning has a single work of urban design brought together and synthesized so many current concerns, including historic preservation, adaptive reuse of obsolete infrastructure, green urbanism, and private-sector funding and stewardship of civic amenities. Furthermore, the economic benefits New York City has reaped as a direct result of the High Line are significant. The first two of the project's three segments cost $153 million, $133.6 million of which came from public funds, with the balance donated by private and corporate sponsors. In a remarkable return on investment, the High Line spurred some $2 billion in ancillary development, primarily housing adjacent to the park, in the first few years after it opened. The "park in the sky" also had a salutary effect on the local crime rate, largely attributable to Parks Enforcement Patrol officers and another, less quantifiable means of crime control—what the influential urbanologist Jane Jacobs termed "eyes-on-the-street": day-and-night pedestrian traffic and a healthy contingent of neighborhood busybodies, she asserted, lead to fewer opportunistic offenses, both major and minor. Because the transformed viaduct threads through such a densely populated district, with many apartments and hotel rooms overlooking the walkway, Jacobs's principle of informal but effective civilian surveillance is confirmed yet again.

The High Line is above all an inspiring case study of how major city-planning initiatives can be realized without either the authoritarian methods of Robert Moses—New York's mid-twentieth-century public works czar, whose pursuit of vast infrastructure and urban-clearance projects often ran roughshod over democratic procedures and working-class neighborhoods—or today's commercially driven redevelopment schemes. When the first of the High Line's three increments opened, the city's picky citizens quickly embraced it, and despite concerns about its environmental bona fides and cavils over some design details, the scheme exceeded expectations in a wholly unanticipated way. Arriving at a time of widespread impoverishment during the Great Recession, this communal enrichment, elevated and elevating, felt like a windfall inheritance. Happily, the same elated reaction that greeted the first segment occurred again in 2011, when the newly completed middle portion of the High Line revealed that the park was evolving into a much more varied experience than many had anticipated.

Diller, Scofidio, and Renfro's transformation of New York's Lincoln Center for the Performing Arts of 2003–2012 has given Manhattan another welcome series of instantly admired gathering spaces, epitomized by the Illumination Lawn, the swooping greensward they built atop the Lincoln restaurant pavilion, set between Eero Saarinen's Vivian Beaumont Theater of 1958–1965 and Max Abramovitz's Philharmonic (now Avery Fisher) Hall of 1958–1962. This 7,203-square-foot expanse of tall fescue and Kentucky bluegrass—rectangular in outline but gently contorted into a saddle-like shape that touches plaza level at the lawn's southwest corner—was immediately embraced by Juilliard students as their veritable campus center and by visitors who luxuriate in its open south-facing vistas and calming purity.

The administrators of Lincoln Center approached Diller and Scofidio shortly after Frank Gehry's controversial plan for revamping the urbanistically flawed sixteen-acre complex—which advocated covering its principal plaza with a vast glass-and-steel canopy—was shelved in 2001. Unlike Gehry, Diller and Scofidio viewed the task as a series of delicate surgical interventions rather than a few large-scale impositions. Although the aging Lincoln Center was in urgent need of repair, a comprehensive overhaul struck some observers, including this one, as throwing good money after bad, considering the dubious architectural quality of the complex and the estimated $1.4 billion price tag.

The original architectural coordinator, Wallace K. Harrison (who designed its ever-garish centerpiece, the Metropolitan Opera House of 1958–1966), envisioned Lincoln Center as an acropolis elevated atop a continuous plinth over the several city blocks conjoined for the ensemble. Owing to the gradually sloping site, the plinth is lowest at the main plaza entry facing Broadway but rises to a height of two stories on West 65th Street to the north and Amsterdam Avenue to the west. Its blank peripheral base walls killed street life around most of Lincoln Center, but this was Harrison's intention. The adjacent neighborhood, which includes low-income housing due west of the

Met, was deemed too dangerous to have any interaction with the new cultural citadel, which unapologetically turned its back on the urban poor.

To make Lincoln Center more welcoming and accessible in a much-changed postmillennial Manhattan, Diller, Scofidio, and Renfro rethought the principal arrival sequence, which from the outset had been complicated by a service road parallel to Broadway. In order to allow a smoother entry, the architects eliminated the service road, repositioned the vehicular drop-off point below street level, and extended a broad stairway (embellished with eye-catching messages from light-emitting diodes on the steps' risers) over the new subterranean driveway, which is short enough not to feel like a claustrophobic tunnel.

The most welcome portion of their scheme is the remaking of West 65th Street between Amsterdam and Broadway. That busy crosstown traffic artery was blighted for decades by the two-hundred-foot-long platform bridge that covered most of the block and linked Juilliard with the grand theaters to the south. Millstein Plaza, windswept and barren atop the span, never caught on as a public space and turned the street below it into an urban abyss. Diller, Scofidio, and Renfro's bold decision to demolish this oppressive overpass was complemented by their creation of street entrances for each of Lincoln Center's thirteen constituent institutions on 65th to increase pedestrian traffic on what had been a dark and forbidding no-man's-land even at noon. Activity is particularly lively at mid-block, with its alignment of the entrance to Juilliard on the north side of the street and, directly across from it on the other side, the Elinor Bunin Munroe Film Center of 2011, designed by the Rockwell Group, with its façade done in collaboration with Diller, Scofidio, and Renfro.

Pietro Belluschi's Juilliard School of Music of 1963–1969, with its longest elevation on the north side of 65th Street, was easily the best of the Lincoln Center buildings. The finest example of Brutalist architecture in New York City, the Juilliard building (with Alice Tully Hall tucked into its lower portions) was hardly an approachable presence, but it did possess an integrity lacking in the sub-Neoclassical Modernism of Philharmonic Hall, the Met, and the New York State Theater. Because Belluschi made Juilliard's principal east-facing front parallel to the city's grid plan rather than lining it up with the diagonal of Broadway, there was a capacious triangular plot left vacant at the northwest corner of 65th Street. It was here that the new architects cantilevered a 50,000-square-foot extension fifty feet over the sidewalk to diminish the bulkiness that would have resulted had the large addition touched down at ground level (see Illustration 17a).

Beneath that new overhang the designers placed yet another of what has become their most familiar and popular motif: rising banks of built-in seats, this time relatively small, made of concrete, facing inward from the street corner to the remodeled building's lobby and adjoining café, and wittily suggesting where the corner of the extension would be if it had been brought down to ground level. The designers made the new façade as transparent and as free of metal supports as possible, exposing, to the full view of passersby on Broadway, dance studios, musical rehearsal spaces, and classrooms, an effect particularly mesmerizing at twilight and after nightfall, when the vast glass elevation comes fully alive with all sorts of motion. This is architectural populism of the very highest order.

The sound quality of Alice Tully Hall was never a problem comparable to the Philharmonic's, but the tonal properties of the smaller hall have been noticeably improved by the architects' collaboration with the acoustician J. Christopher Jaffe. Their subtle, not to say subliminal, reworking of Alice Tully Hall (the performance space has now been renamed the Starr Theater) was also informed by what has been called "psychoacoustics"—the idea that our perceptions of a concert hall's aural qualities are affected by the room's appearance. Here the designers devised an ingenious illumination scheme whereby translucent wall panels of thinly sliced wood veneers are illuminated from behind by LED lights on computerized dimmers that impart an ethereal radiance—or "blush," as the designers term it—to the perimeters of the auditorium. Eschewing the dated gilt-and-crystal of the older Lincoln Center theaters, this elegant space now glows with an inner warmth that seems at once atavistic and timeless, a *Zauberfeuer* (magic fire) worthy of Wagner, that wizard of synesthetic stagecraft.

Apart from their outstanding renovation work, the firm has also executed several start-from-scratch buildings that are as commendable for their economy as for their excellence in design. Their first American building, the Institute of Contemporary Art of 2002–2006 in Boston, offers a superb demonstration of the partners' strongly urbanistic values. The ICA, founded as the Boston Museum of Modern Art in 1936, had occupied a series of converted spaces until it acquired a dramatic waterside site to the east of the city's downtown business center on Harbor Walk soon after the millennium. Before the advent of the ICA, this fifty-mile-long shoreline park, begun in 1984, had been little more than a pathway for joggers and cyclists. Although the derelict waterfront gave Diller, Scofidio, and Renfro a virtual tabula rasa, their client's desire for maximum unobstructed exhibition areas (a must for the unpredictable display requirements of today's new art) inspired the designers to lift the loft-like gallery area to the very top of the structure and create an inviting public space below it on ground level.

This organizing principle gives the pair of large rooftop display spaces—which measure nine thousand square feet each—pellucid natural lighting through thirteen rows of wall-to-wall north-facing skylights. Overhead trusses leave these galleries free of columns and allow the open spaces to be reconfigured as needed, making them among the most adaptable contemporary art interiors in America. The architects' most decisive gesture was to cantilever that uppermost story sixty-four feet out toward Harbor Walk and the bay beyond. They thereby created a large sheltered public space beneath the overhang, where they installed the first version of their urban grandstand, with tiers of wooden bleachers on which pedestrians can sit and observe the passing parade, which has become one of the most popular outdoor gathering places in Boston. The ICA is furthermore noteworthy for its comparatively low price tag. In a period when $100 million museums were not uncommon and many overreaching institutions subsequently suffered the dire consequences of competitive, excessive pre-crash spending on new facilities, the 62,000-square-foot Boston structure was executed for a relatively thrifty $41 million.

Diller, Scofidio, and Renfro acquired a most demanding patron in Eli Broad, the self-styled "venture philanthropist" who hired them in 2010 to design the Broad, a publicly accessible repository for his collection of contemporary art next to Frank Gehry's Walt Disney Concert Hall of 1987–2003 in downtown Los Angeles. The architects' plans for the $120 million structure include the building's intricate exterior, a honeycomb-like wraparound of glass-fiber reinforced concrete. Within, the architects dramatize the sheer volume of the collector's acquisitions—some two thousand works in all—with a looming storage unit they call "the Vault" at the heart of the structure, which suggests vast unseen riches within.

The completion of Disney Hall raised hopes that the environs of Bunker Hill in downtown Los Angeles, isolated by freeways, would at last become an active twenty-four-hour neighborhood instead of an enclave that comes to life only during performance hours, the same problem that plagued Lincoln Center until Diller, Scofidio, and

Renfro's revitalizing makeover. Ambitious plans to transform Bunker Hill through the $3 billion Grand Avenue Project were approved in 2007 but the redevelopment scheme stalled when the Great Recession set in. Though the twelve-acre strip park linking the nearby city hall and other municipal buildings has been completed, well-founded doubts remain about the scheme's prospects for success, given sharp cutbacks in commercial and civic investment. It will take more than a conventional park to establish and sustain around-the-clock street life in what has intractably remained a desolate ghost town after dark. If only Diller, Scofidio, and Renfro had been hired to give Bunker Hill the commonsensical but uncommonly imaginative character of their urbanistic coups in New York and Boston.

More than almost any of their current peers (with the notable exception of the collaborative Norwegian firm Snøhetta), they have repeatedly demonstrated a keen understanding of the social interactions that make for effective and enjoyable public spaces. Thus there was well-founded dismay among their admirers when in 2013 they accepted the Museum of Modern Art's controversial commission to replace Tod Williams and Billie Tsien's former American Folk Art Museum building of 1997–2001, contrary to a long-standing ethical tradition among high-style architects not to abet the destruction of living colleagues' work.

The three New York partners are highly adept architects by any measure, but their keenest design skills are considerably deepened and intensified by a humane outlook of the sort usually ascribed to more earnest urbanists like Jane Jacobs and Lewis Mumford. This dynamic trio has a better feel for the social workings of big American cities than any other designers today, and the way in which these prodigiously gifted late bloomers reliably upend rote responses to contemporary urban conditions makes them our shrewdest yet most sympathetic enhancers of the postmillennial metropolis.

18

SNØHETTA

DESPITE THE PERSISTENT image of the architect as a heroic loner erecting monumental edifices through sheer force of will, the building art has always been a highly cooperative enterprise. Although the parti (basic organizing principle) of a design may sometimes be the product of one intelligence, the realization of a structure of even moderate complexity depends on a broad range of expertise seldom encompassed by any individual, no matter how singularly gifted. As an artistic endeavor, present-day architecture most closely resembles filmmaking, in which the prime creative mover, the director—even the most visionary of auteurs—requires the specialized technical skills of a large cohort of indispensable collaborators. Thus an architectural team today comprises not only the long-familiar roster of structural engineers, HVAC (heating, ventilation, and air conditioning) specialists, acousticians, interior designers, lighting engineers, and landscape architects, but also computer software engineers, environmental impact managers, and (for certain public buildings) security analysts and antiterrorism consultants, positions that did not exist a generation ago. One leading New York architectural headhunter reports an even wider array of new job descriptions, including sustainability director, virtual design coordinator, and digital librarian.

Given the growing complexity of architectural tasks and the ever-advancing technologies available to resolve them, that high degree of interdependence is only likely to increase. As Kjetil Trædal Thorsen, a founding member of the Norwegian architectural collaborative Snøhetta, told me in his Oslo office in 2011:

Architecture is now far too complex to be designed by any one person. It is truly a much more communal process than it ever has been. Our conceptual model is "the singular in the plural," in which all of us are shareholders and each individual takes on responsibility for the company.

Perhaps only a postindustrial social democracy as progressive as Norway—surely among the most enlightened of all contemporary nations, with as good a claim as any to being a humane society—could have produced an architectural office such as this. A self-described nonhierarchical cooperative whose principals avowedly seek to avoid the personal celebrity we associate with Zaha Hadid or Daniel Libeskind, Snøhetta is far different from the top-down model adopted during the postwar period by large American architectural firms, exemplified by Skidmore, Owings & Merrill, that patterned their organizational structure and management methods on those of the large corporations they hoped to attract as clients. Instead, this far more informal group aims to give quite the opposite impression, that of mutually supportive friends who have banded together to come up with ingenious ideas that will make life better for everyone, primarily but not exclusively their sponsors. It is an uplifting ethos that a younger generation of enlightened clients has found irresistible.

Snøhetta promotes a more democratic workplace atmosphere than most other architectural offices. This may merely reflect prevalent employment practices in Scandinavia, but Snøhetta places a stronger emphasis on group participation in the design process than typical high-style firms. Rather than consigning junior assistants to repetitive backroom drudgery like detailing fire stairs and other minutiae of building code compliance, the Norwegian collaborative makes a habit of handing over relatively small commissions to younger associates in order to develop their problem-solving skills. As Thorsen told me, the jobs handled by his less experienced colleagues are carefully monitored "so that they cannot get into too much trouble."

Even the group's unconventional nomenclature works toward egalitarian ends. Snøhetta, which means "snowcap" in Norwegian—a cryptic choice for an organization with such international aspirations—comes from the eponymous 7,500-foot-high mountain that is the tallest peak in the Dovrefjell range 240 miles north of Oslo in central Norway. (As a group "bonding" exercise, Snøhetta employees make an annual pilgrimage to the mountain.) The name was picked in 1987 by the firm's six original organizers, all landscape architects committed to interdisciplinary group practice. The firm's gradual evolution from landscape-architecture specialists to a more full-service operation remains evident in an unusual attentiveness to environmental conditions and an exceptional aptitude for site planning. The only two of the original group still with the organization are Thorsen, who heads the main office, housed in a converted pier-side warehouse on the Oslo harborfront, and Snøhetta's other principal (there are also five partners), the American Craig Dykers, who directs the US office in lower Manhattan near its project at Ground Zero.

Since the turn of the millennium, Snøhetta has risen quickly with a series of well-received schemes that in turn have won it other prestigious commissions. Its meteoric emergence after two decades of practice is a phenomenon on a par with that of its closest American counterpart, the New York firm Diller Scofidio + Renfro, which likewise displays a keen instinct for contemporary urbanism. Although

Snøhetta is based principally in the Norwegian capital—site of its best-known work to date, the Oslo Opera House of 2003–2008 (see Illustration 18)—its increasingly busy branch in New York City oversees its American projects, which include the National September 11 Memorial Museum Pavilion, begun in 2004 at Ground Zero; a 2010 proposal for reconfiguring Manhattan's amorphous and chaotic Times Square, which was finally approved in 2013 by the city's mayoral Design Commission; and an addition to the San Francisco Museum of Modern Art, a job it was awarded in 2010.

As a result of such conspicuous schemes, Snøhetta began appearing on short lists for major projects alongside avant-garde grandees like Jean Nouvel, Jacques Herzog and Pierre de Meuron, and Kazuyo Sejima and Ryue Nishizawa of SANAA—all Pritzker Prize winners. Perhaps because Norway, small and off the beaten path, has been less than central to the narrative of modern architecture, Snøhetta has downplayed its geographic origins to the extent that other Norwegian architects now view the firm as a multinational venture that has priced itself out of the local market for architectural services. That perception may be contradicted by Snøhetta's participation in Norway's admirable government-sponsored National Tourist Routes program (which has underwritten small but exquisite architectural interventions—including rest stations, bicycle shelters, and scenic viewing platforms—in remote locales to encourage tourism to far reaches of the country), yet there is no question that the firm's growing presence in the United States is part of a global-minded strategy intended to combat the lack of recognition experienced by Norwegian architects in the past.

During the mid-twentieth-century heyday of the Modern Movement—which became closely identified with Scandinavia in the popular imagination thanks to that region's widely distributed, user-friendly contemporary household furnishings—Norway had no internationally recognized master until Sverre Fehn won the Pritzker Prize in 1997 (even though Fehn's late-life overnight rediscovery overlooked his youthful coup as designer of the much-admired Norwegian Pavilion at the Brussels Universal and International Exhibition of 1958, which brought to mind a woodsy version of Ludwig Mies van der Rohe's renowned German Pavilion at the Barcelona International Exposition of 1929). This low global profile no doubt had more to do with Norway's relatively small population—in 1940 it numbered just under three million inhabitants, less than half the size of Sweden, a ratio more or less maintained today with five million Norwegians and nine-and-a-half million Swedes—and commensurate level of building activity than with any inherent lack of native talent.

To be sure, Norwegians eagerly embraced International Style architecture, which they call *funksjonalisme* (Functionalism), without any of the conservative resistance to it that has never quite died out in the US. The new architecture of Modernism was ideally suited to the rational, egalitarian tenor of Norway's emergent social democracy, which was further informed by research in the social sciences— specialists called *hvite frakker* (white coats) in Norwegian—and steadily institutionalized as the twentieth century progressed. Since then, Norway has developed one of the most impressive contemporary architectural cultures in Europe, sustaining an overall level of architectural excellence lately equaled on the continent only by Holland and Spain.

Two years after Snøhetta was first organized as a studio called Snøhetta Arkitektur og Landskap in 1987, it produced the winning entry in an open competition for a modern reincarnation of the fabled library of ancient Alexandria, one of the marvels of classical antiquity: the Bibliotheca Alexandrina of 1989–2001. The significance of this prestigious contest—jointly sponsored by the city, the

University of Alexandria, the Egyptian government, UNESCO, and the United Nations Development Programme, among others—which attracted submissions from seventy-seven countries, was further enhanced by the spectacular waterfront site allotted to the scheme, not unlike that which the designers would later enjoy with their acclaimed Oslo Opera House. For the new library, Snøhetta devised a structure that is at once monumental and humane, seemingly contradictory values that on more than one occasion these designers have demonstrated a particular aptitude for combining without the slightest incongruity. The building's most notable aspect is a vast, windowless, slightly tilting, granite-clad cylindrical form that appears like some Ptolemaic vestige as one approaches from the south and enters, either via a narrow elevated pedestrian footbridge that spans the wide traffic thoroughfare in front of it or at street level. Both routes lead to an overscaled, unframed oblong portal cut deeply into the curving stone façade.

As one nears the building it becomes clear that the masonry exterior is densely carved with inscriptions from all known alphabets, ancient and modern, a variation on the traditional practice of engraving the names of famous authors on the outer walls of libraries. This massive, fortress-like, yet propulsive enclosure also serves a practical purpose—to protect the interior from the sandstorms that blow up from the south and toward the Mediterranean just behind it. Viewed from the sea, however, the Bibliotheca Alexandrina presents an entirely different appearance. Instead of the monolithic cylinder visible from the south, the northern prospect is dominated by an immense glazed disc that slopes downward, almost to ground level, toward the water. With its regular pattern of triangular skylights, this gently angled roof brings to mind the composite telescopic mirror of an astral observatory. Beneath it lies the institution's principal space, the great reading hall—a huge, nearly circular room, its roof supported by a modular grid of slender supporting columns that brings to mind the domed and skylit *salle de travail* of Henri Labrouste's Bibliothèque Nationale de France of 1862–1868 in Paris, as well as the forest-like profusion of columned arches in the Great Mosque of Córdoba. With such evocative cross-cultural references and strong civic presence, this Snøhetta scheme deservedly won an Aga Khan Award for Architecture, the triennial prize for outstanding construction in the Islamic world, in 2004.

The work that launched Snøhetta into the architectural big leagues was its Oslo Opera House, which will certainly rank among the firm's highlights whatever else it may do. Although this is by any measure a triumph of city planning, the building itself is not quite a masterpiece, though very fine indeed. It suffers from a clash of mixed stylistic metaphors. The crisply faceted exterior—which is clad with white marble, granite, and aluminum—and the soaring forty-nine-foot-high glass-walled entry hall with gigantic tilting columns have an insistent angularity that seems almost Deconstructivist, to use the word associated with the dislocated and distorted shapes used by such contemporary architects as Peter Eisenman, Zaha Hadid, Daniel Libeskind, and Bernard Tschumi. These elements are in contrast to the undulating vertical-wood-slatted surface of the auditorium's exterior and balcony promenades, which swell into the lobby like a remonstrative visitation from the ghost of Alvar Aalto, Modernism's Mr. Natural.

In the building's frosty-white reception area one encounters the Icelandic artist Olafur Eliasson's *The Other Wall* (2004–2008), among several pieces in various mediums commissioned for the building. This sculptural mural installation, composed of white-painted fiberboard and backed with lime-green LED illumination, is patterned in a molded-and-pierced harlequin motif that gives the lobby a retro-hip air reminiscent of a 1950s resort hotel. Far more successful is Pae

MAKERS OF MODERN ARCHITECTURE, VOLUME II

White's *MetaFoil* (2004), the stage curtain illusionistically woven from cotton, wool, and polyester to mimic an expanse of crumpled metal sheeting. This shimmering silvery *Vorhang*, ingeniously fabricated without recourse to any metallic fibers, provides an ideal foil for the auditorium's somber elegance.

Paneled in dark fumed oak, the grand hall, which seats 1,364, is a superb example of how to give a modern auditorium a sense of occasion without digging into the threadbare grab bag of sham-Classical decor. (Diller Scofidio + Renfro's much smaller Starr Theater of 2009 in New York's Alice Tully Hall does the same.) The most striking feature of the Oslo hall—which also has excellent acoustics—is Snøhetta's reinterpretation of the once-obligatory opera house chandelier. Here, in a minimalist reduction that recalls the roof of the Bibliotheca Alexandrina, a huge disk of 5,800 notched crystal prisms is set flush into the big room's ceiling and backed with LED lights to create a hovering, radiant effect that infuses the majestic space with a feeling of incipient excitement and democratic splendor.

Most important, the Oslo Opera House has given the Norwegian capital one of Europe's most enjoyable and instantly beloved public spaces of the past half-century. This is largely due to the clever massing of the building's exterior, which allows the public to ascend broad ramps that frame the lateral walls and lead uninterruptedly up to the top. The roof thus becomes an extension of the plaza below as well as an observation deck that affords visitors panoramic views of the city and its meandering waterways. In winter it is not uncommon to see skiers schussing down its ice-covered inclines, an utterly captivating spectacle that epitomizes these designers' popular appeal. The paradox that superb urbanism is not automatically synonymous with great architecture underscores the frequent disparity between Snøhetta's knack for effective city planning and some of its structures, which lack either the conceptual audacity of Frank Gehry and

Rem Koolhaas on the one hand or the technical suavity of Norman Foster and Renzo Piano on the other.

The Oslo Opera House is reminiscent of Jørn Utzon's Sydney Opera House of 1956–1973 not only because of their similar white exteriors, sail-like profiles, and waterside sites but also because both have become cherished national symbols in an age when new works of public architecture rarely achieve a high degree of general acclaim, as was achieved by Gehry's Guggenheim Museum Bilbao of 1991–1997. In recent years, new concert halls have become nearly as ubiquitous as new art museums, a surfeit that can only be attributed to the same competitive civic urge that sparked the international art gallery boom a generation earlier, which was motivated in large part by the widespread (if erroneous) belief that cultural tourism is guaranteed to recoup the cost of such sometimes overreaching schemes.

There is no better cautionary example than present-day Spain when it comes to the folly of reckless deficit spending to fund economically dubious, albeit socially beneficial, visual and performing arts projects. The treasuries of Valencia, Santiago de Compostela, and Avilés have been pushed to the brink of bankruptcy thanks to excessive expenditures on large-scale cultural enterprises designed, respectively, by Santiago Calatrava, Eisenman, and Oscar Niemeyer, each venture prompted by the vain hope that these colossal investments would yield "the next Bilbao." Such speculations had no bearing on the $707 million Oslo Opera House, which was subsidized by the most solvent government in present-day Europe, a beneficence made possible by Norway's plentiful offshore oil reserves, the income from which is nationalized.

Snøhetta's biggest American commission to date is its 225,000-square-foot addition to the San Francisco Museum of Modern Art (SFMoMA), scheduled to open in 2016. The selection of the firm for that project is yet another example of the increasingly common trend for museums to seek additions from architects other than the last ones they employed. It used to be almost an ethical imperative to ask the designer of a building to expand it and thus maintain visual continuity with the original structure. Only if the initial architect had died or if the firm did not want the new commission was it considered permissible to seek another practitioner. In an extreme example to the contrary, the original Beaux Arts building of Houston's Museum of Fine Arts was given a discordant succession of modern wings by Kenneth Franzheim (1953), Ludwig Mies van der Rohe (1958 and 1974), and Rafael Moneo (2000), with a further extension by Steven Holl announced in 2012. (Snøhetta was among the three finalists for that job.)

The tendency to seek new architects for expansion schemes began to accelerate in the 1990s, around the time the High Museum of Art in Atlanta decided to add to Richard Meier's building of 1980–1983. Although Meier's eye-catching design gave the small regional institution a dynamic new image, the structure was soon found to be functionally deficient because of light-control problems, skylight leaks, and planning that seemed to favor circulation areas over display space. In a move widely interpreted as a critique of his flawed design, Meier did not get the commission, which went instead to Renzo Piano, whose expansion of 1999–2005 added three wings and doubled the museum's exhibition capacity, but effectively reduced the showy but problem-plagued Meier structure to a glorified entry pavilion.

A similar rejection occurred with Mario Botta's San Francisco Museum of Modern Art of 1989–1995. This ponderous brick-clad Postmodernist pile was quickly deemed both stylistically passé and also too small for the museum's many recent acquisitions, including the coveted collection of Doris and Donald Fisher, longtime benefactors who unsuccessfully tried to build a private gallery designed by Richard Gluckman in the Presidio, the disused military base next to the Golden Gate Bridge. Botta's heavy-handed scheme was nonetheless notable for its stepped-back massing, which gave almost all the galleries natural overhead illumination and took into account the need for future expansion on an adjoining strip of land (used in the interim for staff parking). Given the unpredictable vagaries of architectural taste, it might be argued that the museum's trustees—several of whom had generously contributed toward the Botta design—ought to have had the courage of their convictions and returned to him, however démodé his aesthetic had become. Restricted to a narrow plot at the rear of Botta's five-story structure, the addition could well have become a nearly invisible backdrop had Snøhetta not decided to make its contribution contrast as much as possible with its blocky and stolidly symmetrical precursor.

The ten-story stepped-back expansion, estimated to cost $555 million, is to be clad in striated fiber-reinforced white panels with a cement finish, interspersed with glass, and will rise like an iceberg behind the original. That maritime impression will be underscored by the Botta building's most idiosyncratic feature, a central, smokestack-like cylinder that houses a grand stairway topped by a slanting glass oculus, which, with the icy new addition looming over it, may make *Titanic* buffs think of that doomed ocean liner. Yet the new wing's organization appears logical and likely to much improve visitors' experience of SFMoMA, which heretofore has exuded the sleek and somewhat snooty air of an upscale department store.

Snøhetta's participatory modus operandi was on full and sometimes excruciating view in Eirin Gjørv's revealing documentary film *The Sand Castle* (2007), which follows the firm's senior members as they vie with Rem Koolhaas as finalists in a limited competition for a new capital city for the United Arab Emirate of Ras al-Khaimah, sixty miles north of Dubai. Koolhaas won the master plan commission, but Snøhetta was given the consolation prize of the Ras al-Khaimah

Gateway, the convention center component of the mixed-use project. At one point the cagey client intermediary, Khater Massaad, airily dismisses Snøhetta's initial proposal for a long low-rise structure with a gracefully undulating roof because "it is not an icoon" (icon) akin to the hideously overblown skyscrapers in Dubai that have become emblematic of the emirates, exemplified by Tom Wright's scimitar-shaped Burj Al Arab hotel of 1997–1999, and the world's currently tallest man-made structure, the Burj Khalifa of 2004–2010, by Adrian Smith of Skidmore, Owings & Merrill. As they prepare to meet their patron, Thorsen tells one of his colleagues, "If he doesn't like what he sees tomorrow we'll have to start over," which is more or less what happens.

It is dispiriting to watch the ingratiating and patient Snøhetta team bending over backward to please an obtuse and somewhat ar-rogant client as their subsequent schemes get progressively worse and worse, a syndrome that is not uncommon in the world of architec-tural patronage. Snøhetta's accommodating stance is in marked con-trast to that of the steely Koolhaas, who appears to have carefully and profitably gauged his haughty demeanor to convey an air of com-mand commensurate with those who seek him out, a trick he learned from the past grand master of that power game, Philip Johnson, whose cool take-me-or-leave-me attitude won him far more jobs than it cost him. In any event, the vast undertaking has since been put on indefinite hold because of the emirate's financial woes.

Snøhetta's extreme willingness to adapt to the desires of its spon-sors has never been more evident than in the collaboration between the firm and the New York–based Norwegian artist Bjarne Mel-gaard, for whom the architects are designing a house in Oslo that will be completed in 2014. This strange undertaking was the subject of "A House to Die In," a small exhibition held at London's Institute for Contemporary Arts in 2012. The show featured an intentionally messy-looking installation that centered around a small model for Melgaard's wildly biomorphic house in Oslo—a free-form, blackened, clam-like structure held aloft by sinister, cartoonish doll-like figures (one based on the fashion designer Donatella Versace) apparently meant as contemporary versions of classical caryatids—along with a full-scale mock-up of a portion of the building's exterior, a deeply scarified and scorched swath of lumber that seemed as if a pyromaniacal preteen had run amok with a wood-burning kit, or perhaps was a maquette for a Tim Burton horror tree house. Private patrons of experimental architecture are perfectly free to indulge their whims as they please, but even in a period of unprecedented architectural weirdness, this embarrassment proved that there are necessary limits to unbridled self-expression.

If you had to choose between a pompous grand vizier or a pretentious myth-befuddled artist—both of whom bombard you with endless "suggestions" on how you should design for them—it might drive the faint of heart mad. Yet the project-to-project struggle that is contemporary high-style architecture has rarely been pursued with more equanimity, or better results, than it has been by the happy warriors of Snøhetta. The firm's eagerness (and occasional overeagerness) to please has also been a subtext of its work at Ground Zero, a project that remains mired in disputes over its funding and thus still languishes incomplete almost two years after the dedication of Michael Arad and Peter Walker's magnificent National September 11 Memorial of 2003–2011. (The interiors of the Snøhetta museum are the work of another firm, the New York–based Aedas.)

Even a cursory glance at Libeskind's hypothetical renderings of the former World Trade Center site indicates that Snøhetta—which adheres to no consistent design approach but varies its response from project to project—followed his lead much too readily in its jittery-looking, diagonally scored National September 11 Memorial Museum

Pavilion, which appears to mimic a structure falling down, a dreadful miscalculation on this bedeviled site. The exterior of Snøhetta's wedge-shaped visitors' center is rendered in the sharply angular, diagonally striated Deconstructivist mode originally proposed for the site by Libeskind, who won the competition for the Ground Zero reconstruction master plan but was sidelined from any serious implementation of his ideas by the property's leaseholder, the real estate developer Larry Silverstein. Apart from the pavilion's nervously off-kilter, exaggeratedly slant-roofed form and 1990s deconstructivist aesthetic already looking quite dated, the perforated portions of its metal-panel cladding give the museum entry structure the mechanistic feel of a thinly camouflaged ventilation-equipment housing.

Now, long after Libeskind was unceremoniously shuffled offstage, this vestige of his aborted vision appears even more out of place next to the solemn grandeur and timeless simplicity of Arad's twin memorial pools. If Snøhetta is to advance into the very forefront of the profession, its unquestionably gifted team members must realize that as congenial and nurturing as their sheltered workshop may be, in the rough-and-tumble world of architecture there can be such a thing as being too nice for your own good.

19

MICHAEL ARAD

I WEPT, BUT about what precisely I cannot say. When I first visited Michael Arad's newly completed National September 11 Memorial of 2003–2011 at Ground Zero, which was dedicated on the tenth anniversary of the disaster—the ubiquitous maudlin press coverage of which I had done everything possible to ignore—it impressed me at once as a sobering, disturbing, heartbreaking, and overwhelming masterpiece. Arad's inexorably powerful, enigmatically abstract pair of abyss-like pools, which demarcate the foundations of the lost Twin Towers (see Illustration 19), came as an immense surprise to those of us who doubted that the chaotic and desultory reconstruction of the World Trade Center site could yield anything of lasting value.

Yet against all odds and despite tremendous opposition from all quarters, the design by the Israeli-American Arad—an obscure thirty-four-year-old architect working for a New York City municipal agency when his starkly Minimalist proposal, *Reflecting Absence*, was chosen as the winner from among the 5,201 entries to the Ground Zero competition—became the most powerful example of commemorative architecture since Maya Lin's Vietnam Veterans Memorial of 1981–1982 in Washington, D.C. It is by no means accidental that Arad's scheme derives so directly in several respects from

Lin's epochal monument. As a member of the National September 11 Memorial jury, she was a decisive voice in determining who would receive a commission that could have been hers for the asking had she wanted it. However, the congruities between these two magnificent designs do not in any way lessen Arad's achievement.

It is generally held that great architecture requires the participation of a great client, but just how this stunning result emerged from such a fraught and contentious process, which at several points during its ten-year saga seemed to stall indefinitely or unravel completely, will take quite some time for critics and historians to sort out and properly assess. It is not even easy in this instance to determine who precisely the client was, apart from the American people, an uncertainty raised by the several overlapping municipal and state agencies directly involved in the decision-making process in its early phases, to say nothing of the even larger number of special-interest or pressure groups ("stakeholders," as they came to be called) whose often unsolicited and frequently contentious opinions were brought to bear on every aspect of the complicated undertaking.

When the definitive account of the struggle to bring the September 11 Memorial into existence is written, it seems clear that a good deal of the credit for rescuing the foundering enterprise from further delay, indecision, and dissent will go to New York City Mayor Michael R. Bloomberg and three women whom Arad has described as Bloomberg's "eyes and ears on the ground": First Deputy Mayor Patricia Harris (who had earlier headed public relations and philanthropic affairs for Bloomberg LP, the billionaire mogul's multinational mass media company); Amanda M. Burden, the director of the New York City Planning Commission (whom the architect credits for her dogged attentiveness to small design details that can be of cumulatively huge importance to a scheme); and Kate D. Levin, the commissioner of the New York City Department of Cultural Affairs.

It was only in 2006, when Bloomberg became head of the World Trade Center Memorial Foundation (replacing Gretchen Dykstra) and control of the project passed to it from the Lower Manhattan Development Corporation (LMDC, the joint state-city authority created in the aftermath of the 2001 attack to supervise the reconstruction of Ground Zero), that the project began to gather momentum, in no small part because of the mayor's personal enthusiasm for Arad's design. Though Bloomberg's leadership tactics could often appear peremptory, elitist, and micromanagerial, his forceful takeover of the September 11 Memorial—the city's chief executive essentially made himself the client—was precisely what that organizational mess needed, proof again that one strong architectural patron will get more accomplished more quickly than any building committee, no matter how informed or well intentioned.

During his three terms in office, Bloomberg was widely criticized for city planning decisions that favored commercial property interests at the expense of average citizens, none more so than the Atlantic Yards redevelopment scheme of 2003–2012 in Brooklyn, a vast mixed-use sports arena, residential, and retail complex that critics castigated as socially destructive and a form of corporate welfare for the politically well-connected real estate developer Bruce Ratner. The mayor's unsuccessful bid to win the 2012 Olympic Games for New York City was also perceived as a plutocratic boondoggle, despite his claims that both initiatives would enhance the city's economy by creating jobs and increasing tourism. On the other hand, his backing for the redevelopment of large portions of the city's 578-mile-long shoreline into public parkland, along with his crucial support for the enormously successful High Line and especially the September 11 Memorial, will count heavily in his favor when his urban-design balance sheet is tallied.

Michael Sahar Arad was born in London in 1969, the son of

Moshe Arad, a Romanian-born diplomat who emigrated to Israel in 1950 and served as Israeli ambassador to Mexico from 1983 to 1987 and to the United States from 1987 to 1990. The young Arad lived in Jerusalem for nine years, attended high school in Mexico City, entered Dartmouth in 1987, but took a break after his freshman year to serve in an Israeli commando unit for his obligatory three-year military service. He then returned to college, received a BA in 1994, and went on to study architecture at Georgia Tech. At the age of thirty he moved to Manhattan to work for the large architectural firm Kohn Pedersen Fox, but became disillusioned with corporate practice and after three years took a job in the design department of the New York City Housing Authority, where he worked on neighborhood police stations.

Arad experienced the terrorist attack on the World Trade Center in a very immediate and personal way—from the roof of his East Village apartment building he watched in horror as United Airlines Flight 175, the second of the hijacked jets, slammed into the South Tower. He participated in one of the many public vigils held in the aftermath of the buildings' fall, and well before it was announced that plans would be solicited for an open memorial competition, felt the urge to create a commemorative design, which from the outset featured two square black voids set amid a reflecting pool of water. In due course Arad fleshed out his initial conceptual sketch and proposed a more spatially complex version that expanded the squares into subterranean cubic memorial chambers open to the sky and enhanced with curtain-like vertical fountains. Visitors would have been able to proceed down to the bottom of the pools, which were to have been ringed by walkways, the walls behind them inscribed with the names of the dead, with the central square pools shrouded by cascades of water pouring down steadily from above.

For a variety of insuperable reasons—budgetary, infrastructural, and security concerns high among them—Arad was forced to abandon his initial idea of the below-ground memorial chambers accessible to the public, which he compared to Orpheus's descent into the Underworld, "a vast emptiness that you cannot enter but can only contemplate as you look into the void." From the outset, Arad, who had never had a commission of this magnitude, was wary of making the countless small, bureaucratically imposed compromises—"death by a thousand papers cuts," as he put it—that can sap all the life from a design. But the elimination of the subterranean spaces struck at the very heart of his conception.

Here he was forced to consider either resigning this incomparably prestigious and high-profile commission or coming up with an alternative solution that retained the spiritual essence of his initial idea. "I was incredibly upset," Arad later admitted, "but I had to go from holding onto an idea to finding a way of articulating the same set of ideas in other ways." This he managed to do so well that when one experiences the memorial as it was finally realized, his revised design conveys the same sense of inevitability that one senses with all great art—that it had to be like this, and no other way.

When the memorial first opened to the public, the eight-hundred-foot-long arrival sequence presented a dismal prologue that so closely replicated the security checks of a post–September 11 airport check-in—replete with metal detectors, jacket removals, pat-downs, and conveyor belts for personal property scans—as to verge on black comedy. Because Ground Zero at that time was (and for several years thereafter would remain) an active construction site, visitors were channeled around the rising buildings through a series of fences and barriers that led them toward the south pool, an emphasis that will change when the surroundings are fully completed and the public is free to approach the memorial from any direction at will. After this ad hoc entry maze was negotiated, one came upon the pleasant park designed by Peter Walker, the Berkeley, California–based landscape architect with whom Arad was directed to work by the LMDC, which fretted about the young architect's lack of experience and felt that his scheme needed the softening touch of greenery to make it more palatable to the general public. (The other member in the uneasy troika insisted upon by the LMDC was the architect J. Max Bond Jr., a partner in the large New York firm Davis Brody Bond, who was deemed necessary to supervise the untested young competition winner but died in 2009. The extreme animosity among the three principals, none of whom was shy about speaking to the press, was well documented, and Arad came off for the most part as petulant and abrasive rather than tenacious and principled.)

On the plaza adjacent to the pools, Walker planted a grid of some four hundred swamp white oaks in an intriguing staccato pattern that makes them seem either randomly positioned or formally aligned, depending on one's vantage point. The low-hanging branches of these vigorous-looking specimens have been clipped upward to about half of their approximately twenty-five-foot height, presumably to keep them from touching the heads of visitors, and though those proportions looked somewhat artificial when the memorial first opened, the trees will ultimately form a handsome grove. As one nears the pools, walking across the light-gray granite paving stones installed by Walker, the murmur of rushing water rises from the cascades that pour Niagara-like down all four sides of the sunken fountains. The sound becomes louder and louder, until it reaches such a steady crescendo that the noise of the surrounding city, even heavy construction going on very close by, is drowned out completely.

The veil-like flow of water down the dark-gray granite-clad sides of the recirculating pools is a feat of hydraulic engineering achieved by the installation of weirs (downward-curving comb-like spillways) set all around the upper perimeter of the giant squares. Looking down into the equilateral thirty-foot-deep pits, one sees yet another, far smaller square that extends another fifteen feet below the pool's surface, bringing to mind a simplified, monochromatic grisaille version of Josef Albers's *Homage to the Square* series. With that last, centered quadrangle, the water vanishes into nothingness. The propulsive aural and visual excitement of the three-story-deep waterfall and its mysterious disappearance captures and holds your attention in a way most unusual for the static medium of conventional architecture. That distraction makes one's next perception all the more shocking, as you focus on the names of the victims, incised into the continuous tilted rim of bronze tablets that surround each pool. The initial perspective provided by the cascades mimics a technique employed in classical Japanese gardens, through which one's gaze is briefly diverted by a change in paving, screening, or some other element to dramatize a coming transition.

Here, after you take in the diaphanous waterfalls, you discover spread out before you at waist level the names, the names, the names. Nearly three thousand victims—not only those lost at the World Trade Center, but also those who died at the Pentagon and near Shanksville, Pennsylvania—are memorialized with their names inscribed in Hermann Zapf's classic Optima typeface of 1952–1955 (an elegant, slightly flaring sans-serif font), with the letters cut through the bronze so they can be backlit after dark. This is a typographic tour de force. Phalanxes of firemen are listed, ladder company by ladder company, and cops precinct by precinct; hundreds upon hundreds of Cantor Fitzgerald traders; teams of Windows on the World busboys; an entire family on one plane; and on two of the hijacked flights women with "unborn child." The names are grouped in what Arad termed "meaningful adjacencies" to suggest comradeship among those who died together at work, as first responders in the line of duty, or as travelers who would never reach their destinations.

This was a deeply meaningful concept that Arad came up with in 2004 but that was shelved until Bloomberg took charge in 2006, with letters soliciting information about such interrelationships sent out to the victims' survivors only in 2009. The ecumenical indifference of fate cannot have been more plainly or more movingly put. At times this relentless roll call becomes too much to bear, and your eyes rise up to the buildings that surround the memorial. But in purely architectural terms it is a sorry sight: not a single building of any distinction is to be seen in any direction (one reason why Arad wanted the memorial chambers he first envisioned to be positioned below ground).

Looming over the northwest corner of the site is the 104-story One World Trade Center of 2003–2013, once called the Freedom Tower but later given its current, more market-friendly moniker, which was the original name of one of the Twin Towers. This slick mirror-glass-skinned office building—which retains the symbolic 1,776-foot height first decreed by the site's master planner, Daniel Libeskind—is the work of Skidmore, Owings & Merrill's David Childs, who had been hired to renovate the Twin Towers shortly before they fell. His banal design has attracted less comment than the building's astronomical $3.1 billion price tag, making it by far the most expensive high-rise ever erected in the US. (A class-action lawsuit alleged that One World Trade Center was illegally financed by the Port Authority of New York and New Jersey through steep increases in tolls and commuter fares that could lawfully be applied only to infrastructural improvements, not to real estate speculations.)

No less flagrant in its huge budget overruns is Santiago Calatrava's Transportation Hub, a train station and underground shopping mall linking the trans-Hudson PATH system with New York City's subways. Estimated to cost nearly $4 billion—twice initial projections—it is sited directly to the east of the north pool, across Greenwich

Street. Calatrava likened his design in its original form to doves of peace in flight. After costs began to skyrocket, its wings were clipped, and when it finally opens, years behind schedule, the hub seems more likely to resemble a skeletal dinosaur carcass.

Although much has been made in the press of Arad's manifold battles to preserve the integrity of his scheme, one must also sympathize with Local Projects, a New York–based design firm that performed the daunting task of placing the victims' names in arrangements that would satisfy a seemingly infinite number of demands from many constituencies. An algorithm devised by the software programmer Jen Thorp sped this complex process, but further tinkering was needed to sort out many individual requests from the bereaved. This component of the September 11 Memorial got as close to the heart of the matter for the survivors as the decision to leave the foundations of the Twin Towers inviolate. Because about 40 percent of the victims left no identifiable remains, their survivors look upon the site as an actual graveyard, and thus the site's afterlife became a source of constant contention among the Families (as the next of kin were invariably called). Unidentified remains are to be placed at bedrock level, rendering the site an actual rather than a virtual burial ground.

Perhaps the most vociferous of the mourners was Monica Iken Murphy, a September 11 widow who at one public hearing memorably if bathetically asked, "How can we build on top of their souls that are crying?" Doubtless to the relief of those responsible for the memorial, she spoke favorably to the New York *Daily News* about the results: "My Michael is home finally. They're all home. This is his final resting place. When I come here, I feel him." Predictably, not all among the families felt the same. One survivor complained to a WINS radio reporter that the memorial was "cool"—as in cold, not hip—and said that "there should have been flowers or pictures or something." But of course it is precisely the abstract nature of Arad's design, which eschews all representational imagery, that allows visitors to project onto it thoughts and interpretations of a much more individual nature than if the memorial had been laden with prepackaged symbols of grief.

Although the locations and proportions of the square pools, which measure 176 feet on each side, were determined by the footprints of the Twin Towers, the overall dimensions—especially the relation of width to depth, and the juxtaposition of the two bodies of water to each other—somehow seem so ideally balanced that they might have been determined not by the disaster but by an environmental sculptor of uncommon talent. The only discordant note at the memorial is struck by the freestanding two-story pavilion that will serve as the entry point to the subterranean September 11 Museum. Standing next to but fortunately not between the twin pools, it is the work of Snøhetta. However, in an odd division of labor, the below-ground exhibition galleries were designed by another consortium, the multinational architectural firm Aedas working in association with Davis Brody Bond, a pairing that Arad saw as a conflict of interest because of priorities he believes were given to the museum by his nominal collaborator Bond. (The entire cost of the memorial and September 11 Museum was at least $700 million.)

Whatever one's opinions about the events of September 11, 2001, or their baneful political aftereffects, it seems impossible not to be moved in some way by Arad's memorial. The first time I saw it, I came away with the same devastated feeling that overtakes one after a funeral or memorial service for a relative or close friend, even though I knew no one who perished at the World Trade Center. In creating something at once so monumentally simple and yet so evocatively complex, Arad reconfirmed the radical reconception of public memorial design that Maya Lin set in motion with her Vietnam Veterans Memorial three decades ago. Lin herself was accused at the time by some critics of basing her work too closely on the ideas of Michael Heizer, Richard Serra, and other Earth Art or Minimalist sculptors. The inevitable, and unenviable, question that weighs upon Arad is what can he ever do to top or even equal the precocious triumph of his September 11 Memorial, completed when he was just forty-two, an age when most of his fellow architects are just beginning to find their professional footing.

Daunting as it must be for him to face the possibility of having peaked at such a relatively young age, Arad ought to take another example from Lin, who was a mere twenty-three years old when her Vietnam Veterans Memorial was finished. After being besieged by offers to replicate her masterpiece (much in the same way that Edwin Lutyens was asked to churn out slightly altered copies of his most acclaimed war memorial, the Cenotaph of 1919–1920 in London, for several other cities in Britain and its colonies), Lin was determined not to become typecast as a commemorative monument specialist. She decided after completing several subsequent commissions in that vein to decline further requests for such designs, which is why she exempted herself from the September 11 Memorial project. Since her auspicious debut, Lin has produced a strong body of work that unites architecture, art, and landscape design in inventive and thought-provoking ways that set her apart from the vast majority of single-minded practitioners in those separate disciplines. She is one of those rare creative figures who thoroughly alter the way in which an entire generation reconsiders long-accepted conventions and comes to accept a wholly new conception of how things ought to be. That is a contribution that far outstrips any tally of individual works, no matter how numerous or excellent.

The nature of architectural practice has changed enormously in recent decades, yet it remains much as it always has been in its wild unpredictability. The fates that befall even the most inspired master builders can be so capricious and cruel that one cannot predict whether Arad's youthful masterwork will be seen in due course as his lift-off point or apogee. But just as the test of time has already proven the validity of Maya Lin's insights into the wellsprings of mourning in the modern age, Michael Arad's profound variations and expansions on her themes have in turn ratified him as one of the signal place-makers of our time.

Illustration Credits

Front endpapers: Courtesy of Panayotis Tournikiotis, Greece/© 2012 Artists Rights Society (ARS), New York/ADAGP, Paris/F.L.C

Back endpapers: Eero Saarinen Collection, 1880–2004 (inclusive), 1938–1962 (bulk). Manuscripts & Archives, Yale University.

Frontispiece: Michael Moran/OTTO

1a: Photo © 2012 by Jonathan Wallen. Used with permission of the Preservation Society of Newport County.

1b: Library of Congress, Prints & Photographs Division, HABS Reproduction number HABS NY, 31-NEYO, 78-10

2a: Photograph by Tim Long. Courtesy of the Frank Lloyd Wright Preservation Trust.

2b: Copyright © Franck Mercurio. Photo used with permission of the Frank Lloyd Wright Foundation, Scottsdale, Arizona.

3a: Copyright © Leonard Frank/ /© 2012 Artists Rights Society (ARS), New York/ADAGP, Paris/F.L.C

3b: Copyright © Jonathan Choe/ /© 2012 Artists Rights Society (ARS), New York/ADAGP, Paris/F.L.C

4a: Bauhaus-Archiv Berlin

4b: Thomas Lewandovski

5a: Klaas Vermaas

5b: Digital Image © The Museum of Modern Art/Licensed by SCALA/Art Resource, New York

6a: Fandrade/Flickr/Getty Images

6b: Kjersti Veel Krauss, Norway

7: Egicarte

INDEX

Aalto, Alvar, 46, 91, 112, 119–20, 152, 222, 235, 257
Baker House, Massachusetts Institute of Technology, Cambridge, Massachusetts, 117, 118
Finnish Pavilion, New York World's Fair (1939), 80
University of Jyväskylä, Finland, 151
Abby Aldrich Rockefeller Sculpture Garden, Museum of Modern Art, New York, 184
"Aberrant Architectures of Diller + Scofidio, The," 2003 exhibition, Whitney Museum of American Art, New York, 237–38
Abramovitz, Max, 83
Philharmonic (Avery Fisher) Hall, New York, 245
Académie des Beaux-Arts, Paris, 215
Acedo, Guadalupe, 180–81
Adams, Ansel, 111
Aedas, and Davis Brody Bond,

National September 11 Memorial Museum, 263, 274
Aesthetic Movement, 8, 12
African (Romantic) chair, 49
Aga Khan Award for Architecture, 257
Agoracritus, 195
Agrest, Diana, xix
Albers, Anni, 49, 50
Albers, Josef, 47, 50
Gitterbilder, 52
Homage to the Square series, 271
Alésia Museum Visitor's Center, Burgundy, France, 201
Alfred Lerner Hall, Columbia University, New York, 202–3
Alice Tully Hall, New York, 247–48
Allied Works Architecture, 103
Altman, Robert, The Player, 166
Alton West Estate, London, 37
America First, 24
American Folk Art Museum, New York, 222–23, Illustration 15b

American Transcendentalists, 127
Amery, Colin, 160
AMO, 177
anathyrosis, 11
Anderson, John, *Art Held Hostage: The Battle over the Barnes Collection*, 212–13
Ando, Tadao, 217, 226
Anschluss, xvii
Antioch College, Yellow Springs, Ohio, 116
Applause (film), 4
Arad, Michael, 267–69
  Reflecting Absence, 264–65
Arad, Michael, and Peter Walker, National September 11 Memorial, New York, 236, 263, 264, 265–66, 269–74, 276, 1019
Arad, Moshe, 267–68
Archigram, 129
Arch of Hadrian, Athens, 200
Argot, Don, *The Art of the Steal*, 212
Armand Hammer Museum, Los Angeles, 171
Armour Institute of Technology, Chicago, 47
Armstrong, Louis, 160
Arnold, Anna Bing, 172
Art Deco, 223
Art Institute of Chicago, Modern Wing, 204
Art Newspaper, 166–67
Art Nouveau, 113
Art of the Steal, The (film), 212
Arts and Crafts Movement, 21, 112, 113, 114, 221

Arup, 188
Asplund, Gunnar, Crematorium, Stockholm South Cemetery, 143
Associated Architects, Rockefeller Center, 96
Astrup Fearnley Museum of Modern Art, Oslo, 173–74, Illustration 12b
Atkins, Anna, 53
Atlantic Yards, Brooklyn, 267
Aurora Place, Sydney, 161
Austria, xvii
Austrian Resistance, 71
Avery Fisher (Philharmonic) Hall, New York, 245

Bacon, Francis, 98
Baker, Herbert, 77
Baker, Josephine, 41–42
Baker House, Massachusetts Institute of Technology, Cambridge, Massachusetts, 117, 118
Balmond, Cecil, 188
Banham, Reyner, 106, 157
Barnes, Albert Coombs, 212–17, 218, 220, 224
Barnes Collection, Lower Merion, Pennsylvania, 212–13, 214–15, 217, 218–19
Barnes Foundation Collection, Philadelphia, 211, 216–20, 224, Illustration 15a
Baroque style, xviii, 11, 148
Barr, Alfred F., Jr., 96, 131
Barragán, Luis, 225
Baths of Caracalla, Rome, 2, 3
Bauer, Catherine, 22
  Modern Housing, 61–62

Bauhaus, xvi, xix, 34, 45–58
Vorkurs of, 51, 52
"Bauhaus: A Conceptual Model,"
2009 exhibition, Martin-Gropius-
Bau, Berlin, 45, 46–47, 48
Bauhaus Archive, Berlin, 46, 49
Bauhaus Foundation, Dessau,
Germany, 46
Bauhaus headquarters, Dessau, Ger-
many, 45, 62, Illustrations 4a, 4b
Bauhaus Manifesto, 48–49
"Bauhaus 1919–1928," 1938 exhibi-
tion, Museum of Modern Art,
New York, 47–48
"Bauhaus 1919–1933: Workshops
for Modernity," 2009 exhibition,
Museum of Modern Art, New
York, 45, 47
BCAM/LACMA/2008: The Broad
Contemporary Art Museum at
the Los Angeles County Museum
of Art, 166, 170–71
Beaux Arts style, 2, 19, 95–96, 153,
218, 219, 260
Bêka, Ila, and Louise Lemoine,
Koolhaas Houselife, 180–81
Belluschi, Pietro, Julliard School of
Music, New York, 247–48
Berenson, Bernard, 106
Bergdoll, Barry, 47
Berke, Deborah, xx
Berlin, Isaiah, 156
Berlin Wall, 46
Bernini, Gian Lorenzo, Louvre
expansion (project), xviii
Bertoia, Harry, 118
Beyeler, Ernst, 175

Beyeler Foundation Museum,
Riehen, Switzerland, 56, 164, 173
Bibliotheca Alexandrina, Alexan-
dria, Egypt, 255–57, 258
Bibliothèque Nationale de France,
Paris, 257
Bibliothèque Sainte-Geneviève,
Paris, 2
Bing, Alexander M., 172
Bing, Leo S., 172
Biosphere, Montreal, 129
Black Mountain College, North
Carolina, 47, 125
Blackwood, Michael, 148
Blair, Tony, 162
Blaisse, Petra, 182
Bletter, Rosemarie Haag, 71, 130,
148
Bloomberg, Michael R., 266–67, 272
Blowers, George, 74
Blur Building, Expo.02, Yverdon-
les-Bains, Switzerland, 238
Bo, Jørgen, and Vilhelm Wohlert,
Louisiana Museum of Modern
Art, Copenhagen, 224
Bo Bardi, Lina, "Architecture or
Architecture," 89
Böcklin, Arnold, Die Toteninsel, 144
Böhm, Gottfried, 226
Bond, Max, 270, 274
Booth, George, 113
Bosco, Giovanni (Saint John
Bosco), 84
Boston Architectural Club, 95
Boston Public Library, 2
Botta, Mario, San Francisco
Museum of Modern Art, 260–61

Bourne, Frederick, 107
Box Hill, Long Island, 13
BP Grand Entrance, Los Angeles
  County Museum of Art, 169
Bradbury, Ray, *Fahrenheit 451*, 37
Brasília, Brazil, 77–78, 84–87,
  88–90, 91, 92
"Brazil Builds," 1943 exhibition,
  Museum of Modern Art, New
  York, 80
Brazilian Communist Party, 87
Brazilian Pavilion, New York
  World's Fair (1939), 80
Breuer, Marcel, 3, 131, 200
  Cesca chair, 49
  Whitney Museum of American
  Art, New York, 184–85
Breuer, Marcel, and Gunta Stölzl,
  African (Romantic) chair, 49
Brion, Giuseppe, 143–44
Brion, Onorina Tomasin, 143–44
Brion Family Tomb and Chapel,
  San Vito d'Altivole, Italy, 143–46,
  Illustration 10
Brionvega, 143, 152
British Museum, London, 196–97
Broad, Eli, 165–67, 168, 171, 172,
  175, 249
Broad, Los Angeles, 249
Broadacre City (project), 20
Broad Contemporary Art Museum
  at the Los Angeles County
  Museum of Art, 165–67, 168–71,
  186
Broad Foundation, 165
Bronfman, Samuel, 107
Bronfman family, 163

Bruchfeldstrasse (*Zickzackhausen*),
  Frankfurt, Germany, 62
Brutalism, 99, 247
  New, 36–37, 116
Bryn Mawr College, Pennsylvania,
  117
Bullock, George, 151–52
Bunshaft, Gordon, 90, 225
Burden, Amanda M., 266
Burj Al Arab hotel, Dubai, 262
Burj Khalifa, Dubai, 262
Burle Marx, Roberto, 79–80, 81
Burnham, Daniel, xviii
Busbea, Larry, *Topologies: The
  Urban Utopia in France, 1960–
  1970*, 123–24
Byron, George Gordon, Lord,
  Childe Harold's Pilgrimage, 196
Byzantine Revival, 10

Ca' Foscari renovation, Venice,
  137–38
Caisse Nationale des Monuments
  Historiques, 180
Calatrava, Santiago, 108–9, 119,
  259
  Transportation Hub, New York,
  272–73
California Academy of Sciences
  building, San Francisco, 94
Cambridge University, 156
Camilla, Duchess of Cornwall, 150
Canadian Center for Architecture
  (CCA), Montreal, 133, 136, 140
Canberra, Australia, 77
Canova Plaster Cast Gallery
  addition, Possagno, Italy, 141–42

Captain's Paradise, The (film), 182
Caracas Museum of Modern Art
  (project), 91
Carlton, Julian, 27–28
Casa da Música, Porto, Portugal,
  178
Casino, Pampulha, Brazil, 81, 91
Castelo Branco, Humberto de
  Alencar, 88
Castelvecchio Museum renovation,
  Verona, Italy, 142–43
CBS Building, New York, 107
Cenotaph, London, 275
Center (New RKO Roxy) Theater,
  New York, 96
Central Park, New York, 243
Century of Progress exposition,
  Chicago (1933), 223
Cesca chair, 49
Cézanne, Paul, 217
  The Card Players, 216
  Large Bathers, 215
Chambless, Edgar, 185
Chandigarh, Punjab, India, 38, 77
Charles, Prince of Wales, 150, 157,
  162
Charlie Rose Show (TV show), xxii
Chase-Riboud, Barbara, 149
Chelsea Property Owners, 241
Cheney, Mamah Borthwick, 19, 21,
  26–28
Cheney house, Oak Park, Illinois, 26
Chicago, University of, 223–24,
  Illustration 15c
Chicago Tribune, 26
Chicago Tribune Building, Chicago,
  113

Childs, David, One World Trade
  Center, New York, 272
China, xviii, 188
China Central Television Head-
  quarters, Beijing, 188–91,
  Illustration 13b
Chrysler, Walter P., 107
Church of Saint Francis of Assisi,
  Pampulha, Brazil, 81–82, 91,
  Illustration 6a
Città Nuova, 105
Civil War, US, 7
Classical Foundation, Weimar,
  Germany, 46
Classicism, xviii, 1, 4, 12, 58, 100,
  138–39, 145, 148, 150, 154, 187,
  200, 203
  Beaux Arts, 2, 19, 95–96, 153,
  218, 219, 260
  Stripped, 35, 115, 219
Climatron, Missouri Botanical
  Garden, St. Louis, 128
Cloepfil, Brad, Museum of Arts and
  Design, New York, 103
Clore Gallery, Tate Gallery,
  London, 158
Cohen, Jean-Louis, 36
Collins, Joan, 14
Colonial Revival style, 12
Columbia University, New York,
  5–6, 8, 201, 202–3
Come Fly with Me (record album),
  112
Comme des Garçons, 227
Communism, Communists, xvii,
  xviii, 55, 71–72, 84, 87, 88, 89,
  187

Conceptual Art, 56
Congrès International
  d'Architecture Moderne, 72
Conrads, Ulrich, and Hans-G.
  Sperlich, *Phantastiche Architek-*
  tur, 123
Constantine, University of, Algeria,
  88
Conversations with Elder Wise
  Men (TV show), 18
Cook, Peter, 129
Coop Himmelb(l)au, 202
Costa, Lúcio, 77, 78, 80
  Ministry of Education and Health
  headquarters, Rio de Janeiro,
  Brazil, 78–79
Costa, Lúcio, and Oscar Niemeyer
  Brasília, Brazil, 77–78, 84–87,
  88–90, 91, 92
  Brazilian Pavilion, New York
  World's Fair (1939), 80
Cranbrook Academy of Art,
  Bloomfield Hills, Michigan,
  113–14, 220, 221–22
Cranbrook School, Bloomfield
  Hills, Michigan, 220, 221–22
Crawford, Joan, 43
Crematorium, Stockholm South
  Cemetery, 143
Cret, Paul Philippe
  Barnes Collection, Lower Merion,
  Pennsylvania, 212–13, 214–15,
  217, 218–19
  Folger Shakespeare Library,
  Washington, D.C., 218
  and Jacques Gréber, Rodin

Museum, Philadelphia, 218
"Cronacaos," 2010 exhibition,
  Venice Architecture Biennale, 189
Crystal Palace, London, 4, 80, 121,
  187, 229
Cuzco, Peru, 11
Cy Twombly Gallery, Houston,
  164, 173

Dalí, Salvador, 102
Dante Alighieri, 144
Dassin, Jules, 199
  Never on Sunday, 199
David, Joshua, 241
David S. Ingalls Hockey Rink, Yale
  University, New Haven, Connecti-
  cut, 106
Davis Brody Bond, 270
Davis Brody Bond, and Aedas,
  National September 11 Memorial
  Museum, 263, 274
Debis Haus, Berlin, 161
Deconstructivism, 202, 257
"Deconstructivist Architecture,"
  1988 exhibition, Museum of
  Modern Art, New York, 202
Deere and Company Administrative
  Center, Moline, Illinois, 108
de Gaulle, Charles, 85, 88, 124
De Rotterdam, 178
De Stijl, 148
Deutscher Werkbund, 60–61
  Cologne exhibition (1914), 52, 151
Dewey, John, 220
Diário de Notícias, 89
Dickerman, Leah, 47

Diller, Elizabeth, xix, 237, 239
Diller Scofidio + Renfro, 217, 237, 250, 253
Blur Building, Expo.02, Yverdon-les-Bains, Switzerland, 238
the Broad, Los Angeles, 249
High Line, New York, 239–44, 267, Illustration 17b
Illumination Lawn, Lincoln Center, New York, 245
Institute of Contemporary Art, Boston, 248–49
Lincoln Center for the Performing Arts renovation, New York, 244–48, 249–50, Illustration 17a
Mural, 238
Starr Theater, Alice Tully Hall, New York, 247–48, 258
Dior, Christian, 19
Downing, Andrew Jackson, 11
Downs, Hugh, 18
Drexler, Arthur, 123
Drop City, Trinidad, Colorado, 130
Dubbeldam, Winka, xx
Dudley, George A., A Workshop for Peace: Designing the United Nations Headquarters, 82–83
Dulles International Airport, Chantilly, Virginia, 118
Dulwich Picture Gallery, London, 234
Duveen Gallery, British Museum, London, 197
Dykers, Craig, 253
Dykstra, Gretchen, 267
Dymaxion "2" 4D Transport, 130

Dymaxion Chronofile, 126
Dymaxion Deployment Unit, 131
Dymaxion House, 130–31

Eames, Charles, xix, 114, 131
Eames, Ray, xix, 114, 131
East Africa, xvii, 60, 74–75
École des Beaux-Arts, Paris, 6, 200
École Polytechnique Fédérale de Lausanne, 230, 232
Eisenman, Peter, 202, 257, 259
Elgin, Thomas Bruce, 7th Earl of, 196
Elgin Marbles, 196–98, 199, 208–9
Eli and Edythe Broad Art Museum, Michigan State University, East Lansing, 165
Eliasson, Olafur, The Other Wall, 257
Ellinikon International Airport, Athens, 118
Ellis, Adrian, 166–67
Emma Hartman Noyes House, Vassar College, Poughkeepsie, New York, 117
Emmerich, David Georges, 124–25
Empire State Plaza, Albany, New York, 101, 187
Engineering Building, University of Leicester, 150–51, Illustration 11a
English Baroque, 148
Erdman Hall Dormitories, Bryn Mawr College, Pennsylvania, 117
Erechtheum, Athens, 196
Ernst von Siemens Art Foundation, 49

Esposizione Universal Roma, 110
Euphronios vase, 198
Euralille, Lille, France, 178, 187
Existenzminimum, 55, 65
Expressionism, 48–49, 108–9
Ezra Styles College, Yale University, New Haven, Connecticut, 106, back endpapers

Fahrenheit 451 (film), 37
Falkenberg, Germany, 60
Fallingwater, Bear Run, Pennsylvania, 17, 22–23
Fanning, James, and Philip Johnson, Abby Aldrich Rockefeller Sculpture Garden, Museum of Modern Art, New York, 184
Fascists, 138
Fehn, Sverre, 255
    Norwegian Pavilion, Brussels Universal and International Exhibition (1958), 255
Feininger, Lyonel, 48–49
Fernau, Richard, xix–xx
Finnish Pavilion, Universal Exposition (1900), Paris, 112
Fischer, Theodor, Hermann Muthesius, Richard Riemerschmid, and Heinrich Tessenow, Hellerau, Germany, 60
Fisher, Doris and Donald, 260
Fleischer, Richard, *The Girl in the Red Velvet Swing*, 13–14
Flierl, Thomas, 73
Florida International University School of Architecture, Miami, 201

Folger Shakespeare Library, Washington, D.C., 218
Fondation Le Corbusier, 39
Ford, Henry, 67
Foster, Norman, 259
    Hearst Tower, New York, 235–36
    Reichstag renovation, Berlin, 190, 201
Fox, Charles, and Joseph Paxton, Crystal Palace, London, 4, 80, 121, 187, 229
Fragonard, Jean-Honoré, *Les Hasards heureux de l'escarpolette*, 14
Frankfurt Kitchen, 64–67, Illustration 5b
Franzheim, Kenneth, 260
Frassinelli, Gian Piero, *Monument Continuous, The*, 129
Frederick, Christine, 65
French Communist Party headquarters, Paris, 88
Friedman, Yona, Spatial City projects, Paris, Tunis, 123–24
Fuller, Anne Hewlett, 127
Fuller, Margaret, 127
Fuller, R. Buckminster, xvi, xxii, 31, 121–32
    Dymaxion "2" 4D Transport, 130
    Dymaxion Chronofile, 126
    Dymaxion Deployment Unit, 131
    Dymaxion House, 130–31
    geodesic domes, 122, 123, 126, 127–29
    United States Pavilion (Skybreak Bubble), Expo '67, Montreal, 128–29, Illustration 9

World Game, 126
Fuller, R. Buckminster, and Shoji Sadao, *Dome over Manhattan*, 123, 129
Functionalism, 49
Fung, Hsin Ming, xix
funksjonalisme (Functionalism), 255
Fun Palace (project), 124

Gallis, Yvonne, 41, 42–43
Gandelsonas, Mario, xix
Gang, Jeanne, xx
Garden City Movement, 60, 63
Garnier, Charles, Paris Opéra, 96
Garroway, Dave, 18
Gateway Arch, St. Louis, 110
Gehry, Frank, 108–9, 177, 202, 245, 258–59
Guggenheim Museum Bilbao, xxiii–xxiv, 259
Walt Disney Concert Hall, Los Angeles, xxiv
General Motors Technical Center, Warren, Michigan, 115
Genthe, Arnold, 13
geodesic domes, 122, 123, 126, 127–29
Georges Pompidou Center, Paris, 56, 124, 165, 170, 232, 235
German Pavilion, Barcelona International Exposition (1928–29), 62, 228, 255
German Pavilion, Paris International Exposition (1937), 35
Germany, xvi–xvii, 35, 60, 61, 72, 75, 148
France occupied by, 40

Gesamtkunstwerk, 57, 113
Gesellius, Herman, 113
Gesellius, Herman, Armas Lindgren and Eliel Saarinen, Finnish Pavilion, Universal Exposition (1900), Paris, 112
Getty Center, Los Angeles, 156–57, 171
Getty Villa, Malibu, California, 167, 171
Giocondo, Fra Giovanni, Palazzo del Consiglio, Verona, 2
Giralda, Seville, Spain, 2
Girl in the Red Velvet Swing, The (film), 14
Girouard, Mark, 150, 152–53, 155, 159
Big Jim: The Life and Work of James Stirling, 149
Giroud, Françoise, 124
Giuliani, Rudy, 241
Gjørv, Eirin, *The Sand Castle*, 261–62
Glackens, William, 214
Glancey, Jonathan, 189
Glass House, New Canaan, Connecticut, 229
Glass Pavilion, Toledo Museum of Art, Ohio, 207, 227, 229, 230, 232
Glenn Miller Story, The (film), 160
Goebbels, Joseph, 74
Goff, Bruce, and Bart Prince, Pavilion of Japanese Art, Los Angeles County Museum of Art, 168
Golden Section, 34

Golding, John
"Kandinsky and the Sound of Colour," 57
Paths to the Absolute, 57
Golub, Leon, 170
Goodhue, Bertram, St. Bartholomew's Church, New York, 10
Goodwin, Philip L., and Edward Durell Stone, Museum of Modern Art, New York, 96–97
Gottlieb, Adolph, 104
Gould Memorial Library, New York University, Bronx campus, New York, 5, 6
Govan, Michael, 166, 167, 170–71
Gowan, James, and James Stirling Engineering Building, University of Leicester, 150–51, Illustration 11a
Ham Common Flats, Richmond, England, 152
Grand Avenue Project, Los Angeles, 250
Grand Central Terminal, New York, 3
Grand Comfort chair, 152
Grand-Ducal School of Arts and Crafts, Weimar, Germany, 51
Graves, Michael, xxi
Whitney Museum of American Art, New York (project), 184–85
Gray, Eileen, 71
Great Depression, 21, 23, 96, 133, 138
Great French Paintings from the Barnes Foundation: Impressionist,

Post-Impressionist, and Early Modern, 216–17
Great Mosque, Córdoba, 257
Great Recession, 222, 244, 250
Gréber, Jacques, 218
Gréber, Jacques, and Paul Philippe Cret, Rodin Museum, Philadelphia, 218
Griffin, Walter Burley, 77
Gropius, Ise, 42
Gropius, Martin, and Heino Schmieden, Martin-Gropius-Bau, Berlin, 46–47
Gropius, Walter, 42, 47–48, 50, 51, 54–55, 61, 96, 97, 108, 131
Bauhaus headquarters, Dessau, Germany, 45, 62, Illustrations 4a, 4b
Bauhaus Manifesto, 48–49
Gropius, Walter, and Adolf Meyer, demonstration factory and office building, Deutscher Werkbund exhibition (1914), Cologne, 52, 151
Ground Zero, New York, xxii, 236, 253, 254, 263–64, 265–67, 269, 272
Guardian, 189
Guerrero, Pedro E., 24, 111
Guggenheim Hermitage Museum, Venetian casino-hotel, Las Vegas, 183
Guggenheim Museum, New York, xxiv, 18, 55–56
Guggenheim Museum Bilbao, xxiii–xxiv, 259
Guild of Handicraft, 21

Guinness, Alec, 182
Günschel, Günther, Project for a
  Dome Composed of Hyperbolic
  Paraboloids, 124
Gurdjieff, G. I., 24, 98

Haagse Post, De, 182
Hadid, Zaha, xx, 202, 226, 227,
  252, 257
  Eli and Edythe Broad Art
  Museum, Michigan State Univer-
  sity, East Lansing, 165
Ham Common Flats, Richmond,
  England, 152
Hammond, Robert, 241
Hanrahan, Thomas, xx
Hardenbergh, Henry, Plaza Hotel,
  New York, 19
Hardy, Eric, The Birds of the
  Liverpool Area, 149
Hardy Holzman Pfeiffer Associates,
  Los Angeles County Museum of
  Art expansion, 167, 169
Harris, Marguerite Tjader, 41
Harrison, Wallace K., 82, 83, 96,
  187
  Empire State Plaza, Albany, New
  York, 101, 187
  Lincoln Center master plan,
  245–46
  Metropolitan Opera House, New
  York, 245
Hartford, Huntington, 102
Hartman, Laura, xix–xx
Harvard Graduate School of
  Design, Cambridge, Massachu-
  setts, 47, 192–93

Harvey Mudd College, Claremont,
  California, 94
Haussmann, Georges-Eugène,
  Baron, 124
Hauszinnssteuer, 61
Hawkinson, Laurie, xix
Hawksmoor, Nicholas, 148
Hearst, William Randolph, 13
Hearst Tower, New York, 235–36
Hebebrand, Werner, 73
Hejduk, John, 237
Hellerau, Germany, 60
Henderson, Susan R., "A Revolu-
  tion in the Woman's Sphere: Grete
  Lihotzky and the Frankfurt
  Kitchen," 66–67
Heroic Period (Le Corbusier), 34,
  35, 37
Herron, Ron, 129
Herzog, Jacques, 226
Herzog & de Meuron, 226, 254
  Tate Modern, London, 186
Hess, Thomas B., 142
High Line, New York, 239–44, 267,
  Illustration 17b
High Modernism, 36, 77, 106, 114,
  115, 119, 229
High Museum, Atlanta, 260
Hilberseimer, Ludwig, Hoch-
  hausstadt (High Rise City)
  (project), 86
Hill College House, University of
  Pennsylvania, Philadelphia,
  116–17
History Faculty Building, Cam-
  bridge University, 156
Hitchcock, Henry-Russell, 7, 8

Hitler, Adolf, xvi–xvii, 35–36, 45, 54, 73–74
Hoban, James, President's House, Washington, D.C., 12
Hochhausstadt (High Rise City) (project), 86
Hodgetts, Craig, xix
Hoffmann, Donald, 17
Höhenblick, Ginnheim, Germany, 65
Hollein, Hans, 90, 225
   Aircraft Carrier City in Land-scape, 129
Holston, James, *The Modernist City: An Anthropological Critique of Brasília*, 88
Hood, Raymond, and John Mead Howell, Chicago Tribune Build-ing, 113
Hook-on-Slab system, 74
Hope, Thomas, 151–52
House in Bordeaux, 180
"House to Die In, A," 2012 exhibition, Institute for Contem-porary Arts, London, 262–63
Howard, Ebenezer, 60
Howe, Elspeth Shand, 149–50
Howe, Geoffrey, 149–50
Howell, John Mead, and Raymond Hood, Chicago Tribune Building, 113
Hubbard, Elbert, 21
Humoresque (film), 43
Hunting, Mary Anne, *Edward Durell Stone: Modernism's Populist Architect*, 104
Huntington Hartford Gallery of Modern Art, New York, 94, 102–4
Huxtable, Ada Louise, 5, 102
Hvitträsk, Finland, 112

IBM Research Center, Yorktown Heights, New York, 108
Ictinus, Parthenon, Athens, 195
Illinois Institute of Technology, Chicago, 47, 185
Illumination Lawn, Lincoln Center, New York, 245
Imagist movement, 53
Imperial Villa, Kyoto, Japan, 108
Incas, 11
Indonesia, 181
Industrial Revolution, 118, 121
Institute for Architecture and Urban Studies, 187, 200–201
Institute for Contemporary Arts, London, 262–63
Institute of Contemporary Art, Boston, 248–49
International Style, 23, 47, 86, 97, 101, 102, 108, 115, 117, 134, 157, 255
Iran, xviii
Islamabad, University of (Quaid-i-Azam University), 101–2
Isozaki, Arata, 203–4
Ito, Toyo, 226
Itten, Johannes, 51
   Color Sphere in 7 Light Values and 12 Tones, 51–52

Jacobs, Jane, 244, 250
Jaffe, J. Christopher, 247
James Corner Field Operations, 240

Japan, 8, 108, 131, 179
Japanesque style, 27
Jeanneret, Albert, 38
Jeanneret, Marie Charlotte, 38–39, 40, 43
Jeanneret, Pierre, 34–35, 36
Jeanneret-Gris, Georges-Édouard, 38–39
Jefferson, Thomas, 19–20
Jefferson National Expansion Memorial, St. Louis, 110
Jencks, Charles, 91, 153, 155
  Le Corbusier and the Tragic View of Architecture, 43
JetBlue, 119
Johns, Jasper, 170
Johnson, Philip, xxii, 18–19, 95, 97, 99, 105, 109, 125, 152, 202, 225, 227, 262
  Glass House, New Canaan, Connecticut, 229
Johnson, Philip, and James Fanning, Abby Aldrich Rockefeller Sculpture Garden, Museum of Modern Art, New York, 184
Johnson, Philip, and Ludwig Mies van der Rohe, Seagram Building, New York, 107, 163, 228, 231
Johnson Wax Building, Racine, Wisconsin, 22, 23
Joyce, James, 25
Joyce, Lucia, 25
J. Paul Getty Museum, see Getty Center, Los Angeles; Getty Villa, Malibu, California
Julliard School of Music, New York, 247–48

Jyväskylä, University of, Finland, 151

Kahn, Louis, 93, 95, 100, 117, 126, 133–36, 214–15, 221
  Erdman Hall Dormitories, Bryn Mawr College, Pennsylvania, 117
  Kimbell Art Museum, Fort Worth, 164, 224
Kahn, Nathaniel, My Architect: A Son's Journey, 93
Kandinsky, Wassily, 45, 48, 52, 55–57
  Fugue, 56
  Levels (Etagen), 57
  Untitled (First Abstract Watercolor), 56
Karsh, Yousuf, 111
Käsebier, Gertrude, 13
Kaufmann, Edgar, Sr., 23
Kawakubo, Rei, 227
Keaton, Buster, One Week, 122, 131
Kenwood House, Nairobi, Kenya, 74
Kenya, xvii, 74
Key, Ellen, 27
Kidd, Chip, and Dave Taylor, Batman: Death by Design, 178
Kilgallen, Dorothy, 18
Kimbell Art Museum, Fort Worth, 164, 224
Kimmins, Anthony, The Captain's Paradise, 182
King's Views of New York, 243
Klee, Paul, 52, 55, 57
Knoll, Florence Schust, 114
Kobori Enshu, Imperial Villa, Kyoto, Japan, 108

Kohn Pedersen Fox, 268
Koolhaas, Anton, 181
Koolhaas, Charlie, 182
Koolhaas, Rem, xvi, 32, 93, 105, 147, 177–94, 202, 258–59, 262
"Bigness, or the Problem of Large," 191–92
Casa da Música, Porto, Portugal, 178
China Central Television Headquarters, Beijing, 188–91, Illustration 13b
"Cronacaos," 2010 Venice Architecture Biennale, 189
Delirious New York: A Retroactive Manifesto for Manhattan, 179, 180
De Rotterdam, 178
Euralille, Lille, France, 178, 187
Guggenheim Hermitage Museum, Venetian casino-hotel, Las Vegas, 183
Hollywood Tower (unproduced script), 182
House in Bordeaux, 180
Kunsthal, Rotterdam, 186
Los Angeles County Museum of Art master plan (project), 168, 183, 185–86
McCormick Tribune Campus Center, Illinois Institute of Technology, Chicago, 185
Museum of Modern Art expansion, New York (project), 183, 184
Netherlands Embassy, Berlin, 178
Ras al-Khaimah master plan, United Arab Emirates, 261

S, M, L, XL, 153, 179
Seattle Central Library, 182, 186–87, Illustration 13a
Shenzen Stock Exchange, China, 188
Whitney Museum of American Art addition (project), 183, 185
Koolhaas, Rem, and Hans Ulrich Obrist, *Project Japan: Metabolism Talks...*, 179, 182
Koolhaas, Rem, et al.
Great Leap Forward, 193
The Harvard Design School Guide to Shopping, 192
Lagos: How It Works, 193
Koolhaas, Tomas, *Rem*, 93, 182
Koolhaas Houselife (film), 180–81
Korab, Balthazar, 111
Kresge Chapel, Massachusetts Institute of Technology, Cambridge, Massachusetts, 118
Krier, Léon, 155
Kritios Kouros, 205
Kruger, Barbara, 170
Kubitschek de Oliveira, Juscelino, 80–81, 84, 85
Kuma, Kengo, 217
Kunsthal, Rotterdam, 186
Kurokawa, Kisho, 129

Labrouste, Henri
Bibliothèque Sainte-Geneviève, Paris, 2
Bibliothèque Nationale de France, Paris, 257
Lacayo, Richard, 167
Larkin Company Administration

Building, Buffalo, New York, 21, 23

Las Vegas, Nevada, 2

Lauder, Leonard, 185

Learning from Bob and Denise (film project), 93

Le Corbusier, xv, xvii–xviii, xxiii, 9, 19, 23, 31–43, 46, 54, 55, 78–79, 85, 88, 91–92, 96, 97, 105, 117, 152, 174, 177, 178–79, 200, front endpapers
Chandigarh, Punjab, India, 38, 77
"Five Points of a New Architecture," 32
Heroic Period, 34, 35, 37
Maisons Jaoul, Neuilly, France, 36, 38, 152
Notre-Dame-du-Haut, Ronchamp, France, 35, 39–40, 92, 145, Illustration 3b
Pavillon Suisse, Cité Internationale Universitaire, Paris, 35
Plan Obus, Algiers (project), 79
Plan Voisin, Paris (project), 39
Towards a New Architecture (Vers une architecture), 37
Unité d'Habitation developments, France, West Berlin, 32
Villa Jeanneret-Perret, La Chaux-de-Fonds, Switzerland, 38–39, Illustration 3a
La Ville radieuse, 41
Ville Radieuse (Radiant City) (project), 85

Le Corbusier, and Oscar Niemeyer, United Nations headquarters, New York, 82–84, 187

Le Corbusier, and Pierre Jeanneret, Villa Savoye, Poissy, France, 34–35, 36, 38, 81

Leicester, University of, 150–51, Illustration 11a

Lemoine, Jean-François, 180–81

Lemoine, Louise, and Ila Bêka, Koolhaas Houselife, 180–81

Lenbachhaus, Munich, 56

L'Enfant, Pierre-Charles, 11

Letchworth Garden City, Hertfordshire, England, 60

Levin, Kate D., 266

Liang Sicheng, 189

Libera, Adalberto, 110

Libeskind, Daniel, 90, 202, 203–4, 252, 257
Ground Zero master plan, 263, 264, 272
Spiral, Victoria & Albert Museum, London (project), 233

Lichttoren, Eindhoven, Netherlands, 182

Light Prop for an Electric Stage, 53–54

Lihotzky, Margarete, see Schütte-Lihotzky, Margarete

Limoges Concert Hall, France, 201

Lin, Maya, xx, 189, 275–76
Vietnam Veterans Memorial, Washington, D.C., 265–66, 274–75

Lincoln Center for the Performing Arts, New York, 187, 245–46
2003–2012 renovation, 244–48, Illustration 17a

Lincoln University, 212

Lindgren, Armas, Herman Gesellius and Eliel Saarinen, Finnish Pavilion, Universal Exposition (1900), Paris, 112
Lin Huiyin, 189
Littlewood, Joan, and Cedric Price, Fun Palace (project), 124
Liverpool, University of, 153
Local Projects, 273
London County Council Architects Department, Alton West Estate, London, 37
Long, Rose-Carol Washton, 56
Loos, Adolf, 64
Lorance, Loretta, *Becoming Bucky Fuller*, 127
Los Angeles County Museum of Art, 165–73, 183, 185–86
Louis XIV, King of France, xviii
Louisiana Museum of Modern Art, Copenhagen, 224
Louvre, Paris, xviii, 201, 230
Louvre-Lens, Lens, France, 229–30
Lowell, Robert, xxiv
Lower Manhattan Development Corporation (LMDC), 267, 270
Low Memorial Library, Columbia University, New York, 5–6
Luckman, Charles, Madison Square Garden, New York, 3
Lutyens, Edwin, 37–38, 77
Cenotaph, London, 275
Viceroy's House, New Delhi, 38
Lynn, Greg, 238

MacArthur Foundation "genius" grants, 237

McCarthyism, xviii
McCormick Tribune Campus Center, Illinois Institute of Technology, Chicago, 185
McKim, Charles, 5, 6, 9, 14
Boston Public Library, 2
Low Memorial Library, Columbia University, New York, 5–6
Morgan Library and Museum, New York, 10–11
Pennsylvania Station, New York, 1, 2, 3–4, Illustration 1b
White House renovation, 12
McKim, Mead & White, 1–15
New York Racquet and Tennis Club, 15
Shingle Style houses, 6–8, 13, Illustration 1a
McMillan Plan, 11–12
Madison Square Garden (Luckman), New York, 3
Madison Square Garden (White), New York, 2, 14
Mahler, Alma, 42
Maisons Jaoul, Neuilly, France, 36, 38, 152
Maki, Fumihiko, 129
Mamoulian, Rouben, *Applause*, 4
Manfredi, Michael, xix
Mann, Anthony, *The Glenn Miller Story*, 160
Mannerism, 100, 148
Mansion House Tower, London (project), 157
Marantz, Paul, 216
Martin-Gropius-Bau, Berlin, 46–47
Masieri, Angelo, 139

Masieri, Angelo, and Carlo Scarpa, Veritti Tomb, Cemetery of San Vito, Udine, Italy, 134, 139
Massaad, Khater, 262
Massachusetts Institute of Technology, Cambridge, Massachusetts, 117, 118
Master Plan for Greater Moscow (project), 73
Mastro, Rudy, 241
Matisse, Henri, *The Dance*, 216
Mau Mau uprising, xvii, 75
May, Ernst, xvii, 59–65, 67–68, 72–76, 89
Bruchfeldstrasse (*Zickzackhausen*), Frankfurt, Germany, 62
Höhenblick, Ginnheim, Germany, 65
Kenwood House, Nairobi, Kenya, 74
Master Plan for Greater Moscow (project), 73
Praunheim, Frankfurt, Germany, 62
Römerstadt, Heddernheim, Frankfurt, Germany, 62, Illustration 5a
Siedlungen, 61–63, 64, 66, 72, Illustration 5a
Urban Expansion Plan, Kampala, Uganda (project), 74–75
Westhausen, Frankfurt, Germany, 62
May Brigade, 72
Mayne, Thom, 217
Mazdaznan, 51
Mead, William Rutherford, 1, 5, 14

Meier, Richard, 220
Getty Center, Los Angeles, 156–57
High Museum, Atlanta, 260
Melgaard, Bjarne, 262–63
Melnikov, Konstantin, Rusakov Workers' Club, Moscow, 151
Mendelsohn, Erich, 46
Mendès France, Pierre, 124
Menil Collection, Houston, 164–65, 171, 173
Menil, Dominique de, 164, 175
Menil, John de, 164
Mercouri, Melina, 195–96, 197, 198–99
Metabolists, 129, 179
Metropolitan Cathedral of Our Lady of Aparecida, Brasília, 87
Metropolitan Museum of Art, New York, 123, 198
Metropolitan Opera House, New York, 245
Meuron, Pierre de, 226
see also Herzog & de Meuron
Meyer, Adolf, and Walter Gropius, demonstration factory and office building, Deutscher Werkbund exhibition (1914), Cologne, 52, 151
Meyer, Hannes, 55
Meyer, Russ, 182
Michigan State University, East Lansing, 165
Mies van der Rohe, Ludwig, 9, 19, 32, 40, 46, 47, 54, 62, 96, 97, 138, 147, 187, 260
German Pavilion, Barcelona

International Exposition (1928–29), 62, 228, 255
Illinois Institute of Technology, Chicago, 185
Mansion House Tower, London (project), 157
Neue Nationalgalerie, Berlin, 158, 159
Mies van der Rohe, Ludwig, and Philip Johnson, Seagram Building, New York, 107, 163, 228, 231
Mike Wallace Interview, The (TV show), 18
Milland, Ray, 14
Miller, J. Irwin, 118
Minimalism, 56, 64, 99, 228, 229, 232, 265
Minimalist Modernism, 35
Mitterrand, François, 80, 188, 201
Moderne style, 96
Modernism, xvi–xvii, 23, 37, 47, 57–58, 62–63, 72, 78, 80, 81, 91, 92, 95, 97, 108–9, 116, 118, 123, 134, 139, 148, 149, 150, 153–54, 159, 182, 183, 186–87, 192, 200, 201, 203, 207, 225, 232, 255, 257
High, 36, 77, 106, 114, 115, 119, 229
Minimalist, 35
Modern Movement, 1, 33, 59, 72, 110–11, 121, 123, 131, 147, 151, 178, 254
Moholy-Nagy, László, 45, 47, 52–53
Light Prop for an Electric Stage, 53–54

Mondadori headquarters, Segrate, Italy, 88
Moneo, Rafael, 217, 260
Montauk Association cottages, Long Island, 6
Montebello, Philippe de, 198
Moore, Charles, 167–68
Morgan, J. Pierpont, 10
Morgan Library and Museum, New York, 10–11
Mori, Toshiko, xx
Morphosis, 217
Morris, William, 21
Morse College, Yale University, New Haven, Connecticut, 106, back endpapers
Moses, Robert, 244
Müller-Hummel, Theobald Emil, Untitled (Pillar with Cosmic Visions), 48
Mumford, Lewis, 22, 250
Murano glass, 138
Murphy, Monica Iken, 273
Murphy and Mackey, Climatron, Missouri Botanical Garden, St. Louis, 128
Muschamp, Herbert
Man About Town: Frank Lloyd Wright in New York City, 18
"The Secret History of 2 Columbus Circle," 103
Museum for Applied Arts, Vienna, 72
Museum of Arts and Design, New York, 103
Museum of Fine Arts, Houston, 260

Museum of Modern Art, New
York, 47–48, 65, 80, 96–97, 102,
114, 123, 222
1997–2003 expansion, 183, 184,
186, 204, 222, 234–35, 236
Mussolini, Benito, 110, 138–39
Muthesius, Hermann, Theodor
Fischer, Richard Riemerschmid,
and Heinrich Tessenow, Hellerau,
Germany, 60
My Architect: A Son's Journey
(film), 93
Myers, Victoria, xx

Nash, John, 9
Nasher, Raymond, 175
Nasher Sculpture Center, Dallas,
164, 171, 173, 224
National Archaeological Museum,
Athens, 205, 209
National Gallery, London, 158, 201
National Romantic Movement,
Finland, 112–13
National September 11 Memorial,
New York, 236, 263, 264,
265–66, 269–74, 276
National September 11 Memorial
Museum, New York, 254,
263–64, 274
Nazism, Nazis, xvii, 35, 39, 54, 71,
74, 181, 187
Negulesco, Jean, *Humoresque*, 43
Neoclassicism, 12, 20, 148
Neo-Gothic style, 10, 11, 113
Neoprimitivism, 35, 49
Neruda, Pablo, 87

Nesbit, Evelyn, 13–14, 26
Nestlé headquarters, Vevey,
Switzerland, 200
Netherlands Embassy, Berlin, 178
Neue Frankfurt, Das, 63
Neue Nationalgalerie, Berlin, 158,
159
Neue Staatsgalerie, Stuttgart, 151,
153, 154–55, 157, 170, Illustration
11b
Neutra, Richard, 46
Never on Sunday (film), 199
Nevins, Deborah, 203
New Acropolis Museum, Athens,
195, 197–98, 202–9, Illustration
14b
New Bauhaus, Chicago, 47
New Brutalism, 36–37, 116
New Delhi, India, 77
New Museum of Contemporary
Art, New York, 227–28, 231–36,
Illustration 16b
New Republic, 22
New Towns, 60, 75
New Urbanism Movement, 90, 131
New Wave Planting, 242
New York City Department of
Cultural Affairs, 266
New York City Housing Authority,
268
New York City Landmarks
Preservation Commission, 3
New York City Planning Commis-
sion, 266
New York *Daily News*, 273
New Yorker, 193

New York Herald Building, 1–2
New York Racquet and Tennis
Club, 15
New York Review of Books, xxiv
New York Telephone Building, 113
New York Times, 4–5, 102, 103, 167
New York Times headquarters,
New York, 161, 169, 235–36
New York University, Bronx
campus, New York, 5, 6, 8
Niemeyer, Anna Maria, 86
Niemeyer, Oscar, xviii, 77–92, 105,
259
Casino, Pampulha, Brazil, 81, 91
Church of Saint Francis of Assisi,
Pampulha, Brazil, 81–82, 91,
Illustration 6a
French Communist Party head-
quarters, Paris, 88
Metropolitan Cathedral of Our
Lady of Aparecida, Brasília, 87
Mondadori headquarters, Segrate,
Italy, 88
Niterói Contemporary Art
Museum, Niterói, Brazil, 90
Palácio da Alvorada, Brasília,
86–87
Passarela do Samba, Rio de
Janeiro, 90–91
Plaza of the Three Powers,
Brasília, 86, 91, Illustration 6b
Serpentine Pavilion (2003),
London, 90
Strick house, Santa Monica,
California, 87–88
University of Constantine,
Algeria, 88

Niemeyer, Oscar, and Le Corbusier,
United Nations headquarters,
New York, 82–84, 187
Niemeyer, Oscar, and Lúcio Costa
Brasília, 77–78, 84–87, 88–90, 91,
92
Brazilian Pavilion, New York
World's Fair (1939), 80
Nishizawa, Ryue, 226, 227
see also SANAA
Niterói Contemporary Art Mu-
seum, Niterói, Brazil, 90
North Christian Church, Colum-
bus, Indiana, 118
Norton Simon Museum, Pasadena,
California, 171
Norway, 252, 254–55
Norwegian Pavilion, Brussels
Universal and International
Exhibition (1958), 255
Notre-Dame-du-Haut, Ronchamp,
France, 35, 39–40, 92, 145,
Illustration 3b
Nouvel, Jean, 254
Number One Poultry, London,
157–58

Obrist, Hans Ulrich, and Rem
Koolhaas, Project Japan: Metabo-
lism Talks . . . , 179
Ocatillo Desert Camp, Chandler,
Arizona, 23
Office of Metropolitan Architecture
(OMA), 168, 177, 182
Television Cultural Center,
Beijing, 188
see also Koolhaas, Rem

Office of Ryue Nishizawa, 227
Olbrich, Joseph Maria, 22
Oldenburg, Claes, *Proposals for Monuments and Buildings*, 129, 230
Olin, Laurie, 211, 217
Olivetti showroom, St. Mark's Square, Venice, 137–38
Olmsted, Frederick Law, 6
Olmsted, Frederick Law, and Calvert Vaux, Central Park, New York, 243
Olympic Games (2012), 267
One Week (film), 122, 131
One World Trade Center (Freedom Tower), New York, 272
Organic Design in Home Furnishings competition (1940), 114
Oslo Opera House, 174, 254, 256, 257–59
Ott, Stanley R., 220
Oud, J. J. P., 96, 97
Oudolf, Piet, 240, 242
"Our Towns and Cities—The Future" (Urban White Paper), 162

Packer, George, 193
Pakistan Institute of Nuclear Science and Technology, Nilore, Pakistan, 101
Palácio da Alvorada, Brasília, 86–87
Palazzo Abatellis renovation, Palermo, 140–41
Palazzo del Consiglio, Verona, Italy, 2
Palazzo Querini Stampalia renovation, Venice, 135–36

Paley, William, 107
Palladio, Andrea, 133, 137
Palumbo, Peter, 90, 157
Pan Am Building, New York, 3
Panza di Biumo collection, 56
Parc de la Villette, Paris, 201, Illustration 14a
Paris Opéra, 96
Parthenon, Athens, 195
Passarela do Samba, Rio de Janeiro, 90–91
Pavilion of Japanese Art, Los Angeles County Museum of Art, 168
Pavillon Suisse, Cité Internationale Universitaire, Paris, 35
Paxton, Joseph, and Charles Fox, Crystal Palace, London, 4, 80, 121, 187, 229
Pedestal (Tulip) chair, 114
Pei, I. M., 152
Louvre addition, Paris, 201
Pelli, Cesar, 109
Pennsylvania, University of, Philadelphia, 116–17
Pennsylvania Station, New York, 1, 2, 3–4, Illustration 1b
Pentagon, Arlington County, Virginia, 271
Pereira, William
Los Angeles County Museum of Art, 167–68, 169
Transamerica Pyramid, San Francisco, 162
Perrault, Claude, Louvre expansion, xviii
Perret, Auguste and Gustave, 38

Perriand, Charlotte, 71
 Grand Comfort chair, 152
Pétain, Marshal, 36
Pevsner, Nikolaus, 152
Pfeiffer, Bruce Brooks, 25
Phidias, 195
Philharmonic (Avery Fisher) Hall,
 New York, 245
Philharmonie, Berlin, 158, 159
Philippou, Styliane, *Oscar Nie-
 meyer: Curves of Irreverence*, 91
Phillips, Lisa, 233
Piano, Renzo, xv, 161–75, 203–4,
 259
 Art Institute of Chicago, Modern
 Wing, 204
 Astrup Fearnley Museum of
 Modern Art, Oslo, 173–74,
 Illustration 12b
 Aurora Place, Sydney, 161
 Beyeler Foundation Museum,
 Reihen, Switzerland, 164, 173
 BP Grand Entrance, Los Angeles
 County Museum of Art, 169
 Broad Contemporary Art Mu-
 seum at the Los Angeles County
 Museum of Art, 165–67, 168–71,
 186
 California Academy of Sciences
 building, San Francisco, 94
 Cy Twombly Gallery, Houston,
 164, 173
 Debis Haus, Berlin, 161
 High Museum addition, Atlanta,
 260
 Los Angeles County Museum of
 Art master plan, 168–69, 186

 Menil Collection, Houston,
 164–65, 171, 173
 Morgan Library and Museum
 addition, 10
 Nasher Sculpture Center, Dallas,
 164, 171, 173, 224
 New York Times headquarters,
 New York, 161, 169, 235–36
 Resnick Pavilion, Los Angeles
 County Museum of Art, 169,
 186
 Shard, London, 161–64, Illustra-
 tion 12a
 Stavros Niarchos Foundation
 Cultural Center, Athens, 203
Piano, Renzo, and Richard Rogers,
 Georges Pompidou Center, Paris,
 56, 124, 165, 170, 232
Picasso, Pablo, 87, 216
 Demoiselles d'Avignon, 56, 216
 piloti columns, 32, 36, 79, 81
Piranesi, Giovanni Battista, *Carceri
 d'invenzione*, 4, 105
Plan Obus, Algiers (project), 79
Plan Voisin, Paris (project), 39
Player, The (film), 166
Plaza Hotel, New York, 19
Plaza of the Three Powers, Brasília,
 86, 91, Illustration 6b
Pollock, Jackson, 98
Pompidou Center, *see* Georges
 Pompidou Center, Paris
Pope, John Russell, Duveen Gallery,
 British Museum, London, 197
Porter, Cole, 81
Portinari, Cândido, 82
Portman, John, 225

Portzamparc, Christian de, 226
Postmodernism, 90, 134, 148, 154, 157, 160, 167, 178, 184–85, 260
Prairie Houses, 9, 22, 26–27
Praunheim, Frankfurt, Germany, 62
prefabrication, 64, 66, 67–68, 121–22, 131
Pre-Raphaelites, 102
Presidential Palace, Islamabad, 101
President's House, Washington, D.C., 12
Price, Cedric, and Joan Littlewood, Fun Palace (project), 124
Prince, Bart, and Bruce Goff, Pavilion of Japanese Art, Los Angeles County Museum of Art, 168
Pritzker Architecture Prize, xxiii, 90, 217, 221, 225–26, 254, 255
Project for a Dome Composed of Hyperbolic Paraboloids, 124
Prospectivists, 124
Prouvé, Jean, 131
Pulitzer Prize, 90

Quaid-i-Azam University (University of Islamabad), 101–2

Rabbit, Peter, Drop City, 130
Radburn, New Jersey, 172
Radiant City (Ville Radieuse) (project), 85
Radio City Music Hall, New York, 96
Rampin Rider, 205
Ranalli, George, 136

Rand, Ayn, The Fountainhead, 31
Ras al-Khaimah Gateway, United Arab Emirates, 261–62
Ras al-Khaimah master plan, United Arab Emirates, 261
Ratner, Bruce, 267
Reed & Stem, and Warren & Wetmore, Grand Central Terminal, New York, 3
Reich, Lilly, 71
Reichstag, Berlin, 190, 201
Rem (film project), 93, 182
Renaissance Revival style, 2
Renfro, Charles, 237, 239
see also Diller Scofidio + Renfro
Renwick, James, Jr.
St. Bartholomew's Church, New York, 10
St. Patrick's Cathedral, New York, 10
Smithsonian Institution, Washington, D.C., 10, 11
Resnick Pavilion, Los Angeles County Museum of Art, 169, 186
Reva and David Logan Center for Creative and Performing Arts, University of Chicago, 223–24, Illustration 15c
Rich, Andrea, 166
Richardson, H. H., 2, 6
Richardson, John, A Life of Picasso, 20
Riemerschmid, Richard, Theodor Fischer, Hermann Muthesius, and Heinrich Tessenow, Hellerau, Germany, 60

Rietveld, Gerrit, and Truus
Schröder-Schräder, Schröder
house, Utrecht, 23
Rishel, Joseph J., 217
Robie house, Chicago, 17
Roche, Kevin, 109, 111, 225
Rockefeller, Blanchette, 222
Rockefeller, John D., Jr., 82, 187
Rockefeller, Nelson, 187
Rockefeller Center, 96
Rockwell Group, Elinor Bunin
Munroe Film Center, New York,
246
Rodin Museum, Philadelphia, 218
Rogers, Richard, and Renzo Piano,
Georges Pompidou Center, Paris,
56, 124, 165, 170, 232
Rolex Learning Center, École
Polytechnique Fédérale de
Lausanne, 230, 232
Romanesque style, 9–10
Romantic (African) chair, 49
Romanticism, 11, 101
"Romantic Rationalism," 22
Rome, ancient, 121
Römerstadt, Heddernheim,
Frankfurt, Germany, 62, Illustra-
tion 5a
Romney, Mitt, 220
Ronchamp chapel, see Notre-Dame-
du-Haut, Ronchamp, France
Röntgen, Wilhelm, 53
Roosenburg, Dirk, Lichttoren,
Eindhoven, Netherlands, 182
Roosevelt, Franklin D., 74
Roosevelt, Theodore, 12
Rose, Charlie, 18–19

Rose, Joseph, 241
Rosenberg, Alfred, 54
Rossi, Aldo, 148
San Cataldo Cemetery, Modena,
Italy, 143
Roszak, Theodore, 116
Rotch Traveling Fellowship, 95
Rowe, Colin, "The Mathematics of
the Ideal Villa: Palladio and Le
Corbusier Compared," 37
Royal Academy, London, 215
Roycrofters workshop, 21
Rusakov Workers' Club, Moscow,
151
Russian Constructivism, 55,
147–48, 151, 201
Ryan, Philip, 211

Saarinen, Aline, 106
Saarinen, Eero, xvi, 99
Antioch College master plan, 116
CBS Building, New York, 107
David S. Ingalls Hockey Rink,
Yale University, New Haven,
Connecticut, 106
Deere and Company Administra-
tive Center, Moline, Illinois, 108
Dulles International Airport,
Chantilly, Virginia, 118
Ellinikon International Airport,
Athens, 118
Emma Hartman Noyes House,
Vassar College, Poughkeepsie,
New York, 117
Ezra Styles College, Yale Univer-
sity, New Haven, Connecticut,
106, back endpapers

Gateway Arch, St. Louis, 110
General Motors Technical Center, Warren, Michigan, 115
Hill College House, University of Pennsylvania, Philadelphia, 116–17
IBM Research Center, Yorktown Heights, New York, 108
Kresge Chapel, Massachusetts Institute of Technology, Cambridge, Massachusetts, 118
Morse College, Yale University, New Haven, Connecticut, 106, back endpapers
North Christian Church, Columbus, Indiana, 118
Trans World Airlines Terminal, John F. Kennedy International Airport, New York, 107, 111, 118–19, Illustration 8
Tulip (Pedestal) chair, 114
United States Chancellery, London, 115
United States Chancellery, Oslo, 115
United States Embassy addition, Helsinki (project), 115
Vivian Beaumont Theater, New York, 245
Womb chair, 114
Saarinen, Eliel, 112–13, 114–15
Chicago Tribune Building (competition entry), 113
Cranbrook Academy of Art, Bloomfield Hills, Michigan, 113–14, 220, 221–22
Saarinen, Eliel, Herman Gesellius

and Armas Lindgren, Finnish Pavilion, Paris Universal Exposition (1900), 112
Saarinen, Loja, 113
Sadao, Shoji, and R. Buckminster Fuller, Dome over Manhattan, 123
Sainsbury Wing, National Gallery, London, 158, 201
St. Bartholomew's Church (Goodhue), New York, 10, 15
St. Bartholomew's Church (Renwick), New York, 10
St.-Gilles-du-Gard, Provence, France, 9–10
St. Patrick's Cathedral, New York, 10
Samaras, Antonis, 197–98
SANAA, 227, 232–33, 254
Glass Pavilion, Toledo Museum of Art, Ohio, 207, 227, 229, 230, 232
Le Louvre-Lens, Lens, France, 229–30
New Museum of Contemporary Art, New York, 227–28, 231–36, Illustration 16b
Rolex Learning Center, École Polytechnique Fédérale de Lausanne, 230, 232
21st Century Museum of Contemporary Art, Kanazawa, Japan, 228–29, 230, 232, Illustration 16a
San Cataldo Cemetery, Modena, Italy, 143
Sand Castle, The (film), 261–62
San Francisco Museum of Modern Art, 254, 259–61

Sant'Elia, Antonio, 105
Città Nuova, 105
Scarpa, Carlo, xvi, 133–46
  Brion Family Tomb and Chapel,
  San Vito d'Altivole, Italy, 143–46,
  Illustration 10
  Ca' Foscari renovation, Venice,
  137–38
  Canova Plaster Cast Gallery
  addition, Possagno, Italy, 141–42
  Castelvecchio Museum renova-
  tion, Verona, Italy, 142–43
  Murano glass, 138
  Olivetti showroom, St. Mark's
  Square, Venice, 137–38
  Palazzo Abatellis renovation,
  Palermo, 140–41
  Palazzo Querini Stampalia
  renovation, Venice, 135–36
Scarpa, Carlo, and Angelo Masieri,
  Veritti Tomb, Cemetery of San
  Vito, Udine, Italy, 134, 139
Schapiro, Meyer, 217
Scharoun, Hans, Philharmonie,
  Berlin, 158, 159
Scheeren, Ole, 191
Schinkel, Karl Friedrich, 148
Schlesische Heimstätte (Silesian
  Homesteads), 61
Schmieden, Heino, and Martin
  Gropius, Martin-Gropius-Bau,
  Berlin, 46–47
Schreyer, Lothar, *Death House for
  a Woman*, 48
Schröder house, Utrecht, Nether-
  lands, 23
Schröder-Schräder, Truus, and

Gerrit Rietveld, Schröder house,
  Utrecht, 23
Schultze & Weaver, Waldorf
  Astoria Hotel, 96
Schütte, Wilhelm, 64, 72
  "Grete Lihotzky," 68–71
Schütte-Lihotzky, Margarete, xvi,
  xvii, xix, 59–60, 64–72, 76
  Frankfurt Kitchen, 64–67,
  Illustration 5b
S. C. Johnson Research Tower,
  Racine, Wisconsin, 151
Scofidio, Ricardo, 237, 239
  see also Diller Scofidio + Renfro
Scott Brown, Denise, xix, 93, 100,
  177, 192, 220, 226
Scott Brown, Denise, and Robert
  Venturi
  Learning from Las Vegas, 192, 193
  Sainsbury Wing, National
  Gallery, London, 158, 201
Scully, Vincent, 99–100, 106
  *The Shingle Style and the Stick
  Style*, 7
Seagram Building, New York, 107,
  163, 228, 231
Sears, Roebuck houses, 122, 131
Seattle Central Library, 182,
  186–87, Illustration 13a
Sejima, Kazuyo, xix, 226–27
  see also SANAA
Semper, Gottfried, 22
September 11, 2001, terrorist
  attacks, 162, 222, 268, 271, 274
Serpentine Gallery, London, 90
Serra, Richard, 108
Servan-Schreiber, Jean-Jacques, 124

Seurat, Georges, *Poseuses*, 215–16
Shand, Mary, 149
Shand, Philip Morton, 149
Shard, London, 161–64, Illustration
  12a
Shaw, Richard Norman, 6
Shenzen Stock Exchange, China,
  188
Sherman, Cindy, 170
Shingle Style, 6–8, 13, Illustration
  1a
Shulman, Julius, 111–12
Siedlungen, 61–63, 64, 66, 72,
  Illustration 5a
Silverstein, Larry, 264
Silvetti, Jorge, 140
Sinatra, Frank, 112
Singer Manufacturing Company,
  107
Skidmore, Owings & Merrill, 252,
  262, 272
Smith, Adrian, Burj Khalifa, Dubai,
  262
Smith-Miller, Henry, xix
Smithson, Alison and Peter, xix,
  220
Smithsonian Institution, Washing-
  ton, D.C., 10, 11
Snelson, Kenneth, 125
Snøhetta, 90, 250, 251–64
  Bibliotheca Alexandrina, Alexan-
  dria, Egypt, 255–57, 258
  Bjarne Melgaard house, Oslo,
  262–63
  National September 11 Memorial
  Museum, New York, 254,
  263–64, 274

Oslo Opera House, 174, 254,
  257–59
Ras al-Khaimah Gateway, United
  Arab Emirates, 261–62
San Francisco Museum of Modern
  Art addition, 254, 259–61
Times Square redesign, New
  York, 254
Soane, John
  Dulwich Picture Gallery, London,
  234
  Soane Museum, London, 222
Soviet Union, xvii, 55, 60, 72
Spain, 259
Spatial City projects, Paris, Tunis,
  123–24
Speer, Albert, German Pavilion,
  Paris International Exposition
  (1937), 35
Sperlich, Hans-G., and Ulrich
  Conrads, *Phantastiche Architek-
  tur*, 123
Spiral, Victoria & Albert Museum,
  London (project), 233
Spreckelsen, Johann Otto von,
  Grande Arche de la Défense,
  Paris, 188
Stalin, Joseph, xvii
Stanford University Medical
  Center, Stanford, California, 94
Starr Theater, Alice Tully Hall,
  New York, 247–48
State University of New York,
  Albany, 94, 100–102
Stavros Niarchos Foundation
  Cultural Center, Athens, 203
Steichen, Edward, 53

Stein, Clarence, and Henry Wright, Sunnyside Gardens, Queens, New York, 172
Stephens, Suzanne, 217
Sternfeld, Joel, 242
Stirling, James, xvi, 90, 147–60, 225
"Black Notebook," 149, 160
"Garches to Jaoul: Le Corbusier as Domestic Architect in 1927 and 1953," 37
History Faculty Building, Cambridge University, 156
James Stirling: Buildings & Projects, 1950–1974, 153
Number One Poultry, London, 157–58
Red Trilogy, 150–51
Stirling, James, and James Gowan
Engineering Building, University of Leicester, 150–51, Illustration 11a
Ham Common Flats, Richmond, England, 152
Stirling, James, and Michael Wilford
Clore Gallery, Tate Gallery, London, 158
Neue Staatsgalerie, Stuttgart, 151, 153, 154–55, 157, 170, Illustration 11b
Wissenschaftszentrum Berlin für Sozialforschung, Berlin, 158–59
Stoller, Ezra, 111–12
Stölzl, Gunta, 49–50
Stölzl, Gunta, and Marcel Breuer, African (Romantic) chair, 49
Stone, Edward Durell, xvi, 93–103

Harvey Mudd College, Claremont, California, 94, 98
Huntington Hartford Gallery of Modern Art, New York, 94, 102–4
Pakistan Institute of Nuclear Science and Technology, Nilore, Pakistan, 101
Presidential Palace, Islamabad, 101
Stanford University Medical Center, Stanford, California, 94, 98
State University of New York, Albany, 94, 100–102
United States Embassy, New Delhi, 98, 101
United States Pavilion, Brussels World's Fair (1958), 95, Illustration 7
University of Islamabad (Quaid-i-Azam University), 101–2
Stone, Edward Durell, and Philip L. Goodwin, Museum of Modern Art, New York, 96–97
Stone, Hicks, *Edward Durell Stone: A Son's Untold Story of a Legendary Architect*, 93–94, 98, 104
Stone, Maria Elena Torch, 94
Streamline Moderne style, 23
Strick house, Santa Monica, California, 87–88
Stripped Classicism, 35, 115
Sturm, Philipp, 74
Sukarno, 181
Sullivan, Louis, 2
Sunnyside Gardens, Queens, New York, 172

Tafuri, Manfredo, 106
Taj Mahal, Agra, India, 98
Talbot, Henry Fox, 53
Taliesin, Spring Green, Wisconsin, 21, 27–28, Illustration 2b
Taliesin Fellowship, 21, 24, 98
Taliesin West, Scottsdale, Arizona, 22, 23–24
Tange, Kenzo, 179
Taniguchi, Yoshio, Museum of Modern Art expansion, New York, 184, 186, 204, 222, 234–35, 236
Tate Modern, London, 186
Taut, Bruno, 61, 63, 89, 108
Falkenberg, Germany, 60
Taylor, Dave, and Chip Kidd, *Batman: Death by Design*, 178
Taylor, Frederick Winslow, 65–66
Television Cultural Center, Beijing, 188
Temple of Olympian Zeus, Athens, 200
tensegrity, 125
Tessenow, Heinrich, Theodor Fischer, Hermann Muthesius, and Richard Riemerschmid, Hellerau, Germany, 60
Thatcher, Margaret, 150
Thaw, Harry, 14
Thorne, Martha, 217
Thorp, Jen, 273
Thorsen, Kjetil Trædal, 252, 253, 262
Tiffany, Louis Comfort, 12
Time, 99, 123
Times Square, New York, 254

Today Show (TV show), 18
Toledo Museum of Art, Ohio, 207, 227, 229, 230, 232
Transamerica Pyramid, San Francisco, 162
Transportation Hub, New York, 272–73
Trans World Airlines Terminal, John F. Kennedy International Airport, New York, 107, 111, 118–19, Illustration 8
Tremaine, Burton and Emily, 88
Triumph of Death, The, 141
Truffaut, François, *Fahrenheit 451*, 37
Truman, Harry, 12
Tschumi, Bernard, xvi, 200–201, 257
Alésia Museum Visitor's Center, Burgundy, France, 201
Alfred Lerner Hall, Columbia University, New York, 202–3
Florida International University School of Architecture, Miami, 201
Limoges Concert Hall, France, 201
New Acropolis Museum, Athens, 195, 197–98, 202–9, Illustration 14b
Parc de la Villette, Paris, 201, Illustration 14a
Vacheron Constantin headquarters, Geneva, 201
Tschumi, Jean, 200
Nestlé headquarters, Vevey, Switzerland, 200

World Health Organization
headquarters, Geneva, 200
Tsien, Billie, xix, 220–21, frontis-
piece
Tsien, Billie, and Tod Williams
American Folk Art Museum, New
York, 222–23, Illustration 15b
Barnes Foundation Collection,
Philadelphia, 211, 216–20, 224,
Illustration 15a
"Gallery in a Garden, Garden in a
Gallery," 217–18
Reva and David Logan Center for
Creative and Performing Arts,
University of Chicago, 223–24,
Illustration 15c
Williams Natatorium, Cranbrook
School, Bloomfield Hills, Michi-
gan, 221–22
Tucker, Marcia, 232
Tulip (Pedestal) chair, 114
21st Century Museum of Contem-
porary Art, Kanazawa, Japan,
228–29, 230, 232, Illustration 16a
Twombly, Robert, *Frank Lloyd
Wright: His Life and His Archi-
tecture*, 20

Udet, Ernst, *Fremde Vögel über
Afrika*, 74
Ungers, O. M., 182
Unité d'Habitation developments,
France, West Berlin, 32
United Nations headquarters, New
York, 82–84, 187
United States Chancellery, London,
115

United States Chancellery, Oslo,
115
United States Embassy, New Delhi,
98, 101
United States Embassy addition,
Helsinki (project), 115
United States Pavilion, Brussels
World's Fair (1958), 95, Illustration 7
United States Pavilion (Skybreak
Bubble), Expo '67, Montreal,
128–29, Illustration 9
Unity Chapel, Spring Green,
Wisconsin, 28
Unwin, Raymond, 60
Urban Expansion Plan, Kampala,
Uganda (project), 74–75
Usonian houses, xxi
Utzon, Jørn, 225

Vacheron Constantin headquarters,
Geneva, 201
Vanbrugh, John, 148
van de Velde, Henry, 51
Vargas, Getúlio, 87
Vassar College, Poughkeepsie, New
York, 117
Vaux, Calvert, and Frederick Law
Olmsted, Central Park, New
York, 243
Venice, University of, 137
Venice Association of Architects,
137
Venturi, James, *Learning from Bob
and Denise*, 93
Venturi, Robert, xix, xxi, xxiii, 93,
100, 109–10, 120, 177, 192, 220,
226

Complexity and Contradiction in Architecture, 111
Venturi, Robert, and Denise Scott Brown
Learning from Las Vegas, 192, 193
Sainsbury Wing, National Gallery, London, 158, 201
Vergely, Jacques, and Philippe Mathieux, Promenade Plantée, Paris, 242
Veritti Tomb, Cemetery of San Vito, Udine, Italy, 134, 139
vesica piscis, 145
Viceroy's House, New Delhi, 38
Vichy France, xvii–xviii, 36, 40
Victoria & Albert Museum, London, 65, 233
Vidler, Anthony, 153
Vietnam Veterans Memorial, Washington, D.C., 265–66
Villa Jeanneret-Perret, La Chaux-de-Fonds, Switzerland, 38–39, Illustration 3a
Villa Savoye, Poissy, France, 26, 34–35, 38, 81
Ville Radieuse (Radiant City) (project), 85
Viollet-le-Duc, Eugène-Emmanuel, *Dictionnaire raisonné de l'architecture français du XIe au XVIe siècle*, 22
Visionary Architects: Boullée, Ledoux, Lequeu (exhibition catalog), Metropolitan Museum of Art, New York, 123
"Visionary Architecture," 1960 exhibition, Museum of Modern Art, New York, 123
Vivian Beaumont Theater, New York, 245
Vorkurs, 51, 52
Vriesendorp, Madelon, 182–83
Apres l'amour, 183

Wagner, Martin, 61
Waldorf Astoria Hotel, 96
Walker, Peter, and Michael Arad, National September 11 Memorial, New York, 236, 263, 264, 265–66, 269–74, 276, 1019
Walker, Ralph, New York Telephone Building, 113
Wallace, Mike, 18
Walt Disney Concert Hall, Los Angeles, xxiv
Warchavchik, Gregori, 78
Warren & Wetmore, and Reed & Stem, Grand Central Terminal, New York, 3
Washington, D.C., 11–12
Weber, Nicholas Fox, *Le Corbusier: A Life*, 33, 38–43
Weimar Republic, 58, 61, 75, 89
Weinbrenner, Friedrich, 148
Weiss, Marion, xix
Westhausen, Frankfurt, Germany, 62
What's My Line? (TV Show), 18
White, Pae, *MetaFoil*, 257–58
White, Stanford, xvi, xx, 1, 5, 6, 9–10, 13–14, 26
Box Hill, Long Island, 13
Gould Memorial Library, New

York University, Bronx campus, New York, 5, 6
Madison Square Garden, New York, 2, 14
Montauk Association cottages, Long Island, 6
New York Herald Building, 1–2
St. Bartholomew's Church portico, New York, 10, 15
White House, Washington, D.C., 12
Whitney Museum of American Art, New York, 183, 184–85, 237–38
Widener, Peter, 214
Wiener Werkstätte (Viennese Workshop), Vienna, 50
Wigley, Mark, 202
Wilde, Oscar, *Salome*, 145
Wilford, Michael, and James Stirling
Clore Gallery, Tate Gallery, London, 158
Neue Staatsgalerie, Stuttgart, 151, 153, 154–55, 157, 170, Illustration 11b
Wissenschaftszentrum Berlin für Sozialforschung, Berlin, 158–59
Williams, Kai Tsien, 221
Williams, Tod, 220–21, frontispiece
Williams, Tod, and Billie Tsien
American Folk Art Museum, New York, 222–23, Illustration 15b
Barnes Foundation Collection, Philadelphia, 211, 216–20, 224, Illustration 15a
"Gallery in a Garden, Garden in a Gallery," 217–18
Reva and David Logan Center for Creative and Performing Arts, University of Chicago, 223–24, Illustration 15c
Williams Natatorium, Cranbrook School, Bloomfield Hills, Michigan, 221–22
Williams Natatorium, Cranbrook School, Bloomfield Hills, Michigan, 221–22
Wissenschaftszentrum Berlin für Sozialforschung, Berlin, 158–59
Wohlert, Vilhelm, and Jørgen Bo, Louisiana Museum of Modern Art, Copenhagen, 224
Womb chair, 114
Woolworth, Frank Winfield, 107
World Health Organization headquarters, Geneva, 200
World Trade Center, New York, 162, 268, 270
see also Ground Zero, New York
World Trade Center Memorial Foundation, 267
World War I, 27, 48, 52, 60, 64, 105
World War II, xvii–xviii, 24, 36, 71, 74, 78, 97, 116, 133, 179
Wren, Christopher, 93, 105
Wren, Christopher (son), *Parentalia*, 93
Wright, Catherine Tobin, 25–26
Wright, Frank Lloyd, xv, xx–xxi, xxii, 2, 8–9, 17–29, 31–32, 93, 96, 97–98, 105, 111, 113, 131, 133, 138, 139, 148–49, 200
An Autobiography, 31, 126

Broadacre City (project), 20
Cheney house, Oak Park, Illinois, 26
Fallingwater, Bear Run, Pennsylvania, 17, 22–23
Guggenheim Museum, New York, xxiv, 18, 55–56
Johnson Wax Building, Racine, Wisconsin, 22, 23
Larkin Company Administration Building, Buffalo, New York, 21, 23
Modern Architecture: Being the Kahn Lectures for 1930, 21, 22
Ocatillo Desert Camp, Chandler, Arizona, 23
Prairie Houses, 9, 22, 26–27
Robie house, Chicago, 17, 224
S. C. Johnson Research Tower, Racine, Wisconsin, 151
Taliesin, Spring Green, Wisconsin, 21, 27–28, Illustration 2b
Taliesin West, Scottsdale, Arizona, 22, 23–24
Unity Chapel, Spring Green, Wisconsin, 28
Usonian houses, xxi
Wright house and studio, Oak Park, Illinois, 26, Illustration 2a
Wright, Henry, and Clarence Stein, Sunnyside Gardens, Queens, New York, 172
Wright, Iovanna Lazovich Lloyd (Rosa), 25
Wright, John Lloyd, *My Father Who Is on Earth*, 93
Wright, Miriam Noel, 25

Wright, Olgivanna, 25–26, 28–29, 98
Wright, Tom, Burj Al Arab hotel, Dubai, 262
Wyatt, Edward, 167

Yamasaki, Minoru, 100
World Trade Center, New York, 100

Zapf, Hermann, 271
Zeckendorf, William, 187
Zeilenbau, 62
Zelevansk, Lynn, "Ars Longa, Vita Brevis: Contemporary Art at LACMA, 1913–2007," 166
Zenghelis, Elia, 182
Zenghelis, Zoe, 182
Zumthor, Peter, Los Angeles County Museum of Art (project), 168, 186

Eero Saarinen with the model for his Morse and Ezra Stiles Colleges of 1959–1962 at Yale University in New Haven, a scenographic villagescape of stone-clad student dormitories inspired by the medieval Tuscan hill town of San Gimignano.